Huw. Christmas 1975
Mum & Dad

Huw. Christmas 1975
Mum & Dad

SPIRIT
OF
THE
AGE

ALEC CLIFTON-TAYLOR

ROY STRONG

ROBERT FURNEAUX JORDAN

JOHN JULIUS NORWICH

JOHN SUMMERSON

MARK GIROUARD

PATRICK NUTTGENS

HUGH CASSON

SPIRIT

OF

THE

AGE

—

BRITISH BROADCASTING

CORPORATION

PUBLISHED BY THE

BRITISH BROADCASTING CORPORATION

35 MARYLEBONE HIGH STREET

LONDON W1M 4AA

ISBN 0 563 12897 6

FIRST PUBLISHED 1975

© THE AUTHORS 1975

PRINTED IN ENGLAND BY

JOLLY AND BARBER LIMITED

RUGBY, WARWICKSHIRE

CONTENTS

FOREWORD

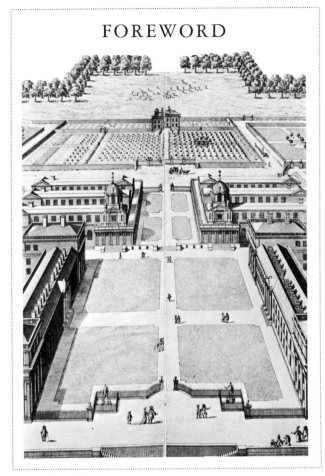

Of all the arts, architecture is the hardest to avoid. Yet, in a curious way, its very omnipresence can make it almost invisible. We take it for granted. Only when we go away from home or visit a place we don't know do we succeed in reopening our eyes to the things that surround us. Perhaps, since so few of us have more than a restricted choice of the kind of building in which we actually live or work, or how that building relates to the others around it, this selective blindness is partly self protection. Perhaps the jumble of buildings of all periods in both town and country makes the overall picture hard to decipher. By placing the architecture of this country in its historical and intellectual context, this book, like the television series on which it is based, encourages us to respond more readily to the Architectural Heritage that we often only recognise exceptionally.

Books about architecture have a distinguished history going back at least two thousand years. Television programmes on architecture are rather more recent and have to contend with a number of problems that don't trouble the reader – problems of size, of scale or atmosphere. Nevertheless, *Spirit of The Age* sought to overcome some of these problems through a real fusion of words and images. Eight outstanding writers, deliberately chosen for the diversity of their approach to architecture, each took a period of our history and related the buildings of that age to the society that produced them; to the ideas, the techniques, the preoccupations of the men who created them. Not just architecture or architects but people.

This approach, perhaps not new, but newly presented, was the result of close collaboration between the writers and the directors of the films. I would like to pay tribute to the writers for the flexibility of their response to the advantages and disadvantages of the television screen. Some of them here regain the dry land of the printed page with, I am sure, a sense of relief.

As producer of the television series I would like to thank three outstanding figures of our time who, though they didn't actually participate in the making of the series, gave me valuable help and advice in its preparation; Sir Nikolaus Pevsner, who has taught us all more about British architecture than we thought there was to know; Sir John Betjeman, who has encouraged us not only to recognise but also to care; and Lord Clark whose own achievements for television gave us a standard to aspire to. To them, and to the many others who also helped, we are sincerely grateful.

JOHN DRUMMOND

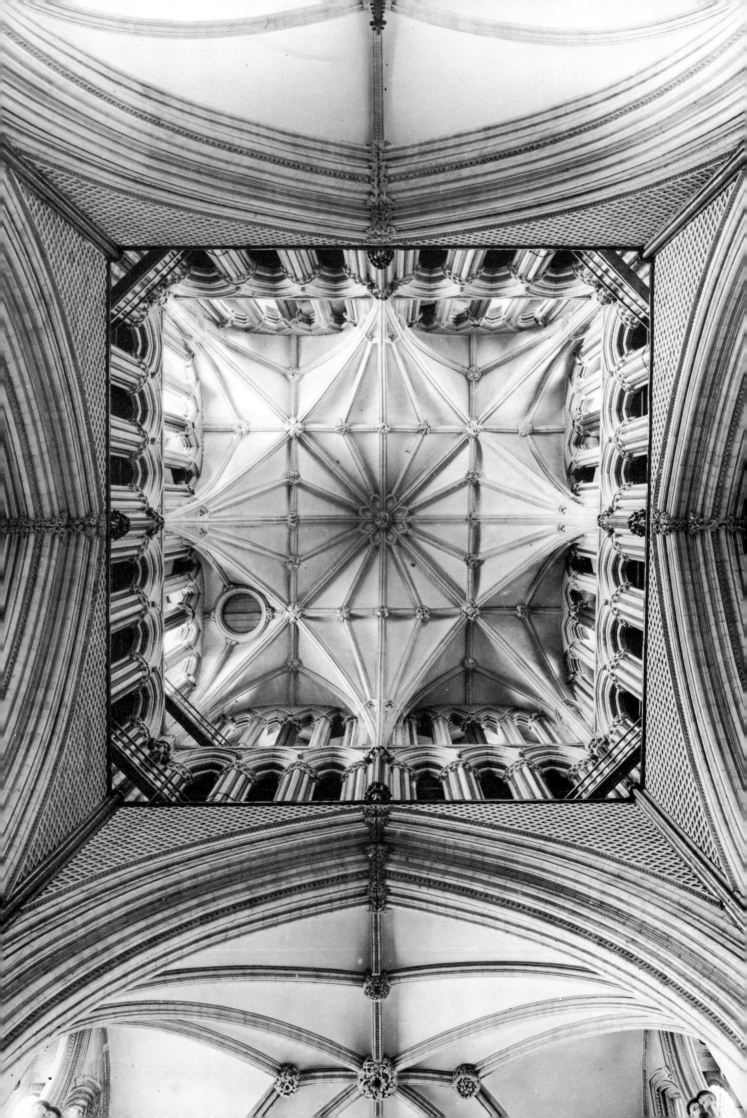

1

ALEC CLIFTON-TAYLOR

THE MEDIEVAL WORLD

Not a dozen miles from Coalbrookdale in Shropshire, the birthplace of the Industrial Revolution, we can still stand upon Wenlock Edge, looking up the vale of the Severn towards Shrewsbury, with the bold contours of the Wrekin, framing the prospect on the right and, to the left, beyond Caer Caradoc, the Long Mynd and the Stiperstones, the last upland bastions of England before reaching the border with Wales – we can still stand here and see no vestige of industrialisation, not even, any longer, the line of railway which used to add a not unwelcome accent to the Severn Valley. If, eight hundred years ago, we had been facing this same panoramic view, we should have seen a great deal more woodland. In the vales and on the less elevated slopes, trees would have been nearly every-where. Farmland had to be wrested from the forest. Before ploughing could begin, trees had to be uprooted, woodlands cleared. The mosaic of fields, fences, farms, with a few larger houses and here and there a church, which is what we see today, was not consciously planned, but nor did it happen by chance. It is the visible outcome of many generations of hard but dedicated work on the land. And so relatively unchanging is the rhythm of life in a rural area such as this that we can still find plenty of buildings which are three or four hundred years old, and some that are considerably more.

The further we go back in time, the more we have to depend upon buildings to provide the clues to man's activities. In this essay the aim will be to try to capture something of that spirit as conveyed by

The vault of the central tower, Lincoln cathedral; the illustration above shows carving around the doorway of Kilpeck church.

Lower Brockhampton, in Herefordshire. The house goes back at least to 1400. The gatehouse in the foreground was a later addition.

what must necessarily be a very small selection of our surviving medieval buildings.

In this matter of survival we in England have been marvellously fortunate. In the whole world there is perhaps only one other country with as much to show from the Middle Ages, and that is Italy. Despite the unrivalled distinction of her most famous cathedrals, it is doubtful whether even France can equal us in this respect. For this there is a variety of reasons, but in the last analysis most of them boil down to luck. Luck in being an island, so that, compared with almost any other country one cares to name, at least in Europe, ours has been very little fought over. Luck in having had comparatively stable political institutions, which have usually

ensured stability in other directions too. Luck, again, in possessing inexhaustible quantities of very fine and durable building materials. This is the aspect upon which, in the pages that follow, I wish specially to concentrate.

For the very large majority of English people in the Middle Ages, the usual building material was wood. In almost every part of the country, even where stone was abundant, most people's houses, when not built just of mud (and the 'cob' still so familiar in Devon and Dorset is in fact mud, which was also widely employed in parts of the Midlands), were timber-framed. For the humblest, most flimsy structures, which have not survived, they may have used inferior woods, such as elder, but all the better

A cruck cottage, at Weobley, Herefordshire. Halves of a curved piece of timber, cut lengthways, make the symmetrical arch of the main frame.

buildings without exception had frames of oak. We should be grateful indeed for our profusion of oaks. Before the days when the trees were felled by the thousand to provide fuel for the iron-smelters, there was so much oak in the Weald that it used to be known as 'the Sussex weed'.

The most primitive type of framed structure was with crucks. The idea was to find a tree with a natural curve and if possible to slice it along its length into two halves, which would ensure a symmetrical arch. If two or three more similar trees could be found, they would be used to make further arches, placed at intervals one behind the other, and linked horizontally at the top by a lighter piece known as the ridge pole. Fill in the interstices with

branches, cover these with straw thatch or perhaps only with heather or brushwood, and you had your house. The basic type was gradually refined and improved, until they built the kind of cruck cottage still standing at Weobley in Herefordshire. Cruck cottages are scarcely ever found in the East, South or South-West of England, but in the West, Midlands and North there are still an appreciable number, although seldom any longer perfect. There are in fact considerably more than is evident, for, in the cause of better insulation, the crucks were often plastered over, if not masked altogether under a stone or brick facing.

With nearly all timber-framed buildings, however, the posts are vertical, the wall areas rectangular, and the roofs gabled, the average angle of the slope being somewhere about 50°. Such houses are not always easy to date. But the large majority of those seen today belong to the sixteenth or seventeenth centuries (or, it would be not unfair to add, to the Victorian period). Only a relatively small number belong to the Middle Ages. One that certainly does is Lower Brockhampton, near Bromyard in Herefordshire, which goes back at least to 1400.

When I first visited this place about 1950, not long after the two-thousand-acre estate had been bequeathed to the National Trust, it was accessible by car, but only just. The track, dropping down into a beautiful wooded valley, was fairly rough, with three or four gates to open on the way. Even today, though the road is now good, the feeling of remoteness and of utter seclusion has not been sacrificed, and suddenly to find ourselves confronted with this venerable moated manor house is to experience a sensation of timelessness. The moat was probably not intended for defence but rather to keep out marauding animals. The house was originally H-shaped but the left-hand wing vanished long ago. The original roof would certainly have been thatch. Now most of it is tiled, but on the right there are some grand sandstone slates. The centre, as in almost every sizeable medieval house, contains the chief apartment, the hall, with windows that go right up to the roof. It is very simple inside, but far more comfortable now than when it was first built. Then the floor would probably only have been of beaten earth, and the hearth for the fire would have been in the centre of the room; the smoke would have had to find its way out as best it could. There would certainly have been no window glass: that was a luxury in 1400. Here they would in all probability have only had wooden shutters. There was also no sanitation at all. But anyone who was still living in a house built in 1400 and who did not want to alter it considerably would, surely, be certifiable. . . .

One of the special delights of Lower Brockhampton is the detached gatehouse, which was added towards the end of the fifteenth century. This has various refinements not much to be seen on the house itself; some of its timbers, for example, are delicately moulded, and all the oak studs (as the vertical members are called) are closely spaced, which always looks better in my view. The fact that the roof of the gatehouse is wholly of heavy sandstone slates is a sure indication of the strength and soundness of the structure. This little building has a

jetty – that is to say, an overhanging upper storey. Jetties are quite common in timber-framed construction, and the structural reason for them I have discussed in some detail elsewhere.* What is not nearly so usual is to find the projection on all four sides. Another feature, seen on the wing of the house too, is the barge-boards running down the edges of the gables. Their purpose was to mask the ends of the roof-rafters but, as so often in the Middle Ages, a useful structural member would be given an attractive decorative form. The pair on the north side of the gatehouse, facing away from the prevailing wind, are somewhat worn but original. The other pair, like those on the house itself, were skilfully renewed by the National Trust in 1952.

The infilling of timber-framed buildings was originally wattle and daub: that is to say, withes or flexible twigs, usually of unbarked hazel or ash, against which were pressed, on both sides, layers of wet clay or mud, often mixed with chopped straw or cow-hair to make it adhere better. Later, starting in about the fifteenth century, the wattles gave place to laths, which were long flat strips of wood – commonly riven oak or beech – fixed on with nails, and covered with properly made lime plaster, which was of course much smoother. Nowadays, alas, the infilling is all too liable to be renewed with a mixture containing far too much cement. A good lime plaster should consist of nine parts sand to two parts lime to not more than one part cement.

In the West of England much of the oak framing is now black and many people love our 'black and white' buildings, but most, if not all, of them have looked like that only since the Victorian period. My own preference is for the natural wood colour such as can be seen at Lower Brockhampton; in East Anglia and the five south-eastern counties, the other principal area for timber-framed houses, the preservation of the natural colour of the oak has always been the normal practice. It is a pleasure to observe that in recent years a certain amount of 'de-blacking' has been going on in the West, as on the Reader's House and the Feathers Hotel at Ludlow.

The roofing material for these buildings, mud as well as timber-framed, was nearly always, in country districts, thatch; this was usually of straw, sometimes of heather, and only in favoured areas – principally Norfolk – of reed. As no thatched roof endures for as much as a hundred years, it is obvious

*See *The Pattern of English Building* (Faber, 1972), pp. 310-312, 315.

Herstmonceux castle, Sussex (now the Royal Observatory). A country house rather than a fortress, showing brick used on a large scale.

that no medieval thatching survives, but I suspect that some of it may have been rather rough and ready. Nowadays, on the other hand, English thatching, whether in reed or in long wheat-straw, is undoubtedly the best in the world.

In towns, however, because of the fire danger, there was a strong preference for baked clay tiles, a form of roofing which had been used in England even in Roman times. In London, as early as 1212, thatch was prohibited; roofs, it was laid down, had to be of tiles, stone slates, wooden shingles or lead. So this introduces another important building material: baked clay, shaped into tiles and also, of course, into bricks.

If we accept the fact that Roman bricks, so called, are really more like large tiles, it is curious to find that tile-manufacture preceded brick-making in England by over a thousand years. There were virtually no native bricks before those to be seen at

Little Wenham Hall, a small fortified house near Ipswich, built about 1275; and England has no wholly brick houses older than the fifteenth century. But from then onwards there are some lovely examples. Herstmonceux Castle in Sussex (now the Royal Observatory) was built, really as a country house, by Sir Roger de Fiennes, an old soldier. He had fought for Henry V at Agincourt, so was able, about 1440, to secure the royal licence to 'crenellate and machicolate', which he did in great style.

In the early days of brickmaking, they did not know how to control with any degree of accuracy the temperature of their kilns. This was aesthetically no disadvantage. It meant that some of the bricks were more burnt than others, and so we find a slight colour modulation over the surface which enhances the richness of the whole. Some are pinker, some redder, and a few are grey. Later, and especially in the Victorian period, bricks could be

Two Norman castles: 1 Rochester, with one of the finest keeps. 2 Richmond, Yorkshire, with probably the oldest of all Great Halls.

made by machinery that were all absolutely identical in colour, in texture, and also in size. This renders possible a precise uniformity which, however valuable from the practical standpoint, can be extremely boring to look at.

During the same years that Herstmonceux was being built in Sussex another, even grander, brick house was going up far away to the North: Tattershall Castle. And go up it certainly did, so high that its tower can be seen for miles, over the flat fields of Lincolnshire. This is only part of a much larger house, the rest of which has vanished. Neither the great hall nor the kitchen was in the tower, which did not contain a chapel either. England had seen nothing like this since the days of the great Norman keeps, which may well have inspired it, although in design and character it is something entirely different. In an increasingly showy age, this was a magnificent piece of ostentation. It was the creation of a very proud, showy man, Ralph the third Baron Cromwell, Treasurer of England for ten years under Henry VI. A modest fortified house had occupied the site since 1231, which Cromwell had inherited; nothing else, surely, could explain why he built so

large a house for himself on this unattractive site. For he also held land in Nottinghamshire and in Derbyshire, where in fact he built another fine house, South Wingfield Manor, which is now much more of a ruin than Tattershall.

Within the tower, the stairs and stair-rail are of stone, and so are the four fine chimney-pieces, which were ripped out about 1911 and very nearly sold to America. It was Lord Curzon who, at the very last moment, rescued them from the dock-side at Tilbury and had them restored to the building which he had just bought, and which in 1925 he bequeathed to the National Trust. But there is plenty of enrichment in carved brick too, notably at the vaults. The tower ceased to be inhabited after 1692 and became ruinous. The floors fell in and have all been renewed, and so have the roof, the battlements, the chimneys and all the window-glass. But many of the dark, slightly brownish red bricks are original, so have endured for well over 500 years. For the tower alone they needed 322,000 of them, and we know where they were made: nine miles away, at Edlington Moor.

Tattershall Castle is certainly the most arresting

3 *Tattershall castle, Lincolnshire, from the east. Like Herstmonceux, this is of brick, and was once part of a much larger house.*

example of brick architecture in England before Wolsey's Hampton Court. What is surprising is to find this material chosen at all here, at this date, in preference to stone. There are parts of England, like East Anglia, which have very little stone, but this is not the case in Lincolnshire. In 1440 Cromwell began building the church; for that Ancaster limestone was floated in flat barges down the little river Slea, from Wilsford, a distance of about twenty miles. It would have been so easy to have used stone, and moreover one of the finest building stones in England, for the castle too. Stone was certainly a labour to quarry and to work, and stonemasons were deservedly among the most highly paid of the medieval craftsmen. But one cannot think that cost would have been a deciding factor with Cromwell. Why he preferred brick remains, in fact, something of a mystery.

For our medieval builders the cheapest stones were those which did not need to be quarried; and in some places they just lay about on the land, or on the sea-shore, waiting to be picked up and used. There were flints, for example, lying everywhere in the fields of the chalk country, and cartloads could

be gathered for the asking; the farmers, then as now, were thankful to be relieved of them. There were also water-washed flint pebbles on the beaches where the chalk reached the sea. There were lumps of volcanic rock in the Lake District, brought down into the valleys by glaciers during the Ice Age (which ended only ten thousand years ago) and easily gathered from the fields and the becks. There were moorstone – lumps of granite on the moors of Devon and Cornwall – and slate, scattered as scree below every rock-face. And on the downs and heaths of southern England there were those strange sandstone boulders known as sarsens, or grey wethers – apparently because in places they looked like flocks of sleeping sheep. All these could be used for rough building with the minimum of cutting; and they were, especially for walls.

But it was the much less hard and far more numerous limestones and sandstones, all sedimentary rocks, which were the great gift to the builders. How amazing it is that in our small island we have almost every kind of useful building stone that exists: even, on the island of Iona, marble, which would otherwise be the one important stone that we

Cathedral cities: Durham and York have overrun their former defences – 1, a Castle at Durham, and 2, city walls at York.

lack. It is no matter for surprise, therefore, that almost all the important buildings of the Middle Ages in England were of stone. And among the many kinds of stone that were employed, the most important of all was the Jurassic Limestone (oolite and lias) which stretches across England in a great ogee curve from Portland Bill to the Cleveland Hills of Yorkshire. Ancaster has already been mentioned: this was but one of a long string of famous quarries which yielded the material for cathedrals, abbeys and parish churches, castles, town walls, bridges, and some houses, all through the period under review.

Worked stone was nevertheless a sign of affluence, and if it had to be brought from a distance, it could indeed prove very expensive. But both for strength and for status, it was much the most desirable building material. With the strange exception of Cromwell at Tattershall, the leading men before Wolsey called for stone almost as a matter of course. In Norman times most of them inhabited stone castles, the visible evidence of the authority of a new ruling class. Later these were either enlarged and adapted for more civilised living, like Warwick and Kenilworth, Warkworth and Ludlow (to mention only a few), or were resorted to only in times of emergency. Almost all of them were 'slighted' at the time of the Civil War, so our castles are today without exception either ruins or restorations.

By world standards, however, Britain was not a very important country for castle-building. We were also late starters. There were no stone castles here when the Normans invaded, which is one reason why the Conquest was so rapidly effected. Between 1066 and 1100 the Normans would appear to have built about eighty-five castles, of which all but half a dozen continued at first to be of earth and timber only. Most of these were rebuilt in stone during the twelfth century. One of the finest was Rochester, which had been granted by the King to the Archbishop of Canterbury. It was he who, in the 1130s, rebuilt the keep in Kentish ragstone, with dressings (mostly gone now) of Caen stone brought across from Normandy, and made it the tallest keep in England: 125 feet to the top of the turrets. This five-storeyed tower is so massive (70 feet square) that there were two rooms, not one, as was usual, on each floor. In the very centre can still be seen a vitally necessary and important feature: the well shaft. This ran up the whole height of the building. Admirably sited on a hill above the Medway, with all its four corner-turrets intact, Rochester Castle still looks attractive.

Another Norman castle which still makes a strong visual impact is Conisborough in Yorkshire. Here the tower keep, built about 1170, was, for purposes of greater security, not square but circular, with six tall buttress-towers projecting at regular intervals from the central core which contained

3 *The Jew's house, at Lincoln: built about 1180, and a rare stone-built house in what was still a town of timber-framed buildings.*

the rooms. Unhappily the battlements here have gone, but the stonework, in the local magnesian limestone, is excellent. The site is the top of a natural mound about 175 feet high. Less than a century ago it was still remote and romantic. Today the appeal is one of poignant contrast with its workaday surroundings.

Apart from their churches it is in these tower-keeps, all stone built, that the architectural legacy of the Normans is seen at its best. Still travelling North, we come to Richmond, where the Castle has a fine hill-top site with a sheer drop on three sides. Only on the fourth, facing the town, was it vulnerable, so the keep went up over the entrance gate. At Durham the keep was not built until the fourteenth century, when one of the Bishops decided that it was necessary, as a defence against the Scots. This one is octagonal, and stands splendidly on its artificial mound. Today it is part of the University.

Townsmen also had their stone walls and gates. These were much less imposing in England than on the continent of Europe or in Asia, but thirty-seven of the leading forty English towns in 1377 were walled, as we know from the poll tax records for that year. The best surviving example is York, where some stretches of the walls stand on lofty earthworks. The stone, for walls and gates, is the same as at Conisborough, that white magnesian limestone which could be brought here quite easily in barges from the neighbourhood of Tadcaster. At

Canterbury good stone was not so readily available, so the walls were for the most part of flint; but here too long sections, rebuilt in the late fourteenth and fifteenth centuries, have survived. The West Gate, dating from *c.*1380, was built, like Rochester castle, of Kentish ragstone, a cretaceous limestone. Erected beside a narrow channel of the Stour, over which there was once a drawbridge, nothing could be more effective than this splendid gate for keeping heavy lorries outside the city centre.

Yet within these walled cities almost every house was timber-framed and thatched. The so-called Jew's house at Lincoln, built about 1180 and among the oldest inhabited houses in England, was a rare exception in this respect. In a troubled world a walled town no doubt seemed to offer the best guarantee of personal safety. Nevertheless, there was in England no strong tradition of town-dwelling. A few towns, like Winchester and Canterbury, survived from Roman times to serve as capitals of petty Kingdoms, Winchester of Wessex, Canterbury of Kent, while London, the largest town in Roman Britain, maintained its primacy. But in the twelfth century nineteen people out of every twenty were still engaged in agriculture. Their Anglo-Saxon ancestors had been farmers, hungry for land; that was why they had come. So they tended to settle in scattered agricultural communities or in small villages. Most of the English villages, but hardly any of the towns, are of Saxon origin.

1 *Stokesay castle, in Shropshire, from the south-west.* 2 *The magnificent interior of the tithe barn at Bradford-on-Avon in Wiltshire.*

Another legacy from Roman times was the network of roads. Most of the roads in medieval England were extremely bad, and many places were completely inaccessible in winter except on horseback; but Roman roads like Watling Street and Ermine Street and Fosse Way survived as main traffic arteries, which were sometimes crowded with travellers, with merchants, and, as we know from Chaucer, with pilgrims.

Bridges were often timber-built, but it is evident from the number which have survived that, owing partly to the initiative and goodwill of wealthy abbeys, stone bridges were not uncommon. With their cutwaters, and in some cases moulded arches, these bridges must have been a delight to the eye. The rare survivors still are. Perhaps the least changed of any is at Standlake in Oxfordshire, at the point where the Windrush flows into the Thames. After six centuries it is still called Newbridge.

It was the abbeys and priories which were also largely responsible for the erection of some magnificent barns of which, miraculously, quite a number remain. A grand example is the tithe barn at Bradford-on-Avon in Wiltshire, once owned by the nunnery of Shaftesbury and now maintained by the Department of the Environment. This is of local stone with beautiful stone slates, and within there is a fine arch-braced roof with no fewer than three tiers of wind-braces to either side. It is 168 feet long and 33 feet wide, and probably dates from the early part of the fourteenth century. They were known as tithe barns because they were built to receive the tithes, the tenth part of the produce of their tenants' farms, to which these ecclesiastical landlords were by law entitled.

But whereas the King, the nobles and the Church could pay to build in stone, even when it might be necessary to transport it from a considerable distance, very few others could afford this before the end of the fourteenth century, and to do so it was certainly necessary for the stone to be readily available locally. One of the earliest English stone houses is Stokesay Castle in Shropshire, constructed of hard Silurian limestone from just across the valley. Dating probably from the 1270s, this house was not built to be defended, even though the Welsh were less than twenty miles away. There were always big windows facing towards Wales. The

1 *Bodiam, Sussex, a country house in castle form.* 2 *Grevel's house, Chipping Campden, a rich man's town house completed about 1400.*

house was bought in 1281 by John de Ludlow, a clothier; and it was his son Laurence who, ten years later, secured from the King the 'licence to crenellate' which enabled him to add curtain walls (since removed) and the tower at the south end. He also constructed the moat. But it still remained virtually indefensible. Laurence de Ludlow, an up-and-coming lawyer who later secured a knighthood, made out that he converted Stokesay into a castle because he was afraid of the Welsh; but by this time Edward I had put an end to Welsh militancy. My own belief is that he did it because then, as now, a castle was a very good address.*

At Bodiam, a century later, it was much the same story. Admittedly the French raid on Rye in 1377 and on Winchelsea three years later had made people in East Sussex a little jittery; but Bodiam, which is among the most picturesque of all our castles and displays to perfection the beauty of Wealden sandstone, here used in very large blocks, cannot be taken very seriously as a piece of military architecture. (Here too there is a good-sized hall window facing outwards.) It was, like Herstmonceux, a country house built in castle form; and here again the builder was an old soldier, Sir Edward Dalyngrigge, who had fought for Edward III at Crécy. It

* The half-timbered gatehouse is a delightful addition made not earlier than the Elizabethan period.

was in the North of England, in Northumberland, Cumberland and Westmorland, that the aspect of defence, against the marauding Scots, really was important. In those counties an entirely different kind of house appeared: the pele tower. Dozens of them survive, looking dour and forbidding. For these people life was much more difficult.

In 1348–9 came the horrifying experience of the Black Death, when about a third of the entire population was wiped out in eighteen months. As a result, there was a grave shortage of labour; and it was this that gave many landowners the idea of turning over to sheep farming. At first the wool was sold, mainly to Flanders. But presently we started weaving our own cloth, and then shipping became another source of revenue. Wool is a recurrent theme in England all through the later Middle Ages. Nearly every county had lands that were good for pasture, so prosperity was widely distributed. But it was where there was plenty of good building stone available locally, as in the Cotswolds, that the numbers of stone houses started multiplying. The money that paid for them nearly all came from sheep. It is as a symbol of what for centuries was to be the principal key to our prosperity that to this day the Lord Chancellor sits upon a woolsack.

If I were asked to name the small English town which gives me the greatest pleasure of any, with

3 *Great Chalfield manor, Wiltshire, the north front. The hall which fills the centre of the house is flanked by richly carved oriels.*

scarcely one false note from end to end, my choice would be Chipping Campden in Gloucestershire. It is still a joy despite the motor vehicles. Almost the entire town is built of a beautiful golden-brown oolite from the Westington quarry up the hill, little more than a mile away. Of course not many of the existing houses are medieval, but one that is singularly unspoiled is the house of William Grevel, completed about 1400. He was, in his day, the richest and most famous wool merchant in the Cotswolds, but he was content to build his house along the main street: there is a garden at the back. Although mainly of rubblestone, the bay window is something very different, with moulded and carved stonework of fine quality; the roof has limestone slates, rich in texture. It is not surprising that in regions less favoured than the Cotswolds, stone long remained a splendid status symbol, a sign of affluence.

Whereas William Grevel was content to have his house in the town, some eighty years later another rich clothier, Thomas Tropenell, chose rather to build his in the country. This was at Great Chalfield in Wiltshire; the property is yet another that is now in the ownership of the National Trust. It is in the heart of the limestone country, and as at Chipping Campden everything is in the local stone. The walls are of rubblestone, now plentifully lichened; the

dressings are of the finest ashlar. The stone, which came from Hazelbury above Box, is one of the group known generically as Bath stone. Then there is the lovely stone roof, with the sizes of the slates again carefully graded, as always until the nineteenth century. Half a dozen large carved finials provide a final flourish. Outside the court-yard is a stretch of water – spotted flycatchers now nest in the reeds and bulrushes – that was not a moat but part of a leat, made by diverting a stream half a mile away to obtain water for driving a mill wheel, which still survives. Nearly facing the house is the small church, which is nominally the parish church of Great Chalfield but in fact the chapel of the estate.

The centre of the house, as in Lower Brockhampton and many others, is occupied by the hall, which rises through two storeys. Here the people who worked on the estate had their meals and here some of them, I dare say, dossed down on straw palliasses. Along the cove of the ceiling run scrolls bearing Tropenell's motto, which, roughly translated, means 'Farming pays'! The family ate in the dining-room to the right of the entrance, and from upstairs could look down into the hall through masks of carved stone with wide-open eyes. Over the dining-room is the most important bedroom in the house, with some little pieces of original

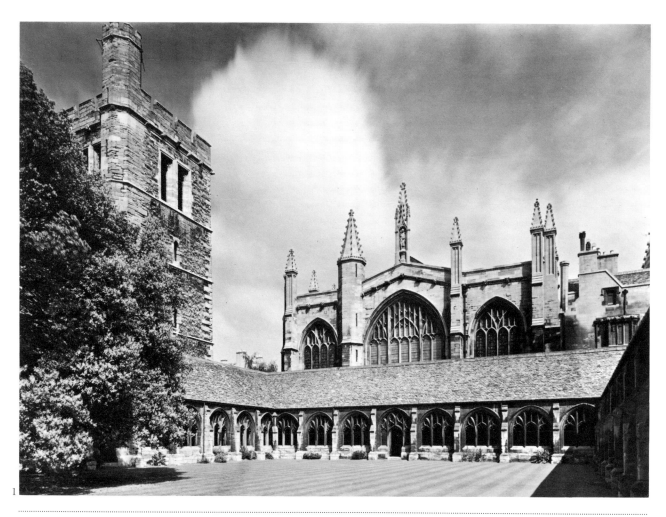

1 New College, Oxford. The chapel rising above the cloisters, with the Founder's bell-tower, dating from about 1400. 2 The chapel interior.

fifteenth-century glass surviving in one of the windows of the oriel. The lovely roof, arch-braced and with wind braces too, is a renewal, but a good one.

Even today Great Chalfield is still remote. Five hundred years ago, this manor had to be completely self-supporting. So it had its pastures, its arable land and its barns, its dairy and its brewhouse, and behind the house, at a lower level, although now in decay, are the fish stews, fed by the stream from a sluice. But what of the inhabitants of a house such as this, and many others like it? We see them occasionally in paintings – in the old dining-room at Great Chalfield is a portrait which may be of Tropenell himself – and we glimpse them on brasses or from the effigies on their tombs. But with a few exceptions it is very difficult to get to know them as individuals. We know that most of them lived in the country all the year round. They were lively people with a fondness for music, for poetry and for songs. The normal squire hunted, fought when required, and served as a Justice of the Peace: for, then as

now, that was the Crown's way of getting justice dispensed on the cheap. By the fifteenth century most people of this class could read and write, but if the family threw up a literary lad, it was very likely that he would go up to Oxford or Cambridge, and probable that he would take holy orders.

Why Oxford and Cambridge should have become the homes of our two most famous universities no one can be sure, but the story goes back, in the case of Cambridge, to 1231, when the university was recognised in a writ of Henry III. At Oxford there were already students in Henry II's time – in 1167. Neither town welcomed hordes of students, usually poor and sometimes undisciplined, and constant quarrels ensued. The colleges originally came into being as halls of residence, first for the teaching staff and before long for students too, who needed protection from the rapacity of landlords. By the end of the thirteenth century Cambridge had one college, Peterhouse, while Oxford already had three: Uni-

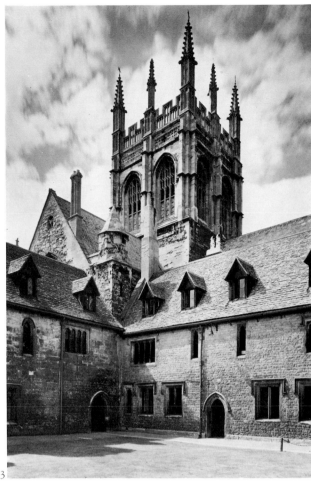

3 The chapel tower of Merton College, Oxford, seen from Mob Quad. This was begun in 1304 and is the oldest quadrangle in Oxford.

versity, Balliol and Merton. These were not sufficient to accommodate all the students, but at least they were a beginning. And fortunately for the growth of the two universities, before long it became quite the thing for rich ecclesiastics, bachelors without direct heirs, to use part of their resources for the endowment of colleges.

Merton College, Oxford, was the first at either university to be officially recognised (in 1274) by the grant of a charter and statutes. Walter de Merton, the founder, was Lord Chancellor under Henry III. The most prominent building is the chapel, which was planned on so grand a scale that it was never finished. The choir was built in 1294, in the early Decorated style. The ante-chapel, a big transept, was not added until the beginning of the fifteenth century and the nave was never built at all because it was not needed. In 1451 they added the splendid tower. Though a little low, it is the finest example of tower design at either university. And, needless to say, it is of stone, like almost every

Oxford university or college building before the Victorians built Keble College. The stone employed at Oxford in the Middle Ages came from Taynton near Burford, whence it was floated down the Windrush into the Thames at Newbridge. The medieval master masons were too good judges of stone to allow themselves to be tempted by the soft limestone of Headington, just up the hill above the city and therefore much more accessible and cheaper. Later builders thought they knew better, an error which has in recent years cost the University millions of pounds to correct.

From the outset three buildings were regarded as essential to every college: a chapel, a hall and a library. At Merton the library dates from 1378. It fills two sides of the Mob Quad, started soon after 1300. Although most of the windows are later, this is the oldest quadrangle in Oxford. A library was of course indispensable; it was the only way that students could get hold of books. For it must be remembered that there were no printed books until

1 The Gatehouse, St John's College, Cambridge. 2 The Divinity School, Oxford: begun about 1420, the vault added some sixty years later.

William Caxton produced his first one, in England, in 1477. Before that, every book had to be hand-written and for some time after remained a luxury. Books were therefore so precious that they were chained to the shelves. At Merton every important book continued to be chained until 1792. Two chains, with a rod and lock, are still preserved, to show how the whole library must once have looked.

Merton, however, grew piecemeal, so its plan is confused. New College, by contrast, was planned from its foundation. Its founder was William of Wykeham, Lord Chancellor under Richard II. He was also Bishop of Winchester and founded Winchester College, the first great English school. So well built were both his foundations that large parts of the original buildings still survive.

New College was conceived on a scale without parallel at the time. The chapel and hall occupy the whole of one side of the Great Quad, both very lofty and built back to back. This arrangement works very well, and other Oxford colleges copied it. The chapel is T-shaped, like Merton's, and the ante-chapel still has most of its beautiful late-fourteenth-century stained glass. Beyond are the cloisters, an abode of solitude and peace because luckily they lead nowhere. They were originally intended as a burial ground for the Fellows, but happily there are no gravestones. In the college garden there is still a long stretch of the thirteenth-century city wall.

Before the advent of the Tudors, two more Oxford colleges had been founded by great

Queens' College, Cambridge: 3 The Cloister Court, with the Hall and timber-framed President's Lodge. 4 The Front Court – in brick.

ecclesiastics who had once been undergraduates at New College, and at both can be seen the New College arrangement of hall and chapel back to back. The founder of All Souls (1437) was Henry Chichele, Archbishop of Canterbury, and of Magdalen (1475) William Waynflete from Lincolnshire, who like William of Wykeham became both Bishop of Winchester and Lord Chancellor. The Tower of Magdalen College, marvellously sited on a curve at the end of the High Street, is famous; most of it is rough and plain, so that the eye is not well prepared for the topmost stage, but the crown is one of Oxford's glories.

Another is the exactly contemporary Divinity School, the earliest university (as distinct from college) building of any size or importance. It was begun about 1420, but not vaulted for another sixty years. We know the name of the architect, although in his own time the word architect would not have been used: William Orchard was then known as a master mason. The vault was a sublime extravagance. It is properly described, like the even more brilliant one over the choir of Oxford cathedral which was to follow it, as a pendant lierne vault. There is a profusion of carved bosses and delicious little figures on the pendants and at the springing points of the main transverse arches. The weight of these pendants can be imagined, and so can the marvellous skill required not only to carve them out of two of the component stones of each arch but to calculate the size and strength of the buttresses needed to counteract the thrust. These pendants, and the abundance of other ornamentation, perform no function. They are there simply for the joy of having them. It is certainly a pity that the vault is not higher, which was impossible because Duke Humphrey of Gloucester's library – part of the Bodleian – was upstairs; but at least there is the compensation that the carved enrichments here can be seen a good deal more easily than in most other buildings with rich vaults.

At Cambridge the oldest surviving quadrangle is the Old Court at Corpus Christi College, finished about 1377; but to get the best idea of what a late-medieval college looked like the one to visit is Queens'. Cambridge is a long way from any good building stone, and here in the Front Court the material is brick. The hall is in the favourite place, between the first two courts. The cosy, domestic-looking character of some of the Cambridge colleges, by contrast with Oxford's, has often been remarked on, and at Queens' it is still more apparent in the second, or Cloister, Court. This is also largely brick, but the north side, containing on the upper floor a typical mid-sixteenth-century long gallery, is timber-framed, which is a great surprise here. Architecturally the finest feature of this college is the great gatehouse of 1448, a striking piece of early brickwork. These gatehouses, no doubt originally associated with fortification but erected at this date mainly for ceremonial purposes, are a feature in which Cambridge easily surpasses her rival. Trinity College has two of them, while St John's has one that is more beautiful than either. Erected in 1510–16, this is again of red brick, but with a lavish outburst of heraldic carving in stone on its outer face. There is also, under the archway of this splendid college frontispiece, a fan vault.

King's College has the grandest building at either University: the Chapel, a masterpiece both outside and in, and incredibly bold in scale. Owing to two long interruptions for political reasons, this chapel took a long time to build: begun by Henry VI in 1446, it was not completed until 1515, and the windows only about 1530. The name of the architect is known: John Wastell, a genius whose name ought to be as familiar to Englishmen as Christopher Wren's, but, alas, is not. He was also responsible for the great central tower of Canterbury Cathedral, and almost certainly for the retro-choir at Peterborough. With its vast windows, this chapel of King's shows the Gothic structural system

carried to its logical conclusion, with the biggest and boldest of all the fan vaults. The stained glass, however confused in design, is truly sumptuous in colour. This chapel was started with magnesian limestone from Yorkshire and finished with oolitic limestone from Northamptonshire. Both these excellent materials had been in use for centuries, particularly for churches.

The churches constitute far and away the most numerous surviving buildings of the Middle Ages. For in those days the Church dominated men's lives in a way that is probably difficult for most people even to imagine today. That domination has gone, went indeed long ago; but the visual evidence of it is still there. Happily for the cause of art, England still has a good many towns, and, it would be no exaggeration to say, thousands of villages, in which the cathedral, abbey, priory or parish church presides over the scene, and helps to bestow upon each place its individual character.

Even in Norman times the churches were generally built of stone, which sometimes had to be transported under difficulties from a considerable distance. Long before the end of the Middle Ages, the achievements of the stonemasons were to become one of the great glories of our civilisation. As builders, the Anglo-Saxons were neither ambitious nor accomplished. But the Normans were. In relation to a total English population of only one and a half millions at the Conquest and not much over two at the end of the twelfth century – less, that is, than the population of Birmingham today – some of the abbey and cathedral churches were designed on a really prodigious scale.

Among the most splendid of the Norman abbeys was Tewkesbury, which was built of Cotswold limestone. Like most of the abbeys located in towns – Tewkesbury is of course an ancient place on the Severn – this one was Benedictine. At the Dissolution of the Monasteries, the citizens of Tewkesbury, who worshipped in the nave, were so proud of their church that, to their eternal honour, they raised £453, which was a very large sum in those days, to buy the choir and transepts from the King. Apart from the cloisters and nearly all the monastic buildings, only the Lady Chapel, at the centre of the east end, was lost. The other chapels surrounding the polygonal east end make a memorable impression, and for England a very unusual one. All this

King's College Chapel, Cambridge, which was completed in 1515, shows the Gothic structural system carried to its logical conclusion.

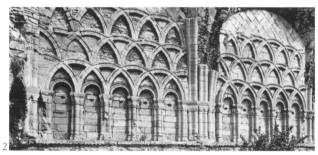

Much Wenlock, Shropshire: 1, The Prior's Lodge, with its roof of sandstone flags, and 2, Arcading from the Priory Chapter House.

part of the church dates from the fourteenth century. The special delight is the gorgeous lierne vault over the choir.

How strange to most of us must seem the idea of spending one's whole life in a monastery. It should, however, be remembered not only that the Middle Ages were a time of faith, a time when it was much easier to believe than it is for many of us today; it should also be realised that this was a period of harsh living, and of great personal insecurity. So, if you were the sort of person who cared for beautiful things, for music and for reading, and who hated roistering and loathed fighting, and had not perhaps much taste for sports either, your one chance of having even a tolerably pleasant life was to enter a monastery. This is not to suggest that even a monk's life in, say, the twelfth or thirteenth centuries was at

all agreeable by more recent standards. He had no personal property, no sexual relations (officially, at least), no freedom; he had to obey implicitly his abbot or prior. Poverty, chastity, obedience: those were his three strict obligations. He had to praise God in an unheated church eight times in every twenty-four hours (including the middle of the night). Often he had also to work in the fields. But at least his life was quiet, for even in a town the monastery was within walls and only accessible through a gatehouse, and there was time for meditation. To some men and women this was worth a great deal.

Great Malvern Priory was a dependency of Westminster Abbey. The fifteenth-century tower, of Worcestershire New Red sandstone, is one of our loveliest. Here too, in 1541, the parishioners had the courage and good sense to buy the church,

4

Tewkesbury Abbey, Gloucestershire: 3 The Norman nave, with the later lierne vaulting, and the apse beyond. 4 The view from the east.

and for once they got a bargain: the price was exactly £20.

The first of the great Benedictine abbeys of the Normans in the North was Selby, founded only three years after the Conquest. Again only the church has survived, and that has had a chequered history; but it is the whole church, and a fine sight it makes since the recent cleaning of the exterior. The stone is that nearly white magnesian limestone which we have already encountered at York and at Conisborough. The abbey shines like a beacon today in the centre of what is otherwise an undistinguished town built almost entirely of brick. All honour, once again, to those citizens of Selby who, more than four hundred years ago, saved it.

At the Dissolution three of the Benedictine abbeys, Peterborough, Gloucester and Chester,

escaped destruction by being turned into cathedrals. So did two Augustinian foundations, Bristol and Oxford. But the Cistercians liked to build their abbeys in remote places, deep in the country: Fountains, Rievaulx, Furness, Netley, Tintern – these are some of the best known. On their once lonely sites the Cistercian abbeys, at the Dissolution, were less likely to be pillaged for their stone; but they nearly all became ruinous, for unless there happened to be someone who was prepared to make a private house out of the domestic quarters, there was usually nobody to buy them. It should perhaps be added that the widespread appeal of the best of our ruined abbeys is something adventitious, which has really nothing to do with the Middle Ages. It is a facet of our deep-seated love of the Picturesque.

It has, moreover, to be admitted that time has not

1 *The little Norman church at Kilpeck in Herefordshire, consisting of nave, smaller chancel and an apse, which is just visible to the right.*

always obliged. Much Wenlock in Shropshire was one of the Cluniac houses. At the Dissolution the church gradually fell into decay; but unfortunately the bits that survive do not make a picturesque composition, a fact much bemoaned by Georgian aesthetes. Here therefore we walk round as amateurs of architecture, enjoying the remains of the Norman chapter house, with its triple tiers of intersecting arcading (pl. 2, p.28), and then the singularly pure Early English design of the South transept. But the principal sight at Much Wenlock is the house which the Prior built for himself just before 1500. Even allowing for the obligation, sometimes irksome no doubt, of offering hospitality to distinguished travellers, one cannot fail to be struck by the imposing character of the residences of some of the abbots and priors of the later Middle Ages. At Forde Abbey in Dorset, a very fine example in Ham Hill stone, the Abbot's tower and great hall were later incorporated into a splendid country house. At St Osyth's in Essex the Prior's residence was the gatehouse, perhaps the finest example of stone and flint flushwork in the country. At Thornton in Lincolnshire the Abbot also inhabited the gatehouse, a towering structure in brick, remotely situated and very little known, and now unfortunately a ruin. At Much Wenlock, on the other hand, the Prior's Lodge has been lived in continuously for nearly five hundred years, and is still a very comfortable home. The walls are of a somewhat friable New Red sandstone from Alverley beside the Severn, but the Hoar Edge flags which cover the roof, from a quarry some eight miles to the west, are of Ordovician

sandstone, one of the oldest and most durable that we have. Three-quarters of them are still the original ones first fixed in position with oak pegs when the house was built. This roof is a splendid sight.

Towards the end of the Middle Ages there can be little doubt that some of the monks grew lax, and one can picture the abbots and priors with their excellent amenities, ample tables and large staffs of servants, all paid for by the establishment. But in addition to the copying of manuscripts, a very valuable service before the invention of printing, which was long performed almost exclusively by monastic scribes, the monasteries fulfilled some of the most essential secular needs of the age. They led the country in estate management, water supply, drainage, forestry, farming and the breeding of cattle, sheep, and (at Jervaulx in Yorkshire) horses. Those situated in the country were, like the manors, usually self-supporting. In addition to growing corn they bred fish, kept bees and made wine. Probably, all the same, there were too many of them. At the Dissolution there were nearly four hundred monasteries, another hundred nunneries and over two hundred houses of Augustinian Canons.

Yet, considered numerically, that was nothing compared with the parish churches. In England alone there are still over eighteen thousand of these, of which well over half are listed as buildings of architectural or historical interest, and something like two thousand are Grade A. It is a mighty inheritance. Travelling around England, one is seldom out of sight of a church for long. In places four, and from hill-tops more, can be seen in a single *coup d'oeil*.

The wealth of sculptural detail at Kilpeck includes 2, the carving of a warrior on the door-shaft, and 3, an unusually fine corbel table.

The only Anglo-Saxon churches to have survived are small and much restored. Many were of wood, so, with one odd exception at Greensted-by-Ongar in Essex, have inevitably vanished. The Normans bequeathed a fine legacy of parish churches, including some, like Castor near Peterborough, surprisingly large. Here the great feature is the central tower, with its profuse surface enrichment, for which the local Barnack limestone was an ideal material. The parapet and spire were added in the fourteenth century. But even when the Norman churches were quite modest in scale, they might none the less be lavishly adorned with carvings. The most enjoyable of the small Norman churches is at Kilpeck in Herefordshire. It is a sequestered spot. Adjacent are the remains of a small motte and bailey castle, but there is no village. One could not have a better illustration of the way in which the builders made use of whatever material was at hand locally. Here, as at Tintern Abbey later, it was Old Red sandstone. The lumps vary greatly in size, so there are no courses and, of necessity, plenty of mortar, which has had to be renewed. But Kilpeck church is a model of sensitive, tactful restoration. The appeal of the rubblestone walls depends primarily upon their rough, peasant texture and their colour, a mixture of pink, buff and grey. The better quality stone used for the buttresses, door jambs and so on, is pink. Running all the way round the church, just under the eaves, is what is known as a corbel table. It is alive with carvings. Those responsible appear to have been free to follow their own fancies. Pagan and Christian subjects seem to jostle each other.

They are bubbling with vitality, and, using the simplest imaginable means, they are remarkably expressive.

The extraordinary carvings on the South door were long protected by a porch; thanks to this and to the hardness of the stone they are so well preserved that it is difficult to believe that they are over eight hundred years old. The outer jambs have, on both sides, coiled serpents biting each other's tails – facing downwards on the left and upwards on the right. The shafts are even more surprising, especially on the left, where among scrolled foliage we find two warriors with peaked hats and tight-fitting trousers, for which it would be very hard to find a parallel. The capital above them has a lion and a fantastic monster with a coiled tail; opposite is a head which looks as if it had been originally conceived in metal, with conventionalised vine-sprigs emerging from its mouth. If this sculpture had any symbolical meaning, it eludes us, but how little it matters. (Incidentally, I have at last used the word 'sculpture', but no one in the twelfth century would have called the creators of these astonishing works of imagination sculptors. They were just stone-masons, assigned to carving.)

A standard plan for village churches in the twelfth century was to have three compartments, nave, chancel and apse, of diminishing size; and that is exactly what we find at Kilpeck. The special delight inside is the chancel arch, with another most original feature. In the angles, instead of columns, we find on each side three apostles, standing one above the other. They are by quite a different hand from

1 Tiverton church: the south chapel given by John Greenway. 2 Cullompton: the fan vaulted south aisle was given by John Lane.

the corbels or the doorway. All have haloes, but only one can be identified: St Peter, with a huge key of heaven slung across his shoulder. This is far more convincing than a more naturalistic treatment would have been.

The parish churches, unlike the abbeys, were built to serve communal needs. Among these the urge to worship no doubt came first, but, especially in the later Middle Ages, it was not by any means the only motive. Human incentives, then as now, were mixed. If piety was one factor, another was certainly fear – fear of what was unknown and not understood.

To most people in those days, when there was practically no education, the concept of Hell was a very real one. All through history, lack of education and credulousness have gone hand in hand. There was certainly, among the church-builders, an element of taking out an insurance policy with the Almighty, as it were. But there were other motives, too, which had little to do with religion: rivalries between the great ecclesiastics, for example, and between rich merchants. Take Cullompton, for instance: a stately town church, the finest in Devon

after Exeter Cathedral. It is mostly built of a delightful plum-coloured local sandstone. But on the south side there is an additional aisle, lavishly adorned with carvings which have decayed badly, because the chalky limestone from Beer, the nearest available, is too soft to withstand the English climate. This was all the gift, in 1525–6, of a local wool merchant, John Lane. Why did he build on this scale, adding to a big church which was already amply large enough for the town? The answer rests a few miles away in the neighbouring town of Tiverton. There, in 1517, one John Greenway added on to the parish church a porch and a two-bay chapel which is a great piece of ostentation. He had made his money in the export trade as well as in wool, and the exterior is plentifully adorned with ships, as well as with his monogram many times repeated and an inscription recording his gift. So across the hill at Cullompton John Lane had been given his cue: he was not going to be outdone. He built not just a chapel but a whole aisle, and inside, with a gesture of splendid opulence, he gave it a fan vault.

There were also rivalries between neighbouring towns and even villages. A medieval contract might

Stone, wood, brick and glass. 1 Kilpeck. 2 A shop front, Lavenham. 3 A vault, Tatershall castle and 4 The Deans Eye, Lincoln

1 The tithe barn at Bradford-on-Avon in local stone. 2 The Gatehouse, Saint Osyth's priory; flushwork of flints and stone tracery.

Long Melford church from the south-east: a brilliant example of flushwork – split flints are used with slabs of dressed limestone.

even stipulate that the new building was to be at least as good as another one which would be mentioned. A church in one town – Higham Ferrers in Northamptonshire may serve as an example – would set a standard for the district: something in fact to live up to. Nearby places like Finedon and, rather later, Rushden had to build stately churches too. The money for nearly all the larger churches came from sheep; at first from the sale of wool, and then, after looms had been set up on a big scale in the fifteenth century, from the sale of cloth and from operating the ships in which much of it was exported.

The materials available locally also played a most important part in shaping the character of parish churches in various regions. For example, nearly all our round towers occur in Norfolk and Suffolk. The explanation is simple: in these two counties flint was usually the only stone they had, and with flint, unlike blocks of masonry, angles are difficult, whereas rounded forms are easy. The development of flushwork, that is, the use of split flint in conjunction with thin slabs of dressed limestone to form decorative patterns, monograms, inscriptions and

so on, brilliantly seen at Long Melford, was equally a by-product of the East Anglian dependence on flint. The absence of elaborate mouldings and of any undercutting in those Cornish and Devon churches which are built of granite is, again, because this stone does not lend itself to such refinements. It is certainly no coincidence that many of our finest parish churches are situated on or very near to the limestone belt.

It would seem to have been a combination of what could be achieved with the stone of a particular area and what can only be termed local fashion which accounts for one feature or another being sometimes singled out for specially lavish treatment. In East Anglia, where there were ample resources, the flint was so intractable that, although the churches were frequently large, their architecture is often somewhat bleak: for flint on its own, to put it mildly, lacks elegance. What is sometimes glorious is the woodwork – the benches, the screens, and especially, as at Woolpit in Suffolk, the angel roofs – on which attention was specially concentrated. The difficulty of working the hard granites and slates of the South-West may largely

Local materials: 1 Wood, for the Angel roof of Wymondham church, Norfolk. 2 Oolitic limestone for the tower of Evercreech, Somerset.

account for the profusion of woodcarving in that part of the country too. On the other hand the exquisite limestones of southern and eastern Somerset, not too hard to carve when first quarried but becoming harder on exposure to the atmosphere, rendered possible, in village after village as well as in a few towns, the erection of some of the most beautiful towers ever built: Evercreech and Leigh-on-Mendip are but two of at least a dozen which for students of tower design prove endlessly fascinating. Even the latest of these Somerset towers are all well over four centuries old, but in the clean country air most of them are still in a splendid state of preservation.

Spires in this part of England are comparatively scarce, but if we travel up the limestone belt into Northamptonshire, Rutland, Lincolnshire and eastern Yorkshire the picture changes completely: we enter the great region for spire-building. There are parts of Lincolnshire, particularly in Holland,

the Fen country, where the spires are focal points in landscapes certainly badly in need of them. Spires were useless. Towers were needed to house the bells. But spires do nothing but point to heaven and – if they are well designed – add to our delight. Most of the stone spires of the north-eastern Midlands date from the fourteenth century. Aesthetically the central spires are no doubt the best, especially when, as at Gosberton in Lincolnshire, the church is cruciform. This church presides over its village with confident authority. At Patrington, in what is now called Humberside but what for me will always be the East Riding, one of the loveliest village churches in England is again cruciform. The tremendous central spire, visible for miles across the flat fields of Holderness, is absolutely plain but plunges towards the sky through a rich Gothic diadem. It is easy here to appreciate the aesthetic value of lofty roofs and pointed gables in relation to the spire form.

Yorkshire was a major wool county long before

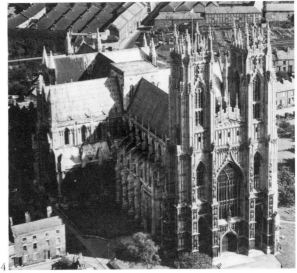

Yorkshire churches: 3 Patrington, 4 Beverley Minster and 5 Hedon – all built of magnesian limestone brought by water from near Tadcaster.

the Industrial Revolution, and the great churches to the north of the Ouse and the Humber make a memorable group: Hemingbrough with another rapier spire, Howden, Hedon and Hull all with proud, lofty towers. These churches are probably among the least known in the country to the general public, but very undeservedly so. For all of them the principal material was again that magnesian limestone, brought without any great difficulty by water from the quarries near Tadcaster – although Hull's Holy Trinity is memorable for having been partly built of brick: this is indeed much the earliest example in the country (*c.*1315–45) of the employment of brick for a major church. Not far away is Beverley, never a big town yet with not one, but two, medieval churches of the front rank. St Mary has a finely designed central tower, a Tudor replacement of the original one which collapsed during a service in 1520. St John, always known as the Minster, is the finest non-cathedral church in

England after Westminster Abbey, and would certainly be a cathedral now if it had been more fortunate in its geographical situation. This great church displays the Early English style, the first phase of our native Gothic, with exceptional purity, while its Perpendicular west front, with twin towers, is also masterly.

Churches like these, and thousands more, in the later Middle Ages highly competent technically apart altogether from their obvious aesthetic qualities, would alone suffice to disprove the ridiculous view, specially current in the eighteenth century, that medieval architecture was a sort of folk art, lacking any intellectual base. Applied to the cathedrals, such a viewpoint becomes still more incomprehensible. Yet, faced with having to choose from among the English cathedrals, where does one go?

When I was invited to prepare the television programme which provided the point of departure

Vicars' Close, Wells: houses built for the minor clergy of the Cathedral in 1348. The most perfect surviving medieval street in England.

for this essay, I was told that, for practical and economic reasons, it would only be possible to light the whole interior of one cathedral, and that it was for me to make the choice. Of course I considered Canterbury, a cathedral which can offer delights ranging from the best display of Norman sculpture in England, on the capitals of the crypt, through our finest collection of stained glass, to the noblest of all our medieval towers, a design by John Wastell (as already mentioned) of great subtlety, and faultless in its proportions. At Salisbury, it is true, the problem of internal lighting did not arise, for the special thrills are outside: the most miraculous of all medieval spires and, in stone, the loftiest (404 feet), soaring above what has rightly been termed England's loveliest lawn – though this we owe not to the Middle Ages but to the ingenuity of James Wyatt, who drained it, and to the invention about 1830 of the mowing machine; and the grandest of all our cloisters, even though this cathedral was

never monastic. It is evident that these cathedral builders were so charmed with the idea of having cloisters that, whenever funds permitted, they could not resist adding them, even where there were no monks to use them and they were therefore purely ornamental. And why not?

Wells is another cathedral which it was specially difficult to pass over, for internally, despite the artistic misfortune of the 'scissor arches', this is among the most poetic of our cathedral churches, especially in the retro-choir and in the chapter house, an astonishing architectural creation, with a tierceron vault dependent upon a central pier from which spring no fewer than thirty-two ribs. Only the wonderful vault of Exeter is comparable. But there is a great deal to be relished here externally too. The setting, with the Mendip hills providing the back-cloth, is unforgettable. And, close to, another immense lawn stretches out before our most memorable west front. This is in many respects a

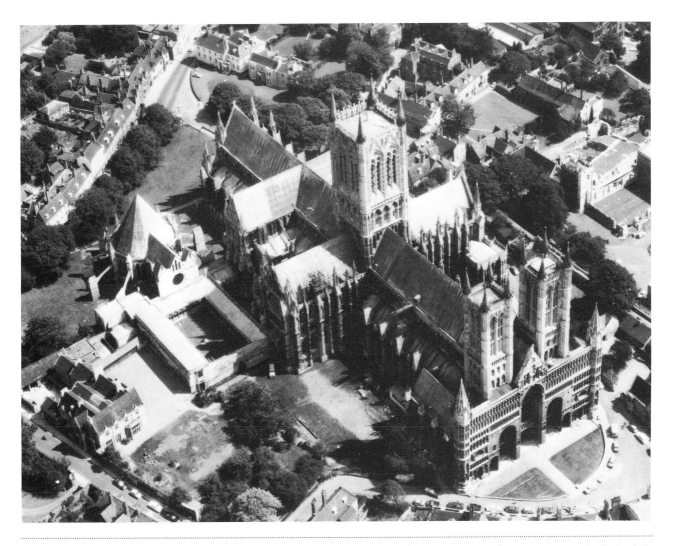

Lincoln Cathedral from the air. The projections at right angles to the main axis – there are two pairs of transepts – are typically English.

classical design, strongly articulated both horizontally and vertically: a façade of immense authority, despite the excessively small doors.

The central tower is outstanding even in Somerset, a song of praise to the glories of English stone: in this case from nearby Doulting. From this point of vantage we can look down on the Bishop's Palace, with its crenellated walls and moat – still an impressive reminder of the power and grandeur of these medieval prelates, even though the great hall is unhappily in ruins. In the other direction is the Vicars' Close, built in 1348, and easily the most perfect medieval street that survives. The vicars were minor clergy who had apparently been having rather too gay a time after dark. So one of the Bishops decided to erect a street of special houses, forty-two of them, for these men, the gate of which could be (and was) locked each evening. They had their own hall and chapel, and access to the cathedral over a bridge known as the Chain Gate.

Then Durham, bestraddling its rocky peninsula high above the Wear: not merely the finest Norman cathedral in England, but the leading Romanesque cathedral in the world. Is not Durham the best of them all? I recall a conversation long ago, when I was hardly more than a boy, with a family friend who had a deep knowledge of our cathedrals and churches and loved them dearly: it was H. Munro Cautley, known for two remarkable books on the churches of Suffolk and Norfolk. I said to him: I suppose Durham *is* our finest cathedral, isn't it? He paused, then shook his head gravely. 'No,' he said, 'no. Durham is superb, but you can see it in two hours. You can't see Lincoln in a week.' He was right. However much time one has at Lincoln, it is never sufficient, because apart from the big things there is an almost infinite number of beautiful and fascinating details.

So Lincoln it was. In medieval times this was the mother church of the largest diocese in England except York, a diocese that stretched from the Humber to the Thames. Today the diocese is much smaller, but in and around the city itself the vast cathedral, on top of its hill, is so dominating as to become, for some, almost an obsession. You cannot look up without seeing it. Even if you want to forget it, it is impossible. Now that it is floodlit every evening (except during Lent), that is even true after dark too. From some angles it hangs lantern-like in the sky, an object of enchantment.

Essentially Lincoln is a creation of the thirteenth century, with some fourteenth-century additions. For an English cathedral it has unusual unity of style. An aerial view reveals that, in contrast to the Gothic cathedrals of France, this is a building with a series of projections stepping out at right angles to the principal axis. Thus the overall effect is not of concentration but of diffusion: a characteristic not only of Lincoln but of English Gothic churches in general. Typical of England is the second pair of transepts to the east of the main ones. Their roofs have a pitch of 73°, which is prodigiously steep.

The limestone came from quarries only a short distance north of the cathedral. They were long ago worked out and have since been built over, but the Dean and Chapter own another, about a mile along Ermine Street, which is still able to supply virtually all the stone that is needed each year for repairs.

It comes as a surprise to learn that the present cathedral originated in an earthquake. Yet, we read in Holinshed, the Tudor chronicler, that

in 1185, on the Monday in the week before Easter, chanced a sore earthquake through all parts of the land, such . . . as . . . had not been heard of in England since the beginning of the world . . . Stone houses were overthrown, and the great church of Lincoln was rent from the top downwards.

Everything had to be taken down and rebuilt except the West end. The front is still partly Norman, and has some lively Norman sculpture too. But in the 1240s it was altered, not altogether to its artistic advantage, when the broad and lofty screen was added.

The central tower collapsed again in 1238. It was then rebuilt in a truly lordly fashion. When it was finished in 1311, it was easily the highest tower in England (271 feet), and the richest: the cathedral's crowning glory. All the three towers once carried wooden spires, the west pair until as late as 1807. The central spire is said to have soared to 525 feet; if this is true, it was the highest in Europe. But in 1548, in a great storm, it came down for ever.

When I visit a cathedral I usually go in first, because that is the way they were conceived – like modern buildings, from the inside outwards, in contrast to the Greek temples and to nearly all Renaissance and Classical buildings. The view from the gallery high up inside the West end is thrilling even though the internal proportions are not perfect. Perhaps the most striking feature of the design is the immense linear elaboration of the stonework. The outer walls are enriched, all the way round the church, with trefoiled blind arcading, above which the lancet windows are all set within shafted frames, while at the clerestory there is yet more shafting in front of the windows. Much of this shafting is of Purbeck marble, which is not a true marble but a dark oolitic limestone that will take a polish. This was brought in ships all the way from Dorset and up the Witham from Boston. In the choir aisles, however, some of the dark shafts are not of Purbeck but Alwalton marble, from beside the Nene near Peterborough. The fossils in this limestone are not of freshwater snails, as in Purbeck, but of oysters, and it has proved decidedly the more durable of the two. There can be no doubt that the thirteenth-century architects liked the contrasts in colour and texture between this dark, shiny stone and the pale yellow of the Lincoln limestone. They handled their polychromatic schemes with the utmost assurance, as is specially well seen in the doorways, dating from about 1250, by which the choir aisles are entered from the transepts. These are among the most exquisite designs of the Middle Ages. The contrasts are manifold: not only between light and dark stone, but also between plain and intricate surfaces, and between abstract and naturalistic decoration. They are conceptions of the most fastidious exactitude, perfect in their proportions.

The first parts of the cathedral to be rebuilt after the earthquake were the ritual choir and eastern transepts, which display Lincoln's earliest Gothic. The Bishop at this time was Hugh of Avalon, a remarkable Frenchman who had been appointed to the see by Henry II and who, twenty years after his death in 1200, was canonised. The shrine of a saint could be a valuable source of revenue in the Middle Ages: Canterbury was already deriving handsome revenues from the offerings of pilgrims

The West towers of Lincoln Cathedral seen from the roof of the South transept: until 1807 they were topped by wooden spires.

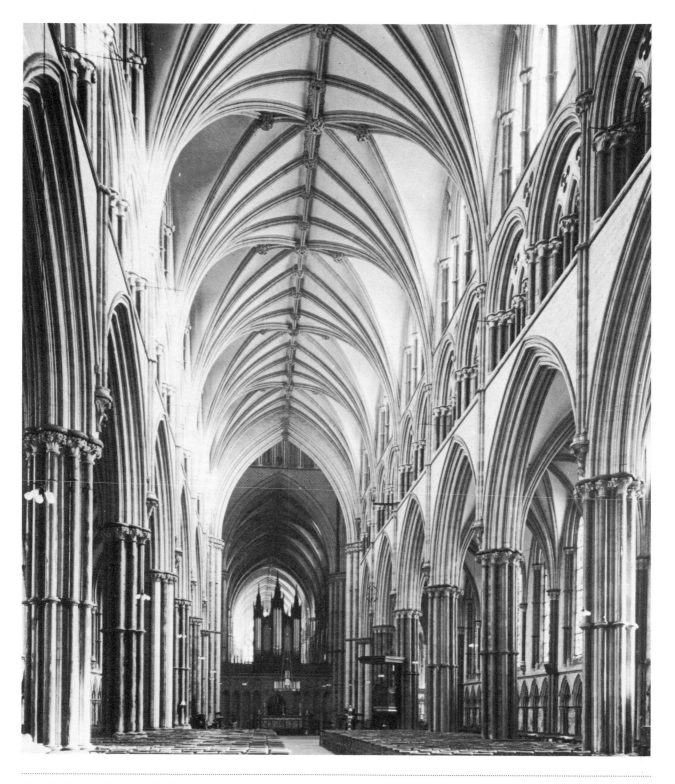

Lincoln Cathedral: the Nave looking east. The dark shafts of Purbeck marble make a contrast with the paler yellow of the Lincoln limestone.

at the shrine of Becket. It was to accommodate the shrine of St Hugh that Lincoln decided, in 1255, to erect a retro-choir. The Angel Choir, as it is always called, took twenty-four years to build, and is the most sumptuous part of the whole building, an exuberant example of that phase of our Gothic architecture which we call Early Decorated. The angels, though, are not the best sculptures here.

Several of the bosses of the aisle vaults are finer.

By the early fourteenth century money was pouring into Lincoln not only from pilgrims at the shrine of St Hugh, but also from the widespread sale of indulgences. Wrongdoers in the Middle Ages had to do penance, but if they contributed generously to the building works they could be granted an indulgence, remitting say forty days of an eighty-

Lincoln, the south transept: the round window, with leaf-like tracery, is known as the Bishop's Eye and was inserted about 1325.

day penance. It will be remembered that the sale of indulgences, which was certainly open to great abuse, was one of Luther's particular grievances. But at least they made it possible for more and more works to be undertaken for the cathedrals: among them, at Lincoln, was the pulpitum or choir screen, another of the marvels. To either side of the central opening are canopied niches, and most of the sur-faces are diapered with rosettes. Specially delicate are the buttresses which separate them, with triplets of tiny gables at three different levels, and a profusion of flowers, leaves and animals. The statuettes half-way up were originally female saints, but their heads were smashed off by the Puritans, and when, about 1765, James Essex gave them new ones, he turned them into Bishops! The whole of this screen

Details of Lincoln: 1 A misericord, 2 North-choir aisle doorway. 3 Carving in the Angel choir. 4 Arcading from south-east transept.

was undoubtedly coloured, and indeed traces of the original colours remain. Personally, though, I do not regret their disappearance. The stone is too beautiful to be hidden under paint.

The superb display of wood carving in the choir has survived with relatively little damage. The stalls date from the 1370s. There are carvings everywhere, including sixty-two misericords of exceptionally high quality, each carved out of a single block of oak. Yet the quantity of oak used ornamentally was minute compared with what was needed for structural purposes. The great oak beams of the cathedral roof, if placed end to end, would stretch for over four miles. A vast amount of other wood

was also required. Much of it is still in excellent condition.

Very different has been the fate of the windows. Lincoln once had magnificent early-thirteenth-century stained glass; but the losses have been far worse even than at Canterbury. Especially in 1644, appalling damage was done by the fanatical and vandalistic Cromwellian soldiers. About 1788 what was left was collected together and inserted, unhappily without much skill, into eight windows. The rose window in the north transept known as 'the Dean's Eye', which goes back to *c*.1210, has more of its original glass than any other. But the finest window at Lincoln is 'the Bishop's Eye' in the

5, 6, 7 Roof bosses: two old men, a man fighting a monster and a queen playing with a dog. 8 Capitals from doorway to south choir aisle.

south transept, inserted *c.*1325: another gorgeous extravagance. It is not a rose but a tracery design based upon two huge leaves, which is unique. This lovely window shimmers with rich colour, and it is all old glass; yet it is nothing but fragments collected together about 1788 from the battered remains of many windows in different parts of the building.

We do not know who designed Lincoln, but this cannot diminish our enjoyment. As with all the medieval cathedrals, many minds and hands contributed, and some of them were obviously consummate artists. After 1400 there was really nothing more to be done here, yet the Middle Ages were far from over. No more new cathedrals were built, no more abbeys, no more priories. But for the parish churches, as we have seen, some of the most exciting years still lay ahead, and this was even truer of secular and domestic architecture. When, at the Reformation, what we call the Middle Ages came to an end, it was not, architecturally nor in any other way, to a dying close; there was simply a change of direction. It cost us, within a century or so, nearly all our stained glass, the destruction of which is surely the greatest calamity that has befallen art in Britain. But, especially when we remember how small was the population that created it, the architectural legacy is a wonder.

Henry VII's chapel, Westminster Abbey, with the tomb by Torrigiano. The engraving of Nonsuch Palace is from John Speed's map of Surrey.

2

ROY STRONG

A NEW HEAVEN, A NEW EARTH

The glorious fan-vaulting of Henry VII's Chapel in Westminster Abbey is one of the triumphs of late medieval English architecture. It hangs like frosted lace above a wall of glass and yet when we look beneath at the tomb of the man who built it and that of his wife, Elizabeth of York, we sense something different, we recognise what we think of as renaissance as against middle ages. They are no longer formalised images of a king and a queen but portraits of human beings with definite physical features and characteristics. No one in 1485 could have guessed that the victory at Bosworth Field of Henry Tudor over Richard III was to herald the long peace of the Tudor and Elizabethan ages, the end of the Wars of the Roses. This truly was to be England's Golden Age. Its greatest symbol lies in one of the side chapels, Henry's granddaughter, Elizabeth Tudor. People still come to lay flowers on her tomb. She seems to symbolise across the centuries the proudest moment of our history. That mask-like face, and beautiful long fingers clasping orb and sceptre, conjure up an heroic age: Drake sailed around the world, Raleigh founded Virginia, the English navy defeated the great Armada of Spain and in the forty-five years of peace she brought her people there occurred the most astounding flowering of the arts we have ever known. Above all men built as never before.

Compton Wynyates, not far from Banbury in Warwickshire, gives one a good idea of the earliest domestic architecture produced by the new Tudor age. The house as we see it today is still largely the work of Edmund Compton and his son, William.

Westminster Abbey: 1 Effigies of Henry VII and his wife Elizabeth of York on the tomb. 2 The effigy of his grand-daughter, Elizabeth Tudor.

William was First Gentleman of the Bedchamber to Henry VIII and rose so high in the King's favour that he was actually allowed to wear his hat in the royal presence. Henry VIII as a young man loaded William with honours and came, together with his first wife, Katherine of Aragon, to stay at Compton Wynyates. Over the entrance porch there are the royal arms and the motto in Latin 'My Lord King Henry VIII' with the Beaufort portcullis, badge of his grandmother, the Lady Margaret, Countess of Richmond, on the right and, on the left, badges of the Queen, the ship of Castile, a sheaf of arrows and a pomegranate. As a house, however, it is still basically a castle, more so then than now because it was encircled by a moat.

Looking at the outside one is struck by the domesticity of it, soft rose red brick, windows cautiously letting light stream in but also giving a view out for those within, battlements reduced to decorative crenellation and a forest of twisted chimneys marking the new luxury of the fireplace. It is still a medieval house, the style and details are Gothic, but it is an incidental Gothicism and not a structural one. In spite of all its picturesque rambling beauty, evocative of romance, it is a style from which the guts has evaporated.

Compton Wynyates is a courtyard house and to build courtyards is to think in castle-like terms, of layers of defence which could be shut off one from another against invaders. But the courtyard windows are something new, both in their number and in their size. Being on the interior of the house, they assume a dominance beyond those on the exterior. In a corner of the courtyard at one end of the great hall there is a huge oriel window running from floor to ceiling. Under the impact of French Renaissance architecture this late-medieval detail, here caught in its infancy, was to multiply until, by the close of Elizabeth's reign, houses were to be almost nothing except arrangements of bay windows.

3

3 *Compton Wynyates, in Warwickshire, was still basically a castle – it looked more so when the moat had not been replaced by lawns.*

Within there is the great hall (or Big Hall, as it is known at Compton Wynyates), which was built in Sir William Compton's time. The disposition of the rooms is characteristic of an early Tudor great house. There is a screen at one end, a feature which lasted until well into the next century, and the one at Compton Wynyates is of typical early Tudor linenfold panelling (wood carved to look like the folds in carefully arranged fabric). Above it, there is a gallery, another feature which continues into the Stuart age. The present fireplace is a recent insertion, for up until the close of the Victorian period the fire was lit, as it had been in the Middle Ages, in the centre of the floor and the smoke made its way up through the beams of the roof and out of a hole in the centre of the ceiling. In the hall the family and their retainers ate together, the family seated at one end on a dais, and the retainers at long tables stretching the length of the room. It is an arrangement followed in any Oxford or Cambridge college,

and in the Inns of Court, to this day. Throughout the Tudor and early Stuart periods the hall remained the focal point of any palace or house. It bridged the sphere of master and servant. Through the doors in the screen there lay the world of the household offices, the kitchen, the pantry, the brewhouse, the laundry, the bakery, the stables. Through the door at the dais end lay the domain of the family. As the century progressed more and more rooms were created for their use until the hall gradually took on the character it has today, that of an axial space and waiting room. In the 1520s all this lay in the future. The creation of these new rooms reflected a move away from the communal living of the Middle Ages and a desire for privacy. In architectural terms it expressed the hierarchical structure of the household where every single person had his or her place, not only socially, but in terms of building.

Compton Wynyates distils the quintessence of

Compton Wynyates. The size of windows looking onto the courtyard (1,2) was something new. 3 The hall with its screen and gallery.

what we know as Early Tudor. How remote it seems from the achievements of Renaissance Italy! The hall took its present form in 1512. It reminds us that England was on the cultural fringes of Northern Europe, far away from the dramatic developments of High Renaissance Florence or Rome. There, under the impact of the rediscovery of classical antiquity and of Renaissance neoplatonic philosophy, architecture was held to be a science which involved complex principles that integrated each part of a building, inside as well as out, into one and the same system of mathematical ratios. This basic tenet was not to reach England until a century later in the dynamic figure of Inigo Jones.

Henry VIII was certainly not particularly interested in such subtleties. What he required

George Clifford third Earl of Cumberland from a miniature by Nicholas Hilliard

Hilliard's miniature of Queen Elizabeth 1, and details of embroideries and plaster work from Hardwick.

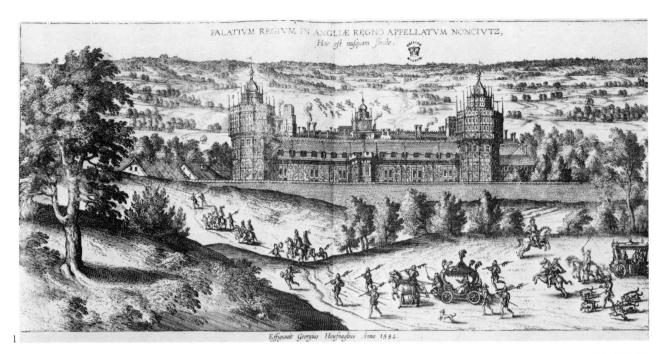

Two of Henry VIII's palaces: 1 Nonsuch, from Joris Hoefnagel's engraving. 2 A drawing of Whitehall Palace by Anthonis Wyngaerde.

above all was an architectural style which would provide a setting of the utmost magnificence and splendour for the Crown. In this he followed the patterns of patronage and opulent taste laid down by his great minister, Cardinal Wolsey, whose palaces of Hampton Court and York House he took over when Wolsey fell from power. Next to George IV Henry VIII was the greatest builder ever to sit on the throne of England. Two of his most fantastic palaces, Whitehall and Nonsuch, have vanished, and we can now only gain some impression of these extravagances from old prints and drawings, but

their impact on Tudor, and subsequently on Elizabethan, architecture was, we know, considerable. Of his palaces Hampton Court alone has survived. Here a majestic gateway enhances the approach to the King, roundels depicting Roman Emperors inset into it remind visitors of the tribute owed to Caesar, spacious courtyards succeed one another to establish distance and eventual climax in the royal presence. It is a building massed to pierce the skyline from afar with a riot of twisted chimneys, vanes, turrets and cupolas. In Hampton Court we see the palace and the country house begin to

Hampton Court. 2 The entrance, flanked by (1 and 3) busts of Roman Emperors. 4 Wolsey's closet: typical early Tudor palace decoration.

take over the assertiveness on the landscape once reserved for the cathedral, the abbey and the church.

Hampton Court speaks of the Tudor peace. The windows are not defensive. They are meant to let in light and give the inmates views of pleasure gardens. There is a new interplay between interior and exterior. Unfortunately no complete interior survives so that we must always add with the eye of imagination to what remains. Walls were lined with linenfold panelling, above this they were encircled by a painted frieze and over all hung a ceiling of gilded plaster. In the Great Hall at Hampton Court, the setting for banquets, revelry, and spectacle, the

The Great Hall at Hampton Court: the roof is gilded and the walls are hung with tapestries. It was the setting for banquets and revels.

hammer beam roof is covered with gold leaf and the walls are hung with tapestry. We only have to add to the scene the people of Holbein's portraits, nobles, ladies and gentlemen, ablaze with brilliant fabrics and swagged with jewels, and we have the essence of what Henry VIII most sought, *Magnificence*. Magnificence not only to impress his own subjects but the rest of Europe. In all, Hampton Court is the aesthetic expression of the new power of the Tudor Monarchy, born of the greatest upheaval of the century, the Reformation.

Henry's palaces and the great houses of the Elizabethan aristocracy that followed celebrate that power, which came from a revolutionary transfer of control from Church to State. It was a rejection of over five hundred years of Catholic Christianity entailing vast changes in the fabric of English society.

The monasteries were the first to suffer. In the Middle Ages abbeys such as Glastonbury were havens of piety and faith. Thousands of people had found a vocation and a way of life in monastic communities. They worshipped, ate and slept together, they and their employees farmed the land around, they were the earliest form of social service acting as lodging houses for travellers, giving medical aid to the sick and alms to the poor. They were also seats of learning and education. Their buildings and contents represented some of the greatest triumphs of medieval English art. At the opening of the sixteenth century they were in decline but it could have occurred to no one in 1520 that by 1540 they would not even exist. In a period of just five years they were all to be smashed to the ground. As a result of Henry VIII's desire to marry Anne Boleyn, the King was forced to break with the Church of Rome and declare himself Head of the Church of England, more than that, he and his Protestant advisers set about the reform and despoliation of the medieval Church. In 1536 all except the greatest monasteries were dissolved. Three years later even these went under. The monks were driven away, given state pensions or allowed to go abroad. The King's commissioners came and carted off to the Royal Treasury the plate, jewels and rich furnishings. These, melted down, paid for Henry's palace building. The land too passed into the hands of the King and as a result there occurred the greatest change in land ownership since the Norman Conquest. Land soon after passed from the Crown to its new servants cementing them firmly into an alliance, of sovereign and subject, in the interests of the new Protestant faith. These new rich were to be the builders of the arrogant houses of the Elizabethan and Jacobean periods. English creativity in the visual arts ceased abruptly to be mainly ecclesiastical. For the next three hundred and fifty years it was to find its supreme expression in the country house.

Worse was to happen. Catholic Christianity was a faith which expressed its devotion by means of images, statues of the saints, of Our Lady, of Christ on the Cross, stories from the bible and from lives of the saints enshrined in stained glass in church windows or painted in brilliant colours over the walls of both nave and chancel. Ten years after the abbeys and monasteries were destroyed, all this was to go too. Under Henry's son, the boy King Edward VI, England went decisively Protestant and in 1549 an order was issued to empty the churches of all images. In the holocaust which followed everything went, vestments, banners, statues, paintings, relics, all the trappings of late medieval christianity in which liturgy had reached an apogee of splendour. Often these treasures of medieval English art were dragged out into the churchyard or town street and burnt in public. Shiploads of vestments and manuscripts left the country and learning, through the dispersal of libraries, suffered a terrifying blow. Pages from illuminated manuscripts were reported as literally being used by shop owners as wrapping paper. In some areas of England the attack was savage, as we can see to this day in the Lady Chapel at Ely Cathedral where chisels were taken to the bosses which were literally hacked off. (Elizabeth, when she came to the throne in 1558, stopped this wave of destruction but what had not gone by then was to be broken to pieces by Oliver Cromwell's troops in the great Civil War.) Every single person in Tudor society lived through this horrifying experience in which most of what everyone had always taken for granted was suddenly swept away. It was the end of English medieval art, more than that it was the end of the centuries old alliance of Church and Art. Henceforward art became, above all, the servant of an omnipotent State.

And what replaced it? Rycote Chapel near Oxford gives one a very good idea of what it was like to go to church in the reigns of Elizabeth and her successor, James VI of Scotland and I of England. Rycote is a marvellous expression of the blanket solution to the extremes of Catholic and Puritan which was epitomised by the Anglican Church as formulated by Elizabethan and Jacobean divines. The medieval rood screen has been kept, so has the chancel and the altar in the form of the communion table. Some of the pews face that way but others emphatically face the pulpit, reminding us that Protestantism was fundamentally a religion of the word and not of the sacraments. The Latin Mass had gone. There were no more colourful processions and ceremonies, instead the congregation heard the words of the Book of Common Prayer, the Bible in English, the Homilies, and John Foxe's *Acts and Monuments*. They sang psalms and listened to sermons. The walls were whitewashed, sometimes

The interior of Rycote chapel, Oxfordshire, showing the Norris family pew (to the left) and that built for Charles I (to the right).

1 *Two peeresses: Lady Burghley and her daughter. 2 Obelisk of fame with trophies from the Hunsdon tomb in Westminster Abbey.*

they were covered with biblical texts, occasionally the ceiling was painted with a star-spangled unoccupied heaven. In place of the figure of Christ on the Cross flanked by Mary and John, the royal arms were erected over the chancel arch reminding every worshipper that the blessings of true religion rained downwards upon them from the Imperial Crown of England.

Plumb in front of the rood screen at Rycote there are two elaborate pews, one built for King Charles I to sit on, the other, earlier one, for the family who lived in the mansion house a hundred yards away, the Norrises of Rycote. We are looking at a microcosm in building terms of Tudor and Stuart society. This tiny building sums up the social hierarchy of the age: God, His representative on earth, the King, and the new aristocratic and gentry families who were the supporters of this rigid ladder which stretched from earth to heaven. These families were the new dynasties, up and coming ones who had fought with Henry Tudor at Bosworth, and served Henry VIII and his children as officials implement-

ing their revolutionary policies. The close of Elizabeth's reign and the Stuart age saw them become the arms of the new establishment. Sir Henry Norris of Rycote is typical of hundreds of men who carved out careers in the service of the crown. He served Elizabeth as her ambassador in France and his six sons became soldiers who fought bravely for their Queen in the Low Countries, France, and Ireland. His wife was one of Elizabeth's closest women friends. She called Lady Norris her 'Crow' because of her raven black hair, and to Rycote she came on progress. Sir Henry and his wife now lie side by side in the great monument they erected in the north transept of Westminster Abbey. Around them kneel their six sons described as 'a brood of spirited, martial men'. Such tombs too, in their way, celebrate the Tudor triumph of State over Church. In churches up and down the country the new aristocracy and gentry erected these vast pantheons to themselves, placed without any consideration for the medieval buildings they stand in, sited deliberately for all the world to see

Burghley House: 3 The court looking towards the clock tower and hall. 4 The house seen from across the park. 5 The view across the roof.

and marvel at. They trumpet achievement. The faces of the dead are not humble and resigned as they make their pious journey from this world to the next, but satisfied and proud of their success in this life. Obsessed with status symbols – robes and attributes of office, and rich costumes – as only the *nouveaux* could be. Above all these are monuments to family and connexion, some are virtual explosions of coats of arms, actual and mythical, speaking of noble descent and grand alliance. Rows of children kneel in prayer, ensuring a continuance beyond the grave of all that the monument stood for. Careys, Cecils, Knollys, Hattons, Howards, Thynnes and a hundred more such families established themselves as the governing classes of England – a position they were to enjoy until the Reform Bill of 1832 began to strike the death knell of aristocratic privilege. In the second half of the sixteenth century and through into the opulent opening decades of the seventeenth they were the builders of vast palaces. These arose all over England from 1570 onwards, expressing a confidence in

the right to rule, and in the future, unknown to us. Palaces these great houses truly were, for they were conceived from the outset as shrines to receive Gloriana and her court.

Burghley and Hardwick are houses that sum up this prodigality and lust for splendour. Burghley was one of the two country houses built by Elizabeth's great minister William Cecil, Lord Burghley, mostly during the decade 1575 to 1585. It rises out of the landscape like some fantastic town, still working within the visual premises of Hampton Court and Nonsuch with a skyline pierced by a forest of pinnacles, cupolas and spires. It follows them too in still being a courtyard house approached through a massive ceremonial gateway. Burghley is the architectural masterpiece of the middle of the reign – the years leading up to the Armada of 1588. Building fever was to reach its real peak however in the nineties, and to continue unabated to the close of the second decade of the next century.

To this era belongs the greatest glory of

Hardwick Hall. The High Great Chamber, with its tapestries depicting the story of Ulysses hanging below the painted plaster frieze.

Elizabethan architectural creativity, Hardwick Hall in Derbyshire. Built between 1591 and 1597 it is the supreme expression of the palace house and the crowning jewel of the age. As a building it can hold its own against the finest produced by the architects of Renaissance Italy. Like all Tudor and Jacobean houses it is first and foremost a statement by one person, in this case a grasping, difficult woman with indomitable willpower and a peculiar flair and taste in the visual arts: Elizabeth Talbot, Countess of Shrewsbury, known to posterity as 'Bess of Hardwick'. The daughter of an obscure Derbyshire squire she rose over a period of thirty years to be the second lady in the land, next only to Elizabeth herself. Throughout her life Bess had building fever, Hardwick was her last and most remarkable creation. Typically its extravagances were made possible by the money which came her way when her last husband, the Earl of Shrewsbury, from

whom she had been estranged for many years, at last died.

To understand how to look at Hardwick is to understand how to look at almost any of the great Elizabethan and Jacobean houses. In the first place it asks to be seen. It is built on a prominence and visible for miles around. Its crowning balustrade celebrates its owner and her rank, ES – Elizabeth Shrewsbury, and above it is a countess's coronet. Approaching the house from afar one could, at first glance, mistake it for a castle in the form of a rectangular box with four great corner towers. But if indeed it is a castle, it is not like any medieval castle we know, it is instead one of glass. Hardwick expresses the fruits of the Elizabethan peace in terms of light. Nature is tamed by art. The occupants of such houses look out and feel no threats, no fear of marauding armies, nor of hostile nature. Instead they look out upon the earth's surface made

Hardwick Hall, the greatest building of the Elizabethan age – The West front. The E.S. on the balustrade stands for Elizabeth Shrewsbury.

pleasant in the form of gardens and formal walks. Hardwick takes this architectural statement to an extreme unknown in any other building. The windows at the top of the towers, for instance, have no real function, and some windows below actually run right across changes in floor level. Such was Bess's obsession with light and symmetry.

Hardwick is a palace, and Bess probably built it with her grandchild, the Lady Arabella Stuart, whose claim to the throne was seriously being canvassed in the nineties, in mind. The interior is of the utmost magnificence, deliberately designed for splendid ceremonial. It has a great hall as at Compton Wynyates but that is no longer important. By 1590 the really grand rooms are the state and private ones for the family, approached by what was still an architectural novelty, the staircase. The staircase is one of Hardwick's great glories. It unfolds its way dramatically upwards to the state rooms in a way which can only be described as breathtaking. The staircase was the artery leading to the new rooms, but from the outset it can never have been conceived as purely utilitarian. It was carefully articulated to suggest and establish, within the mind of both occupant and visitor, grandeur and distance as the ascent was made towards the royal or aristocratic presence. Up these stairs each day Bess's servants would bear her food in procession. The colourful ritual of the medieval Catholic church was replaced by the secular etiquette of the great house.

The stairs lead to the High Great Chamber which Sir Sacheverell Sitwell once described as 'the most beautiful room, not in England alone, but in the whole of Europe'. This is the most magnificent of the state rooms to which the staircase gives access. They follow a Tudor palace sequence fit to receive a queen, the High Great Chamber is the Presence

---

1 Bess of Hardwick – in old age. She was the greatest needlewoman of her time. 3 and 5 show embroidered cushion covers from Hardwick.

Chamber for formal receptions, beyond lies the Privy Chamber for less formal encounters and beyond even that the Royal Bedchamber. Elizabeth and James never came to Hardwick but such state found vivid expression when Bess's immediate successors sat here beneath a canopy enthroned in splendour as Earl and Countess of Devonshire. These allusions to royalty are developed in the coat of arms of Elizabeth I over the fireplace, with its lion and wyvern supporters, and the marvellous painted plaster frieze by a certain Charles Williams who was specially imported by Bess as being a 'cunning plasterer'. At the end of the room, where Elizabeth would have sat had she come, runs a celebration of her as the chaste goddess of the hunt, Diana. Elizabeth-Diana sits enthroned surrounded by her nymphs, trees symbolic of virtue like the palm grow near her, animals emblematic of virginity such as the elephant gravitate towards her, while the Cavendish supporters, the roebuck, chase away the vicious lion and tiger. How Elizabeth would have loved this celebration of her rule! Below, splendid Brussels tapestries are swagged around. Bess purchased them two years before she began Hardwick and the room was built to fit them.

These tapestries depict the story of Ulysses. By

ANIMI MAGNITVDINE MVLTA PERPESSVS TANDEM A
PVDICA VXORE EXCIPITVR NON SINE NOTICE SIGNO

2 The Staircase at Hardwick leads ceremonially to the state rooms above. 4 Ulysses' return – a tapestry from the High Great Chamber.

reading their story we catch another clue as to how to look at Hardwick. Like Elizabeth I Elizabeth Shrewsbury cast herself into various mythological roles, and Ulysses's virtuous wife, Penelope, was one of them. The only subject picture Bess owned, one still in the house, depicts Penelope, the pious and faithful wife at her loom. She it was who unravelled each night what she had woven during the day to stave off the suitors who sought her hand. In this way she remained constant to her husband until he returned to her. Bess's optimistic idea of her own married life was in this saga given dramatic form and no figure from classical legend could have

better suited a lady famed for her ability with the needle. Penelope indeed recurs in one of the famous wall hangings at Hardwick flanked by Patience and Perseverance, attributes needed more by Bess's husbands than possessed by the lady herself. The other hangings at Hardwick are filled with the figures of other virtuous ladies, Zenobia, Artemesia and Lucretia. Those who saw them knew that it was Bess that they celebrated. These hangings are made up in appliqué from old church vestments. What a marvellous glimpse of the new art rising out of the old! *Opus anglicanum* was one of the glories of medieval English creativity, and embroidery

Hardwick Hall, the Long Gallery. Bess of Hardwick's ultimate extravagance was to hang pictures over the sumptuous tapestries.

became one of the great art forms of the Elizabethan age.

Hardwick was built by the greatest needlewoman of the age. Furniture in Elizabethan houses was sparse, little more than chairs, tables and cupboards, and it is easy to forget that the quintessence of interior decoration consisted of plasterwork, panelling, tapestry and, above all, needlework. This covered upholstery, beds, cushions, curtains and hangings, and was made in rich fabrics – cloth of gold and silver, velvets, damasks, all embroidered and fringed and tasselled with yet more gold and silver. In their pristine glory the state rooms at Hardwick would have glistened and glittered like some enchanted place. At Hardwick the surviving cushion covers alone give us a stunning insight into

this staggering sumptuousness. Like everything else needlework was covered with cryptic images meant to be read by the educated eye.

The Long Gallery, a vast corridor off the state rooms, is perhaps the new room which, above all others, gives expression to Tudor magnificence and opulence. From 1580 onwards no house of any pretension was without one. It became the status symbol of the age. It was, to use a later term, essentially a room of parade, used for walking in: as such it was ideal for festive occasions, for displaying jewel-encrusted costumes to advantage as ladies and gentlemen perambulated its length. The Long Gallery at Hardwick contains something unique in any house I know, a kind of defiant ultimate extravagance: pictures are hung over sumptuous

Lady Dorothy Cary by William Larkin: 'Carpets and rush mats tip upwards beneath the sitter's feet. The figures are placed like dolls in a box.'

tapestries. Icons I would think of them, rather than as pictures in our sense of the word. The painted portrait was relatively new to the Elizabethan age. It gave expression to egocentricity and pride as tombs did in churches. Like them, portraits expressed family achievement, social connexion and patronage. Along the walls of the long gallery hang these votive images, stern-faced Bess with her children and their wives, and the great with whom she claimed friendship and kinship: Burghley, Leicester, the Queen of Scots and, of course, Elizabeth of England, the sun around whom these lesser planets revolved.

In Bess's day the gallery would have been virtually devoid of furniture. Two fireplaces gave warmth to the inmates. Over these are another Elizabethan form of 'portrait', the figures of Justice and of Mercy. Such abstractions of virtue in human form were not conceived purely as arbitrary decoration. They were designed for contemplation, in a sense a secular replacement within the walls of the great house of the statues of Christ and his saints which had once filled the churches. Elizabethan houses are full of such moralities in the form of figures and mottoes. They are part of a lost way of thinking about a building. An Elizabethan would think of Justice when he saw such a figure over the fireplace. He would look at the family portraits in exactly the same way, as images of virtue and vice, human folly and passion. There is something immensely strange and powerful about Elizabethan portraits. They seem hardly human these compilations of hands and face, lace and embroidery, jewels

and rich fabrics. We are immediately made aware that they are superior beings, remote and grand, withdrawn into themselves yet exhibiting their status within the social hierarchy by means of attributes of office and splendour of costume. The picture surface does not open into another world, rather it is governed by its own irrational principles. Carpets and rush mats tip upwards beneath the sitters' feet, chairs stand and curtains are looped at seemingly impossible angles. The figures are placed like dolls in a box, with emblems and inscriptions scattered across the background surface; there is no sense of the ordered nature of pictorial space as evolved by the theorists of Italian Renaissance art. As a result there is a unique fantasy about Elizabethan and Jacobean painting and to let one's eye wander over these brilliant mosaic-like surfaces is to come closest to the visual essence of the age.

And the house joins these portraits: it is itself a huge icon, a portrait in stone of the woman who created it, requiring 'reading' as much as any other visual artefact of the age of Elizabeth. The plan of Hardwick is a square imposed on a Greek Cross doubled. Any educated Elizabethan would have obtained great satisfaction from spotting that this was the 'device' of the house. 'Device' is a key word for Elizabethan architecture. From the 'device' came the building and almost without exception the 'device' came not from the architect but from the patron. Architects as we think of them did not exist in the Tudor and Jacobean periods. Surveyors did, and the greatest of these was a man called Robert Smythson. He was almost certainly responsible for Hardwick but his task would have been to make practical, and orchestrate, the arrogant symmetrical vision or 'device' of the aged Countess. It is an indication of the status of the Surveyor in society that we have no portrait of Smythson, nor is there surviving material which gives us any glimpse of him outside his official role as an organiser of the building of houses. Yet Smythson's career takes us to most of the great houses of Elizabeth's reign. He began, over twenty years before Hardwick, at another great mansion, Longleat in Wiltshire, a house with a complicated building history stretching through the 1560s and 70s. What we now see is the accumulation of several buildings but the final result, which Smythson worked on for Sir Thomas Thynne, made it the seminal building, above every other, for the development of the country house under Elizabeth. Thynne himself was a favourite of Edward VI's Protector, the Duke of Somerset, which takes the story of Longleat and its style back into the middle years of the century and to a group of men, centring on Somerset, who promoted a new more strictly classical style under the impact of influences from France. To this Thynne added a touch of personal idiosyncracy, a delicate multi-

Bolsover, near Chesterfield in Derbyshire. Smythson's last great work and the last great architectural expression of Elizabethan chivalry.

plication of bay windows – a feature derived from French châteaux but now increased so that no less than thirteen great bay windows run the height of the façades of Longleat. The result is a compact angular composition, the direct ancestor of all those shimmering castles of glass that were the glory of Elizabethan architecture. We can see what happened to this initial statement a decade later by looking at Smythson's Wollaton Hall in Nottinghamshire, built for Sir Francis Willoughby, and begun in 1580. It is Longleat again but made more fantastic both by the scrolling and strapwork in the heavy mode of Flemish mannerism and by the crowning touch of inserting the great hall into the centre of the house and lighting it by raising it up like a gigantic lantern above the level of the rest of the building.

Smythson's Longleat and Wollaton tell us a great deal about the ideas that motivated house builders for the next fifty years. Bolsover Castle near Chesterfield, Smythson's last masterpiece begun in 1612, shows him responding to another patron and another set of ideas. This is a fantasy castle. One expects ladies to be imprisoned within it and knights in shining armour to storm the keep and rescue them. As a building it is the supreme and final architectural statement of Elizabethan and Jacobean chivalry. What an irony that in the new hard world of the *nouveaux riches* there was a delib-

erate revival and cult of chivalry! Chivalry in the medieval sense of the word had, of course, gone but it was replaced by a new revivified form, assiduously cultivated by the Tudor dynasty, with sovereign and subject as knight and lady, which was essential for the idealisation of Elizabeth.

An yearely solemne feaste she wontes to hold,
The day that first doth lead the yeare around,
To which all knights of worth and courage bold
Resort to heare of straunge adventures to be told.

These are lines from the greatest poetic epic of the Elizabethan era, Edmund Spenser's *Faerie Queene*, the first part of which was published in 1590. This huge unfinished saga, of Gloriana and her Knights and their struggle against vice and the forces of the Antichrist of Rome, is a handbook to the assumptions of the age. Indirectly it explains a house such as Montacute near Yeovil in Somerset which was built in the last decade of Elizabeth's reign by an up-and-coming young lawyer, Sir Thomas Phellips. Across the main façade are monumental statues of the Nine Worthies, heroes of chivalrous romance, including Charlemagne and King Arthur. Montacute is fairy-tale architecture. Spenser's *Faerie Queene*, written to glorify Gloriana herself, was described by its author as a 'dark conceit'. It is patriotic, romantic, it is protestant and anti-Catholic, it is imbued with all the riches of Renais-

1 *Montacute House, 'the Fairy Queen's castle'. 2–6 Four portrait miniatures and a self portrait (6) by Nicholas Hilliard.*

sance learning and philosophy. Montacute is the Fairy Queen's castle. Its forecourt is a pasteboard castle, the defensive walls have become light and airy balustrading, its castle towers are transformed into garden pavilions or pepper pots of stone scrolling, the whole of it a preface to the main façade over which the knights preside, guarding a shimmering wall of glass, fit to enshrine a goddess.

This house and others like it which went up during the last decade of the sixteenth century and the first decade of the seventeenth century are visual expressions of Elizabethan and Jacobean chivalry. The splendours and rituals of chivalry enhanced the crown. Henry VIII had wished to emulate the Dukes of Burgundy who had set the pace and style for the rest of the courts of Europe in the late fifteenth century by staging gigantic chivalrous spectacles. A more correct visual image of Henry VIII than the brute of Holbein's famous portrait is the golden-haired youth astride a horse wearing fantastic fancy dress as he hurtled along the tiltyard, lance in hand. Such courtly magnificence found its greatest fulfilment in the legendary Field of Cloth of Gold in 1520. Ostensibly a round-table conference between the monarchs of France and England it became the vehicle for vast festivities. A strange castle was erected to house the King, his Queen and his attendants, a fantasy which recalls what was to happen later in Henry's palace of Nonsuch. Henry VIII's daughter became an even greater focus of chivalry in a later revival. So integral was it to the Elizabethan way of thinking that annually, on 17 November, the anniversary of her accession to the throne, a fancy-dress tournament was held in her honour; thus the rites of medieval chivalry were linked with a celebration of the triumph of Protestantism. We catch glimpses of this cult of chivalry in the portraiture of the period. Men are not depicted

as knights in armour only to give them the status of gentlemen, but also because they are champions of the Queen. A portrait of the young Earl of Sussex shows him as the White Knight, a colour complimentary to a Virgin Queen. By his side rests a helmet from the crown of which arise, like the branches of a tree, wings encrusted with jewels. Elizabeth's Champion, the sailor Earl of Cumberland, wears star-studded armour in his miniature by the court artist, Nicholas Hilliard, and the Queen's glove is pinned to his hat. In the next reign Lord Herbert of Cherbury, painted by Hilliard's pupil, Isaac Oliver, reclines by a babbling brook, a melancholy knight seeking the solace of the greenwood tree. This mood of arcadian romance and drama was an essential part of the spirit of the age; to be aware of it is as essential for the understanding of Hardwick or Bolsover as it is for the poetry of Sidney or Shakespeare. It was also promoted by the court as a political principle. We can trace it in the presentation of Elizabeth to her people as the Virgin Queen in countless masques and entertainments.

In spite of the fact that chivalry could cut across the religious barriers of Catholic and Protestant, Tudor and Stuart, England was an absolutist state which did not allow for exceptions. It was not, of course, as intolerant as those on the continent. There were no civil wars, the Anglican umbrella was a pretty capacious one, and a blind eye was turned on those who did not cause trouble. But as the state felt increasingly threatened by the might of Catholic Spain penal laws were introduced involving heavy fines and even imprisonment and death for those who would not conform. Catholics survived, for the majority were loyal to the Queen, but they could not express the faith openly or, if they did, it now had to be in a cryptic language. Traces of this

The Triangular Lodge: an image in stone of a forbidden faith. 1 South-east. 2 North. 3 South-west. Drawings made in 1730 by S. Buck.

frustration of expression can be found in recusant architecture.

The Triangular Lodge at Rushton in Northamptonshire was built by a loyalist Catholic, Sir Thomas Tresham. Lord Burghley regarded him as a first-class subject and Tresham was among the first to offer to defend Elizabeth at the approach of the Spanish Armada. But he was also a devout Catholic convert, which excluded him from office at court, and meant that he had to live on his own estates in Northamptonshire. Tresham managed to express his faith in a remarkable series of esoteric buildings. Before building the Triangular Lodge, he erected in 1584 Lyveden New Build, a garden pavilion in the shape of a cross, with a five-sided window bay bearing the instruments of Christ's passion. The whole structure was once crowned by a lantern, long since gone, which shone out across the countryside reminding one of the Light of the World. Originally it was also surrounded by an elaborate symbolic garden.

The Triangular Lodge continues these themes and the result is one of the most curious buildings in the country. If one knows how to read it one sees that it was, at the time, preaching high treason, yet on the surface it is a harmless celebration in stone of the doctrine of the Trinity. The triangle is the traditional symbol for this and it is followed throughout: it is triangular in shape and the exterior is covered with every form of triangular allusion. It has three floors and there is a typically Elizabethan play on the name Tres-ham, the Latin word for three being *Tres*: his coat of arms is three trefoils.

But what really needs to be studied is the chimney, which arises from the centre of the building (even though the fireplace is in one of the side walls,

4 Entrance to the Lodge: The arms and motto of Sir Thomas Tresham, and mystical numbers, over the doorway. 5 The Lodge today.

a technical triumph serving emblematic emphasis if ever there was one). If we start on one face of the chimney we see the date of the building, 1595; it has the sacred monogram, IHS with a cross, above it and the three nails used on the Cross below. All are enclosed in an octagon and the Latin legend, *esto mihi*, which is a contraction of Psalm XXXI which begins 'Be thou my rock, for an house of defence to save me'. Read aright these and the emblems on the other faces are symbols of the Mass. We can follow them round. On the north side in a square representing the four Evangelists, there is the Lamb of God, with the word *Ecce* (Behold): the opening word of the sentence the priest first speaks when giving communion at Mass (*Ecce Agnus Dei*, Behold the Lamb of God). On the south-west side of the chimney there is Tau ('T') Cross within a chalice, enclosed in a pentagon, which usually signifies sal-

vation. The Latin word on this side is *SALUS* (Salvation), a reference to the words the priest speaks just after he has eaten the Host, and before he drinks from the Chalice, *Calicem salutaris accipiam* (I will take the chalice of salvation). And, needless to say, the T of the Tau Cross stands also for Tresham himself. What an astounding building! It preaches across the countryside the high treason of the banished Roman Catholic Mass. Who at the time would have guessed it?

The Triangular Lodge may seem to us an odd 'device', to use the Elizabethan word, but Tresham's way of thinking is only an extreme instance of the norm for the Tudor and Jacobean periods: it is one virtually lost to us. Although the images of Christ and his saints had been cast out of the churches as so much rubbish, there were others, of Gloriana, for instance, which needed highly educated minds to

1 *Robert Cecil, builder of Hatfield, by John De Critz. 2 Icon of the end of an age: the 'Rainbow Portrait' of Elizabeth by Gheeraerts.*

understand them. One needed to know, when look-ing at the Ermine portrait of Elizabeth at Hatfield House, that the little creature resting on the Queen's sleeve was an ermine, an animal, which, it was believed, would rather die than soil its pure white fur. For the Elizabethans and early Stuarts, under the impact of the fashions and philosophy of the Renaissance, the whole of art and nature, was one vast series of meaningful images intercon-nected by layers of allusion. Take, for example, the work of the artist who epitomises above every other the Elizabethan achievement in painting, the miniaturist, Nicholas Hilliard. It is just as difficult to unravel the meaning of these pale images as of any building. Who is the famous *Young Man Among Roses* and why is he leaning, love-sick, in the midst of a bush of white roses? Who is the Youth who holds a hand let down from heaven and what is the Attic love to which the motto refers. The arts of the period are a riot of vanished meaning: monsters,

mermaids, mythological characters, virtues and vices animate costume, silver, ceramics, jewellery and embroidery. At the time they were meant to be 'read', so were the houses which they adorned. One portrait seems to sum up the whole Elizabethan myth and at the same time usher in a new era, the Rainbow Portrait at Hatfield. It depicts Elizabeth at the age of almost seventy, but her features are rejuvenated to those of a young girl. An assemblage of attributes celebrates the golden age she has brought her people. The crescent moon adorns her headdress alluding to her role as the chaste moon goddess, Diana; virgin pearls are everywhere; a jewelled gauntlet hangs on her ruff reminding us that she is the sovereign of her knights; she clasps a rainbow as the bringer of peace after storms ('No rainbow without the sun' as the motto reads); the serpent of wisdom encircles her sleeve; Fame with its many eyes and ears to see and listen besprinkles her golden cloak, and her bodice is embroidered

3 *The Marble Hall, Hatfield House. Its elaborate decoration is a final fling of Jacobean splendour and shows a style in exuberant decline.*

with spring flowers of the Golden Age she has brought to England. But in 1603 the subject of this apocalyptic vision suddenly vanished. Elizabeth I died and was succeeded by her cousin of Scotland, King James I.

The Rainbow Portrait hangs in the house built by his chief minister, Lord Burghley's son, Robert Cecil, Earl of Salisbury. A new reign brought a new court – extravagant, over-indulgent and vulgar. This last fling of Jacobean splendour is summed up in Hatfield House. The staircase, with its gates to keep the dogs from going upstairs and its florid strapwork and plump cherubs, exemplifies this restless flamboyant style. Above all we find it in the Marble Hall.

Robert Cecil built Hatfield between 1607 and 1612. He was forced to give Theobalds, his father's great house nearby, to the King, who, in return, gave him the old Tudor palace of Hatfield. Within a stone's throw of it Cecil erected a magnificent house. It embodies the triumphant swan song of a

style: here, in its extreme form, it produced images of barbaric, almost nightmare, intensity. Bearded men with breasts, and grotesque harpies: obscene images which recall the medieval past. Such insularity of style was doomed. Cecil was already patronising the man who was to sweep away all this overblown decoration, the first Englishman who consciously described himself as an architect, Inigo Jones. Just seven years after Hatfield was completed, Jones introduced the austere disciplines of the Italian Renaissance to England.

This revolution can be succinctly summed up in one building, the Whitehall Banqueting House. More than any other we have looked at so far it epitomises an ideal and a revolution. It stands as a monument to the claims of the first two Stuart Kings, James I and Charles I, to be the representatives of God on earth, and it was built by Inigo Jones as a setting for the magnificent acts of state of these god-kings. It is the only remaining part of the old

Inigo Jones's masterpiece, the Whitehall Banqueting House, symbol of an artistic revolution. 1 The interior from the throne. 2 The exterior.

palace of Whitehall (the rest was burnt to the ground at the close of the seventeenth century) and is not in fact a banqueting house, but a ceremonial hall, where the monarch sat enthroned, flanked by his court in gala costume, receiving ambassadors, ratifying acts of government or responding to the graceful homage of dancers in a court entertainment. We should imagine it at night, lit by a hundred torches, the windows obscured by tapestries swagged along the walls, the sides thronged with courtiers ablaze with rich costumes and glistening with jewels.

Inigo Jones was a man deeply imbued with the ideals of the Italian Renaissance; not just with the surface details but with the philosophical-cosmological and mathematical assumptions which underlay the architecture of Alberti, Brunelleschi, Palladio and Serlio. He believed that buildings reflected in their proportions the harmonic structure of the universe: the Banqueting House is first and foremost two cubes standing side by side. Like Stuart kingship it allowed for no exceptions. The ill-digested quotations and excrescences of the Elizabethan age are an attempt at comprehensiveness, the mathematical exactitude of Jones's architecture mirrors the rule of the cavalier Charles I, every detail perfect, a defined arcadia inflexible to those who did not conform exactly to the royal will.

The building went up with great speed between 1619 and 1622. At the time it must have looked quite extraordinary, a palladian palace from Vicenza arising abruptly amidst the Tudor red brick and ramshackle black and white of Jacobean London. Inigo Jones was not only an architect, he was an author, a theorist, an antiquarian, a painter and, above all, the first man in the history of the arts in Britain to develop his talent as a draughtsman in order to express his ideas. For almost forty years he *was* the arts at the Stuart court. He designed the royal palaces and their interiors, gardens, and garden buildings; he helped Charles I build up his huge collection of Italian paintings and classical antiquities; he catalogued the royal antique coins; he even wrote a book on Stonehenge; and each year he designed the scenery and costumes for the great spectacles in which the King and Queen danced, the Stuart court masques. Above all Jones taught people to look at the world around them in a way unknown to the Elizabethans. He introduced scientific perspective and the picture frame stage. For the first time people began to think in terms of aesthetic depth. The proscenium arch became a boundary through which the eye, conditioned by its acceptance of the new rules of optical illusion, travelled into another world. It happened at the same time in painting: Sir Anthony van Dyck's cavaliers and ladies glide dreamily through a world of their own, they don't stare at us out of a box like an Elizabethan icon. And here, in the Whitehall Banqueting House, we have the supreme example of this new vision, Sir Peter Paul Rubens's ceiling decorations. It bears no relation to an Elizabethan plaster ceiling with its pendants and plaster emblems. Here it is as though certain areas of the roof had been taken away, and the eye is looking up beyond into the sky above, witnessing an apocalyptic vision. This was something utterly new, the use of illusionistic painting to destroy the very architecture of walls and ceiling, to sweep them away as though they were not there. It was to become a standard motif and in the end a cliché of what we call the baroque.

The court assembled below could study the Platonic ideas (for such they were) hovering above them, spelling out in paint the claims of the Stuart kings to rule with the sanction of heaven. Above all they were for contemplation by the King who sat on the throne. Furthest away Charles I could see himself as a baby, the infant Great Britain. His father gestures with a sceptre commanding two ladies, England and Scotland, to unite the crown into one, and Hercules with Minerva, Valour and Wisdom, remind the King of the attributes of a monarch. The eyes of a visitor would rise up from an initial contemplation of the present occupier of the throne to his father on the ceiling above him, bearing down War and Rebellion under his feet and ushering in Peace and Plenty. Finally the eye would move on to the central panel in which James I is swept up to heaven in a secular assumption.

The new architecture entered England allied to a fatal political creed. The buildings of the Tudor age, court and country, had been in a boisterous unified style, reflecting the comprehensive government of Elizabeth. There was no style for the court as against a style for the rest of the country. But by 1630 there was. The Banqueting House expresses a divisive political philosophy, that was the spirit of the age of Charles I, perfect, exquisite, arrogant and finally disastrous. No wonder that the policies which had created this brief arcadia led to civil war, no wonder too that the victors cut off the head of Charles I in front of the one building which summed up his most extreme assertions of power, the Whitehall Banqueting House. Almost the last thing he saw was Rubens great painting of his father crowned as he was carried up to heaven, and Charles's own last words were 'I go from an earthly to a heavenly crown'.

The King ascends to heaven. Peter Paul Rubens's 'Apotheosis of James I' expresses in paint the political creed of the Stuart kings.

One of Vanbrugh's grand interiors – the Saloon at Blenheim seen from the ante-room. The engraving is of the main front of Seaton Delaval.

ROBERT FURNEAUX JORDAN

THE CULT OF GRANDEUR

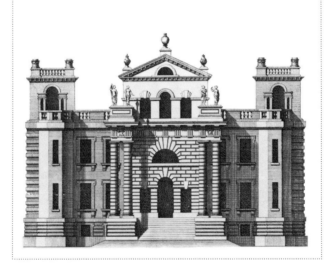

In the early seventeenth century, beneath an apparently unchanging pattern of landscape and architecture, a placid façade of old villages, old market towns, and farms, England was a country moving towards a crisis. Although the ordinary ploughboy, draper or squire might be quite unaware of it, such grave issues as how the Church should be governed, or how the country should be ruled and taxed, had created tension that for years had seethed not far below the surface. Now it was to break out. As was the eighteenth century for France or the twentieth century for Russia, for England the seventeenth century was the Age of Revolution. The great confrontation of powers reached its climax in the Civil War – a confrontation of Parliament and Crown, culminating in 1649 when King Charles died upon the scaffold. He died outside the Whitehall Banqueting House that Inigo Jones had built for him.

On a cold winter morning, to the tap, tap of Puritan drums, Divine Kingship came to an end. Eleven years later, it is true, Kingship came back, but on very different terms. Its Restoration, moreover, gave us something more than a new king; it gave us new ideas and new men who could turn those ideas into reality.

The England of the Tudors – of King Henry and of Gloriana – was dominated by a Cult of Sovereignty; the England of the Stuarts and Hanoverians, less happy about absolute monarchy, by a Cult of Grandeur.

That grandeur suffused the whole visual world: the world in which a gilded coach and six, with its outriders, could roll between incredibly carved Hensington Gates at Blenheim Palace, over the

Baroque Bridge, and so on to where that monstrous pile, the epitome of English Baroque stands high and magnificent above the Lake; the world where one could pass beneath a Roman Arch of Triumph and so up the great Avenue to where that serene colonnade of Stowe still stands among groves, pools, temples of the Olympian deities, and grottoes glimpsed among the foliage; the world where Seaton Delaval stood dramatic and gloomy on lonely northern moors.

Nor did it stop at great exteriors. There were the Battle Tapestries at Blenheim, or the marvellous Hall at Castle Howard – gallery above gallery. There was Rysbach's great flourish – his equestrian statue of William III at Bristol, and marine paintings showing the massed masts and rigging of the men of war below Greenwich Reach. There was Greenwich itself as in Griffier's view of it – the domes half-built and, beyond the huge curve of the river, the steeples of London, and St Paul's, like Greenwich itself, still unfinished, with the hills of Highgate and meadows of Kensington further off still.

There was always the landscape which, by chance or design, was also part of this Cult of Grandeur. Not just parks or gardens or town squares; but, say, Chevening seen from the slopes above the Park, the Lake at Harewood, or the Lake at Prior Park with its Palladian Bridge. There were avenues and lawns, but there were also long belts of trees against the sky, with the farms and villages of the tenants nestling in the wooded valleys. As well as the irregular chequer-board pattern of the older medieval landscape, there were the broad acres, the vast fields of, say, Lincolnshire or the Ridings.

The style was seen in small things as well as large ones – in an almshouse with almsmen and women in velvet caps or starched bonnets, in a fountain among the yew trees at Hampton Court, in the scrolls and curls upon a thousand tombstones, or the red coats of the Pensioners at Chelsea. In the huge four-poster – ostrich-plumed – of a state bedroom, in the Royal Barge or in a Herald, a Judge, a Lord Chancellor, or even a town-crier, in full fig. In a gilded chair by Kent, or, back to Greenwich and architecture, in the gods on Thornhill's ceiling.

England was a land first of castles, and then of mansions in great parks. Even into this century many of them were the homes of territorial landlords living more royally than royalty – Marlboroughs, Devonshires, Howards, Bedfords, Thynnes, Cecils and the rest – ruling their fifty thousand acres as despotically as any king.

France was different: a land of the palaces of Renaissance Princes, of François Premier or Louis the Sun King. To live at Court, rather than to own land, was a man's ambition. Fontainebleau, the Louvre, the Tuilleries, Saint Cloud, or Versailles, were among the biggest buildings in Europe – only occasionally rivalled in Rome, Vienna or Petersburg – while even the slightly smaller but rather more fantastic châteaux of the Loire Valley had been the palace-homes of kings or their mistresses.

England, indeed, has never had palaces – except in name – only very big houses, which are not the same thing at all. A real palace can be small, perhaps no more than a pretty pavilion, but it must have perfection; it must be sophisticated and artificial: as the monarchy is itself. It must be like a Dresden shepherdess or a jewel, the product of the cosmetician rather than the architect. Such were the Belvedere in Vienna, Sans Souci at Potsdam or the Petit Trianon in the Park at Versailles. Now we, in England, have nothing like that, only the homes of great country gentlemen, with their horses, their dogs and their undisturbed libraries.

A pattern of building was part of the system or, as we would call it, the Establishment. It began when William of Normandy parcelled out England to his Norman subjects. It was confirmed by King John at Runnymede – Magna Carta being not the bastion of our liberties, only a landowners' guarantee. Kingship lived on to build its last and most glorious symbol, that royal mausoleum, Henry VII's Chapel at Westminster; after that the way was clear for the biggest single event in our agrarian history – the distribution of all monastery lands to the Tudor millionaires. These landowners – merchants now rather than barons or earls – built themselves the superb mansions discussed in the last chapter. As we have seen, Henry and Elizabeth built very little themselves.

Even when Kingship came back after the Civil War, there was little palace building. English kings had lost the habit. The new king tried to pick up the threads, but it was the Cavaliers – men who had risked their necks for his father – who had to be rewarded with lands and estates. There were some dreams of palace building, but apart from a little at Hampton Court hardly anything was realised.

Inigo Jones had been dead for eight years. His loyal amanuensis, John Webb, lived on to build a few big houses in the Inigo manner and also, his one real achievement, the King Charles Block at Greenwich. But then all the men who through two generations served the Crown in architecture – Inigo Jones, John Webb, Christopher Wren, John Vanbrugh, Nicholas Hawksmoor – had their share in Greenwich, that gallimaufry of English architecture.

By 1660 the generation of Inigo Jones was dead or dying. And in any case the England of Charles II was seen to be something quite different from that of Charles I. Divine Kingship had gone, to be replaced by Divine Landlordism – the rich man in his castle, the poor man at his gate. The King might have a place in this, but he had to know his place. For the next two centuries England was to be ruled by great Whig landlords, and they at any rate needed grand houses. And for Grandeur what more appropriate style than that which had come to us, by way of Paris, from Michelangelo and Bernini – the Baroque?

And what is this Baroque? It is, as always, the precise expression of that which gave it birth. These palaces, these curving colonnades, these tall porticoes, these pediments, these gods painted upon ceilings, these enormous beds in which to conceive heirs, these avenues and lakes, these wigs and red-heeled shoes and coaches – these things are the Baroque. They are all children conceived to flatter their makers – Italian popes, French kings, Spanish hidalgos, English dukes – assuring them that in creating such things they themselves acquire – or very nearly – the divinity that belongs to a Creator.

However, in little agricultural England, with its seven or eight million people, there was still the peasantry. Nothing much had changed for them. Still the blue wood smoke rose from the dozing thatched cottages, still there was glass in the windows only if you were lucky, still the middens stank, still life was short. Also, there were still the clergy – everywhere – but now around the old monastic cathedrals they were building palaces for married bishops, quiet but spacious houses for the canons, choir schools, while in the villages a vicarage secured for every parish – or so they said – at least one scholar and gentleman, to baptise the babies when he was not coursing hares.

Now, instead of merchants venturing overseas on their own account, there were great trading companies – like the East India Company – with warehouses, bourses and exchanges in London, Antwerp, Danzig, Boston and Madras. Even the ordinary traders – grocers, cordwainers, fishmongers and the rest – had their great Livery Companies with Halls in the City of London, and were founding and building schools and buying gold plate. Alongside them, ousting the old usurers and moneylenders, were the banks, emulating the Medici in Florence or later the Rothschilds in Nuremberg, issuing letters of credit as well as merely guarding gold. As for Oxford and Cambridge, instead of schooling a few hundred boys for the celibate priesthood they were now burgeoning into great seats of learning with new colleges and fine libraries.

In this Age of Renaissance, this rebirth of the culture and learning of Ancient Greece and Rome, there had, ever since Shakespeare's day, been something of an obsession with the Classical and the Italianate, in verse and drama and even, after a fashion, in architecture. That obsession was now to be reflected also in music and the pleasures of the Town. Our period will see the building of the first Opera House and of the coffee houses that would become the clubs of Pall Mall. In regional capitals – as they truly were – in Bristol, York and Norwich, they were building their own theatres, assembly rooms and fine squares. The fashionable spas were yet to come, but the provinces were no longer parochial.

In the summer months trains of coaches, baggage carts and wagons would move along the high roads, from one great country seat to another, so that when, for instance, my Lord of Carlisle went north each year to Castle Howard, some forty carriages might make their way, very slowly, through the mud of the Great North Road, to arrive eventually to where liveried servants awaited them in the huge Court of Honour.

The Birth of the Establishment, then, and the Birth of Learning, is the theme of this Age: that and Glory. On 16 March 1661 King Charles II founded the Royal Society – an event which Lytton Strachey would one day call 'the birth of the Modern World'. It was certainly an extraordinary recognition that wisdom and knowledge were no longer the sole prerogative of the Church. If the term 'philosopher' still meant a man who loved all wisdom, then wisdom itself must now include all of what we call the sciences and they called 'Experimental Philosophy'. Experiment, observation, measurement and rational thought were at last beginning, just beginning, to take the place of witchcraft, astrology and magic spells. The foundation of the Royal Society was one of the acorns that would one day give us the oak trees of Marconi, Lister and the astronauts. Emanating mainly from Wadham College, Oxford, that

London before the Great Fire. This section of Visscher's panorama of 1616 shows old Saint Paul's standing high above the medieval city.

brilliant coterie, the first members of the Royal Society, included such immortals as Newton, Boyle and Harvey and also that 'miracle of a youth', as Evelyn called him, Oxford's young Savilian Professor of Astronomy, Christopher Wren.

Christopher Wren is certainly the most famous of English architects. Whether he is the greatest must be a matter of opinion. He has been built into our nostalgic English legend – possibly for the wrong reasons. There were many in his own day who might have put him lower than, say, Talman, now quite an obscure figure. Equally we, today, may sometimes feel that he was a less imaginative artist than Vanbrugh – a man despised by the Victorians.

Wren was never in his own lifetime officially styled an architect. He was one of that succession of 'Surveyors to the Crown' – Inigo Jones, Christopher Wren, John Vanbrugh and Nicholas Hawksmoor – who, from the office in Old Scotland Yard, dominated the architectural scene for over a century – from the time when Inigo Jones built the Queen's House at Greenwich in 1619 to the day when Nicholas Hawksmoor died in 1736, with the great Mausoleum at Castle Howard still unfinished.

Christopher Wren, the son of a Wiltshire parson, may have become interested in science by looking at a sundial in his father's garden. Thereafter he looked at the stars, made models – including one of the moon – and dials, stained marble crimson and dissected dogs. If he had died in his thirties he might just be remembered as an astronomer, certainly not as an architect. However, in those days a philosopher *was* a philosopher, a master of all wisdom, and a man who could make a model of the solar system could certainly make a model of a cathedral.

His friend, Archbishop Sheldon, asked him to build the Sheldonian in Oxford, that Ceremonial Hall that still stands as a marvel of construction, owing much to the Theatre of Marcellus in Rome but most ingeniously roofed in timber. Christopher Wren then read the works of Vitruvius and Vignola. He never saw Rome but he did visit Paris just when the architects of Louis XIV were making it one of the glories of the world.

He came back to London, at the age of thirty-three, to be involved in discussions about the decayed and ruinous state of the old medieval cathedral of St Paul. After much talk he was asked to sketch out a dome, or a rotunda, or suchlike, to cover the central space when the old tower should collapse – which, it seemed, might be any day.

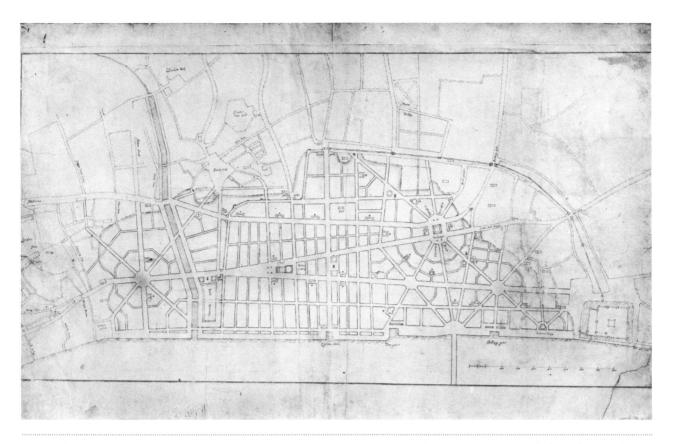

Wren's plan for London. The approach, up Ludgate Hill, dominated by a new Saint Paul's, goes on to a piazza with the Exchange and Mint.

They could have saved their breath. The year was 1666, and a week later the old City of London, with its labyrinth of plague-ridden lanes and wooden houses, was almost utterly destroyed by fire – from a point near the Tower of London westwards to Fetter Lane. If this was, at the time, a tragedy, it was also an event of hygienic importance and a great architectural opportunity.

Within a few days – literally – Wren had presented to the King his Plan for a new London. This was an astonishing achievement. Wren, on his Paris visit, must have seen Le Nôtre's avenues in the great Park at Versailles. He must have seen engravings of the Rome of Sixtus V with those three broad boulevards fanning out from the Piazza del Popolo. City Planning in this Grand Manner, however, was not, and never has been, a very English thing. Wren's fine boulevards, his piazzas, his spacious riverside quay and his marvellously sited churches, were never to be. The City merchants and the shopkeepers would have none of it. Like bees who possess their own hive they knew what they wanted: to build quickly on their own bits of land – some of them even put up tents while the ashes were warm – and get back to business.

And so, it is always said, Wren's famous Plan was lost to us. That is not wholly true. Town Planning does not just mean mapping streets. It is, above all things, a three-dimensional art – heights and masses as well as widths and lengths. Wren's concept of a new City was lost to us in width and length, but not in the third dimension of height and mass, of silhouette and skyline. He gave us, in fact, a miracle of a City, founded like Venice upon the Tide, and not less fair. The old medieval labyrinth might remain down below, but up in the sky the fifty-one steeples all paid court to that riding, redoubtable dome.

The new London that arose from the flames was a City of little houses of brown brick, only two or three storeys high. The new churches, which had to be fitted onto their old cramped sites, were now just protestant preaching houses – ingenious and elegant but plain – with plain towers for their bells. But once those towers were clear of the chimney pots they blossomed out with steeples of Portland stone, carved and shaped into pure fantasies, temple upon temple, pagoda, flèche and obelisk. And always in the foreground, with its traffic of wherries, barges and skiffs, was the green and busy Thames.

From far off, from across the river or from Highgate Hill, those steeples must have seemed like an

1 Wren's London: the new skyline, dominated by the dome of Saint Paul's and the towers of city churches. 2 Saint Stephen's, Walbrook.

armada of white galleons sailing upon a brown ocean. Wren had, therefore, at all costs to raise the dome of St Paul's high upon a drum, to give it a tremendous silhouette, so that it would – like Brunelleschi's dome seen across the Arno or Michelangelo's seen from the Pincian Mount – dominate the whole town, a little higher even than the highest steeple. That panorama was Wren's greatest achievement. Successive generations have been hiding or destroying it ever since so that, in its

entirety, it is something no living person has ever seen. Planning in the Grand Manner might be an un-English thing but somehow here, more almost than anywhere in Europe, the vision of the Courtly City was achieved. It was the opening chord of that great symphony, the Heroic Age.

Book upon book has been written about Wren's architecture – Palladian, High Renaissance, Baroque, he lived through all these styles, but would, quite simply, have called them Roman. His plans,

The spires of city churches were pure fantasies – temple upon temple, pagoda, and obelisk. 3 Saint Mary-le-Bow and 4 Saint Bride's.

proportions and details have been analysed again and again; but in fact much of that work had to be handed to others, to Hawksmoor or to many long-forgotten craftsmen. What must not be forgotten, because it is no longer before our eyes, is that Wren, like Vanbrugh and Hawksmoor, was also a designer of landscape – in his case the urban landscape, in theirs the landscape of great romantic houses.

Well, how did Wren do it? How did he create the centrepiece of the skyline of that new City of Lon-

don? He started with two great handicaps. First, he had hardly ever seen a dome. One may assume that he knew about Santa Sophia in Byzantium and about the Pantheon in Rome, but both those, for all their great size, were just saucer domes. True, St Peter's and the Duomo in Florence were real Baroque domes such as Wren would want to build, standing high on drums and each carrying a weighty lantern or cupola on its apex. The Baroque domes of Les Invalides or of Le Panthéon in Paris were still far

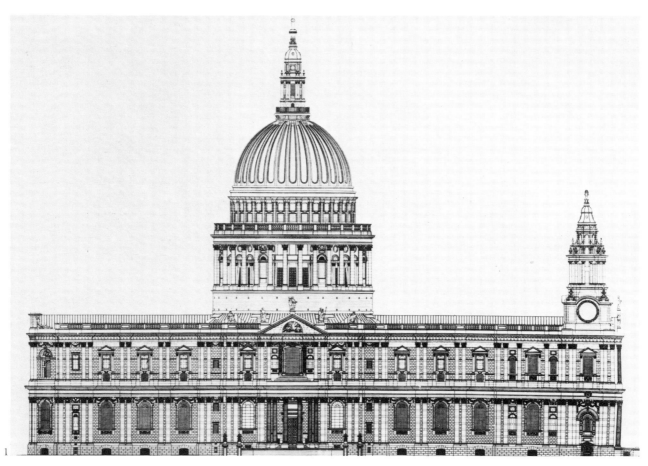

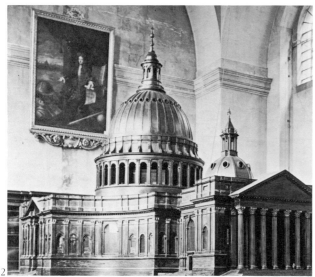

1 The north elevation of Saint Paul's shows the long nave and choir. 2 The Great Model – which Wren preferred – a great octagonal hall.

over the horizon. The structural problems were immense, moreover they were clean outside Wren's experience or, indeed, that of any living Englishman.

His second handicap was that the St Paul's they made him build was not the St Paul's he wanted to build. He had started – 'if only', as he said, 'for discourse sake' – by designing a great octagonal hall, rather like one of his own City churches, although on a vaster scale. It was simply a preaching house with all the emphasis upon the pulpit rather than the altar, with a huge central space for a congregation but no dim and distant chancel for a mass. All Wren's churches were virtually without chancels, all very protestant and Anglican and secular. His first design for St Paul's was no exception.

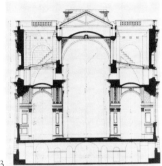

3 *A cross-section through the choir of Saint Paul's.* 4 *The second 'storey' masks flying buttresses.* 5 *Nave and aisles from under the dome.*

The big model that Wren made of this 'assembly hall' – for that is what it is – may still be seen. It is always known as 'the Great Model' and is big enough for a man to walk inside it. Like his plan for the City itself, however, it was not to be realised. The clergy were as conservative and timorous as the shopkeepers. 'The generality', as Wren said, 'were for grandeur' but they also wanted 'something more cathedral-like' – in other words, long nave and choir, big chancel and processional aisles. It was over a century since the Reformation but the clergy had forgotten nothing. In short they wanted a Gothic cathedral in Classic dress.

The whole building, therefore, became a compromise – between Wren's vision of Roman Baroque on the one hand, and clerical obscurantism on

Saint Paul's. 1 Carving in the choir. 2 The staircase in the south-west tower from below. 3 Carving from the north corner of the west front.

the other hand. A dome is, in essence, a device for covering a great central space, a circle or an octagon. It now had to be used at the central point of a traditional cruciform plan. It also had to dominate the whole City, to out-top those steeples. Wren had to use every device, artistic and structural, to achieve his end. It is all a great tour de force – and yet, in a way, it looks so easy.

From Cannon Street we can look up at those cliff-like walls – with the dome above them – their massive solidity all the greater for the rich carving that is a foil to the plain surfaces. From paving to cornice these walls are about one hundred feet high, about the same as the big vault of Notre Dame in Paris. It was in the creation of this impressive bulk, these high walls, that Wren played his first trump card, a card that was either a very naughty dodge or a stroke of genius – you take your choice.

He had been instructed, in effect, whatever its outward style might be, to build a medieval cathedral. A Norwich or an Ely – with a high nave, lower aisles on each side, and flying buttresses to take the thrust of the nave vault. It is an arrangement we can see in a score of Gothic buildings, but here at St Paul's the aisles and the buttresses have all

vanished. What on earth has Wren done with them?

These walls are sheer for a hundred feet – no aisles, no buttresses – but look more closely. The whole affair is designed, superficially, as if it were two storeys. But we soon notice that the upper range of 'windows' are not windows at all. They are blank niches. They are framed very nicely with decorative pilasters and pediments, but they are *not* windows. They can't be because there is nothing behind them. The whole of this upper half of St Paul's is in fact nothing but a screen wall – in effect a great sham for the sake of grandeur. Or, as that Victorian and arch-Gothicist Augustus Welby Pugin put it, 'one half of St Paul's is built to hide the other half'. It is glorious urban scenery but is it glorious architecture?

Why was it done? First and above all because that full unbroken height was necessary to the design, not only of St Paul's but of the whole City of London and its skyline from distant villages. Second, because flying buttresses – lovely things in the fretted and picturesque romanticism of Gothic – are just not part of the Roman or Baroque vocabulary. If an Italian architect ever had to use them he would do almost anything to disguise them. Longhena, for

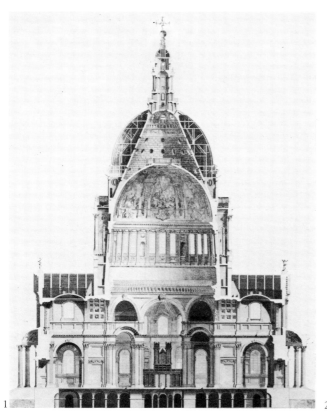

1 A section shows how the weight of the cupola rests on the brick cone. It is thus supported independently of the wood and copper dome.

instance, in his splendid church of Santa Maria della Salute at Venice, actually transformed all his flying buttresses into enormous scrolls. There could never be anything quite as high-flown from Wren but, behind those screen walls, between them and the high nave, the flying buttresses are there all right. After all the building would collapse without them. Never meant to be seen at all, they are shamefaced little things, just sticking up above the leaded roofs of the aisles. They can be seen only from above, by the tourists high up in the Golden Gallery of the Dome.

The two-storey theme for the design of the walls had, of course, to be taken right round the cathedral. Even the columned West Front, with its impressive portico, is designed as if it were two-storeyed. Perhaps here, at the top of Ludgate Hill, Wren would have liked a one-storeyed portico with columns eighty feet high. It is said, however, that the drums of stone for such gargantuan shafts could not be dragged from the quarries at Portland to the barges which would bring them through the Channel and so round to a Thames wharf.

The West Front of St Paul's, with its lovely towers and its flight of steps – a Victorian addition, these steps – is a fine piece, but to demand, as was done after the War, that it should be given a Piazza in the manner of St Peter's in Rome was a very ignorant idea – a misconception both of function and scale. The Piazza of St Peter's is, in a warm climate, a deliberate outdoor extension of the Church, designed for big crowds. The modest forecourt of St Paul's is quite different; it is the place where funerals begin or end, the place where the Dean says how d'ye do to the Queen. There is no Pope on the balcony to bless the multitude and so there is no multitude. Moreover, such is the contrast in scale between Rome and London, that a Piazza like that of St Peter's would land us somewhere in Fleet Street. It would not be grand, it would be grotesque. If we had had Wren's great boulevards, planned when the ruins of London were still smoking, that would be a different matter, but all that went with the wind three hundred years ago.

When we come to the real glory of St Paul's – the dome itself and the stone cupola surmounting it – we once more find Wren's genius at work. The cupola carries the golden ball and cross; its last stone was laid by Wren's son when his father was nearly eighty – but even then Wren had himself

2, 3 The two-storeyed elevation is carried round to the main front, although the choir, 4, and nave rise to the full height of the building.

hauled to the top in a basket. Now that cupola – or lantern or whatever you like to call it – is no mere ornament. It is eighty-eight feet high, just on a quarter of the height of the cathedral – as if Wren had put one of his church steeples on top of his dome. The cupola weighs eight hundred tons – eight hundred tons of solid Portland stone.

Now to put a weight like that on the apex of a convex dome is to defy the laws of nature. The dome, even if itself of solid stone, would simply burst outwards somewhere near its base. It must be held in. Brunelleschi, in Florence, crowned his dome with a stone cupola, and tied the dome in with a massive chain of timber balks bolted together. Michelangelo, in Rome, crowned his dome with a stone cupola, and tied the dome in with seven iron chains all buried in the dome's stonework. Wren did none of these things; he solved the problem neatly and ingeniously – by evading it.

How? The dome is, undeniably, crowned with all those eight hundred tons of stone, but the dome itself is *not* of stone. It is an affair of timber and lead and – as a sort of insurance – has only one rather apologetic chain round its base. Yet the cupola still stands. How come? Is the cupola suspended from heaven by a golden chain? Why did Wren's eight-hundred-ton stone cupola, perched on a timber dome, never come crashing on to the floor of the nave three hundred feet below? (It is worth noting, in parenthesis, that in all the cracks from which St Paul's has suffered in its time, the inherent trouble has usually lain underground, in the foundations. Nobody has ever seriously questioned the stability of the dome itself – only of the piers supporting it.)

The dome is only of wood – pretty massive beams admittedly, covered with thick lead – but still only of wood. It is when we go inside that we discover Wren's stroke of genius. This is the famous brick cone, nearly one hundred feet high, a sort of giant oast-house. It is punctuated by holes – rather like big portholes – to reduce its weight somewhat, but it is in fact very strong: the cone is a strong form. This one carries the entire weight of the stone cupola, and is hidden from the world by the outer dome of wood and lead. If, in 1940, they had dropped two or three incendiary bombs in the wrong place and the actual dome had been consumed by fire, the people of London – for the first time in history – would have seen the cupola of St Paul's safely perched upon its oast-house.

Now this was not just technique for its own sake. It shows how technology and building served, as they always must serve, the Spirit of the Age. Wren had to design a city, the skyline of which should have weight, mass, style and grace. It was to this end that he used every architectural device and strained every technical nerve.

To walk down the nave of St Paul's is to feel the very essence of the heroic, grand, or – if you feel that way – pompous. Generations of Lord Mayors, Sheriffs, Aldermen, Judges, and Masters of Livery Companies, with their sword or mace bearers, have passed this way. Grandeur is very worldly, and this – the City of London at Prayer – is a worldly church.

And yet, for all its grandeur, this is not the nave Wren wanted. Had he had his way it would not be a traditional 'nave' at all, but rather the vast octagonal hall of the Great Model, a positive auditorium. All the same it is magnificent. We are rewarded here for those massive walls towering above Cannon Street. These piers between the arches, for instance, are not mere columns or shafts but solid ten-foot chunks of masonry, with that counterpoint of carving and smooth surface we think of as medieval.

The clerestory windows, above the roofs of the aisles, flood light down into the centre of the building, but if one climbed up and looked out through them one would see nothing but little shamefaced buttresses and the back of the sham walls which give the extra fifty feet or so of height Wren the City designer needed so badly if the building was to achieve the right mass.

Looking out from the Golden Gallery – just below the Cupola and just above the dome itself – it is tempting to wish the skyscrapers away and to imagine London as it was at the end of Wren's long life when St Paul's was finished. There would be lovely white steeples – fifty-two fountains of stone in the sunlight. As for St Paul's itself, until it was cleaned a couple of years ago one had to imagine away the soot of centuries that had blackened the first forty feet or so – the part that had always been sheltered by the little houses from the wind and rain. The steeples must always have been white, although a little whiter where they got the full force of the sou'westers. Today, between chunks of property built by 'developers', one can still see two of the loveliest silhouettes of all – St Mary-le-Bow and St Bride's, Fleet Street. Farther away still are Wren's twin domes at Greenwich.

Quite close to anyone in the Golden Gallery, rising above the roof ridge, are the two western towers of St Paul's, each over two hundred feet high. If the steeples are courtiers to the dome, these are the Lords-in-Waiting. They use the Baroque vocabulary of good Roman detail to make lovely fantasies, at once chinoiserie and classical. It is said that Wren's faithful aide, Nicholas Hawksmoor, or even Wren's successor in the Surveyorship, John Vanbrugh, may have had a hand in the design of these towers. Wren was getting old – he lived to be ninety-two – so it is quite possible. It is inconceivable that the three men did not often put their heads together over the same drawing-board.

Of these three giants of the English Baroque Wren is the most famous. But Hawksmoor – what of him? He might have been the best of the lot; too often, however, he was content to be a loyal assistant, taking the load off Wren, and making Vanbrugh's fantasies possible. It has been said of him that, when acting as an architect in his own right, he was always trying to interpret Wren in terms of Vanbrugh. This is clear in his fine church towers – Christ Church, Spitalfields, St Anne's, Limehouse, or St George's-in-the-East. In a superficial sort of way, with one classic element piled upon another, they are all Wren towers. Equally, however, in their robust chunkiness, their Baroque coarseness, they are pure Vanbrugh – High Renaissance changing under our eyes into English Baroque. At St George's, Bloomsbury, for instance, Hawksmoor simply topped his tower with a stepped pyramid. It was a cheeky solution. Wren, always so gentlemanly, would never have done anything so amusing, but once, in the Park at Stowe, Vanbrugh had built a stepped pyramid just for the fun of it.

There were occasions, too, when – obedient to his client's wishes – Hawksmoor could turn (as he would have put it), from Good Roman to Rude Gothic. How many of the millions of tourists who look at the West Front of Westminster Abbey, for instance, ever realise that Hawksmoor designed it a few years after the death of Wren, and almost a thousand years after the Abbey was founded. It was the same at Oxford, at All Souls, where, presumably because it was thought more collegiate, he designed the charming exterior of the Codrington Library in Gothic; the interior, out of sight of all other college buildings, is impressively Classic – all very odd. We

Christ Church, Spitalfields, by Nicholas Hawksmoor. His city churches, built late in his life, show the full development of his style.

1 The tower of Saint George's, Bloomsbury. Three makers of the English baroque: 2, 4 Wren and Vanbrugh, by Kneller. 3 Hawksmoor.

may, therefore, call Hawksmoor an eclectic. We owe much to his genius: for instance, it was he who kept Vanbrugh's ebullience in order, and that was asking quite a lot. I have called Wren's City of London the opening chord of a great symphony – an urban symphony. With Vanbrugh we come back to the other major theme-shapers of this Age of Grandeur – the landowners. Everywhere, they were building mansions and making landscapes.

Wren and Vanbrugh make a marvellous contrast. Wren, with his equable, serene mind, the parson's son, dying quietly in the retirement of old age – the typical English gentleman except that he had a first-class brain. Vanbrugh – or Vanbrook – the son of a Dutch refugee, born somewhere in the alleys of the old City the year before the Fire, one of nineteen children, was a soldier of fortune, playwright, man-about-town, and architect. A man of the theatres, the coffee houses and the brothels, living on his wits and his amiability. 'A sweet-natured gentleman', they called him. In the Kit-cat Club – that collection of dissolute aristocrats and racy intel-

Hawksmoor's Codrington Library at All Souls, Oxford: 5 The Classic interior. 6 The Gothic exterior of the Hawksmoor quad.

lectuals – it was not long before he was, as he said, 'on nodding terms with the lords'. As the author of 'The Relapse, or Virtue in Danger' he was the rightful heir of Congreve. On a rapturous night at Drury Lane, with the applause in his ears, he knew he had arrived. He was thirty-one. Wren's genius was mathematical and pragmatical, Vanbrugh's was dramatic, romantic and imaginative. Whatever we may mean by the word 'great' Vanbrugh was probably the greater of the two. He had no training; his practical knowledge, such as it was, must have

been picked up as he went along – he knew that Hawksmoor would keep things straight.

We shall never know why or when Vanbrugh turned from the theatre to architecture. All we have is Swift's couplet of 1699:

> Van's genius, without thought or lecture,
> Is hugely turned to architecture.

By that date Vanbrugh, fully armed like Athene from the head of Zeus, had already sprung into the arena and designed a huge mansion, for the most

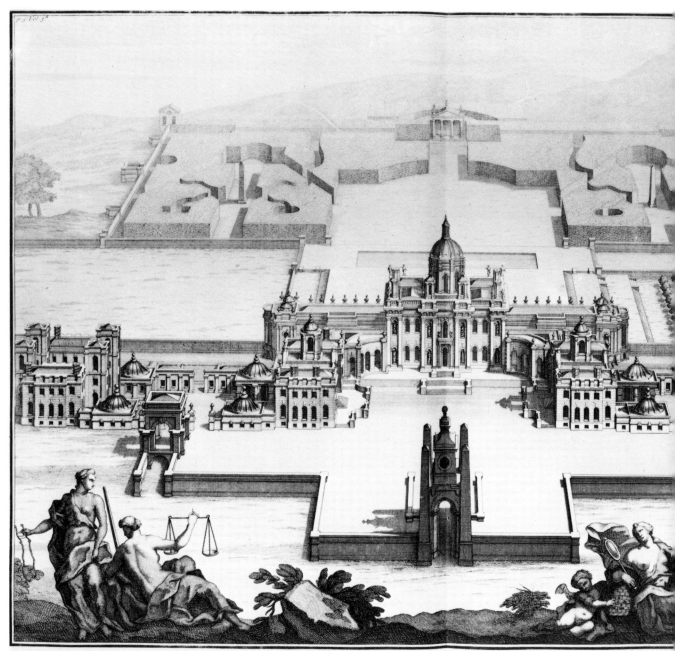

Castle Howard by Vanbrugh. The engraving, from Colen Campbell's 'Vitruvius Britannicus', shows Castle Howard from the North.

exalted of the circle of great Whig landowners. The King could never have afforded such a palace. It was Charles, third Earl of Carlisle, who asked Vanbrugh to replace his old and ramshackle Yorkshire castle with something grander and more fashionable. If the commission caused surprise, it was nothing compared with the surprise caused by the design itself. Perhaps even more surprising, however, than what he had done – sensational as that might be – was that he had done it at all. One moment John Vanbrugh was an upstart playright of Drury Lane, the next moment, after a brief tour of what he called 'the great houses of the North', he had produced the design for Castle Howard – one of the greatest houses in England.

Moreover, while one may argue endlessly as to whether Wren was a Baroque architect at all – is St Paul's Baroque or merely High Renaissance? – with Castle Howard Vanbrugh established himself overnight as one of the same fellowship as Michelangelo, Borromini or Bernini. A master of true Baroque – of what Edwin Lutyens called the 'High Game'.

What then is Baroque? When we look at the

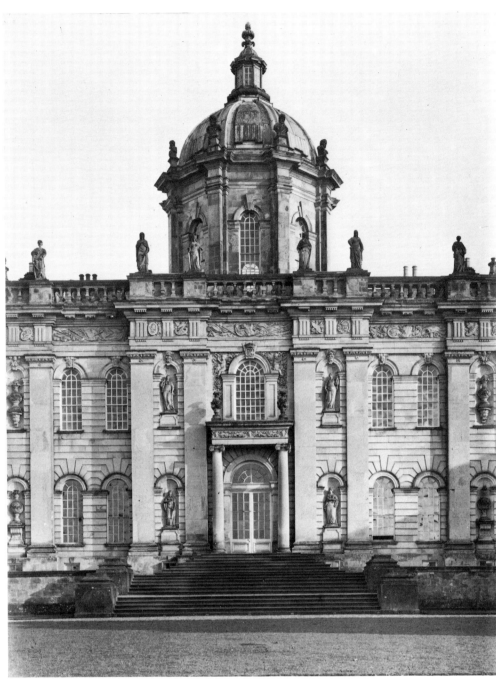

Castle Howard: the centre of the entrance front with its giant order of pilasters. It is topped by the dominating central cupola.

sculptural quality, the modelling of, say, the City steeples, we may be tempted to call Wren a Baroque architect. The play of smooth surfaces and carving is brilliant, and once his towers are free from the plain masses below they have tremendous verve. There is still, however, little or no sculptural massing of the parts of the building; no relationship like that of Bernini's curving colonnades to St Peter's, for instance, or of the three blocks of Michelangelo's Roman Capitol to each other and to their setting. It is a fallacy to think that Baroque is necessarily a richly carved style. Bernini's colon-

nades, the main adornment of St Peter's, are themselves utterly unadorned. This interplay of parts is the essence of Baroque. Compare, for instance, the foursquare block of Wren's Hampton Court – non-Baroque – with the far-flung masses of Castle Howard or Blenheim Palace. Every scrap or ornament can be stripped from those latter buildings and what remains would still be Baroque. It is the corner towers, the curved linking colonnades, the outriding courts and pavilions, that are the essence of the matter – they are built sculpture, the most sophisticated style in the world.

Castle Howard: 1 The South front. 2 The mausoleum, built by Hawksmoor after Vanbrugh's death, was incomplete when he himself died.

For centuries, if only for protection and warmth, the English house had been compact about its centre – even such large Tudor houses as Longleat or Wollaton are compact about some kind of hall or court. But now we have a revolution – the plan of Castle Howard. There had never been anything like it in England. The colonnades and the wings and pavilions are like so many tugs about a liner. So, too, are the kitchens, laundries, and brewhouses, all around their own courtyard, and the stables, with coach-houses and some fifty loose-boxes. The Court of Honour – the big entrance court – approached on all sides through triumphal arches, was in itself yet one more piece of abstract sculpture, everything subordinate to the high cupola. The house itself, with that cupola at its centre, spreads over more than seven hundred feet. It spreads, not sprawls, for the whole design is beautifully controlled – a complete unity. Versailles sprawls. But then Castle Howard is not so much a very big building, or even a group of buildings, but rather an enormous piece of sculpture within which one may, incidentally, live. It was unprecedented and is, most emphatically, of the Baroque style.

Why? First, because it was grand, heroic, and intensely romantic. This was how a great lord should live, should want to live and was expected to live by his peasants. Second, and above all, this was a house that held its own in the landscape. It dominated those broad Yorkshire acres exactly as St Paul's dominated the City of London. And so the landscape – all gay ornaments and pyramids among solemn woods – was no less than the house itself, part of the Baroque.

Castle Howard, like Blenheim or Stowe, was designed to be seen from far off. The great vista, the temple and the mausoleum, arches, lakes, bridges and lawns inspired Horace Walpole, gazing upon it all from Exclamations Gate, to write: 'Nobody informed me that I should at one view see a palace, a town, a fortified city, temples on high places, woods worthy of being each a metropolis for the Druids, the noblest lawn in the world fenced in by half the horizon, and a mausoleum that would tempt one to be buried alive; in short I have seen gigantic palaces before, but never a sublime one.'

The Tudor Garden, with its topiary and its parterres, belonged to the past in the history of land-

3 *The Temple of the Four Winds, Castle Howard. Vanbrugh designed a landscape of lake and lawns, ornamented with temples like this one.*

scape. The romantically casual glades and winding lakes of Capability Brown were still in the future, but John Vanbrugh, for one brief generation, had established the Grand Manner, not only in English architecture but in the English landscape.

By the year 1706 the central cupola of Castle Howard was finished. It is a few years older than the dome of St Paul's. Meanwhile something else had happened. On 13 August 1704, to the beat of drums, the armies of Prinz Eugen and of John Churchill, Duke of Marlborough, were fanning out with all their cannon, in the morning mist. By evening, between the Danube and the little village of Blenheim, the French armies had been defeated and the war in Europe almost won.

The banners and the trophies were borne through the streets to Westminster Hall, but Marlborough had to have his own reward – in Europe a Principality of Empire, at home the gift of that Baroque castle set upon the gentle slopes of Oxfordshire – Blenheim Palace. Marlborough wanted a reasonably stately ducal house; his wife wanted a comfortable home quickly; Vanbrugh wanted to build the finest palace in the whole

world; while the Government, sometimes Whigs and sometimes Tories, were the paymasters. It was a recipe for disaster. Therein, for over twenty years, lay a tale of blood and sweat and tears – so sad a tale that when the great house-warming did come, and the trumpets were playing upon the terraces, the Duchess Sarah shut the gates upon her bitter but immortal architect.

In 1704 Marlborough was free to choose his own architect. It was never in doubt, which of the triumvirate at Old Scotland Yard – Wren, Vanbrugh or Hawksmoor – he would ask for. Wren was old, Hawksmoor the eternal second fiddle, but when John Churchill came home from the wars, John Vanbrugh was the talk of the town. In the end he received his commission quite casually one Christmas night in a box at the theatre.

All around Castle Howard, Vanbrugh had created a landscape of marvellous artificiality; at Blenheim he had to place the house with exactitude in a landscape already beautiful. Now, to the real architect, his site – the whole *genius loci* – should be almost everything, or at least the starting point dictating the design. Almost all may be won or lost by

1 *The sunlit south face of Vanbrugh's Blenheim Palace.* COLOUR *One of the tapestries in Blenheim celebrating Marlborough's victories.*

that first throw of the dice – the placing of the building.

The Park at Blenheim, for almost half a mile back from the Oxford Road, is a level plateau; then it falls steeply to a little stream, the Glyme. Vanbrugh could have set his palace in mid-plateau, with a French style of Cour d'Honneur to the road – all cobbles and coaches in the manner of Versailles. Or he could have set it picturesquely in the valley or on the far slopes, with a long winding approach through the woods as, say, a Paxton might have done a hundred and fifty years later. He did none of these things. He set the Palace facing north and south at the very edge of the plateau just before the land falls to the valley. From the south, therefore, Blenheim is seen sunlit across level lawns; and on that side, the sunlit side, the façade – except for surface adornment and the slight projection of the corner towers – is flat in the sunlight, a very serene building seen across serene lawns.

Seen from the north, however, a broken composition of courts, towers and pinnacles stands high above Vanbrugh's Brobdingnagian bridge – it then spanned the stream which, a generation later, Capability Brown would turn into a winding lake. From here, against the light, especially when there is a fierce or cloud-racked sky, the flamboyant silhouette with all its intricate groupings may be seen in thunderous darkness against silver clouds. This marriage between landscape and building, between the English Cotswolds and a Roman style, is the stuff of genius. It gives Vanbrugh his title to greatness.

As we walk round Blenheim, making our way back from the lake to the level lawns, we notice that, like Castle Howard, it is a house with, on either side the entrance portico, far-flung wings – stable court and kitchen court – embracing a forecourt. This is so deep – some three hundred feet – that the house is, as it were, thrown back from the rest, to which it is joined only by the colonnades, and becomes an almost independent foursquare block. It was to give life to this central mass, otherwise so austere, that Vanbrugh devised those four corner towers. It is these, with their thirty-foot-high pinnacles – each carved by Grinling Gibbons with a fleur-de-lis

COLOUR *A detail of the drum of the dome of Saint Paul's.* 1 *Vanbrugh's bridge at Blenheim, now spanning Capability Brown's lake.*

crushed beneath a ducal coronet – that create Blenheim's fantastic skyline and, like so many banners in the breeze, give movement to the massive pile. From half a mile away across the Park that great broken silhouette holds its own. We know that there was a strange martial streak in Vanbrugh. After all he had trailed a pike in the Low Countries, and somewhere deep inside him was some nostalgic desire to build ancient and highly romantic castles – monuments of chivalry. Here, at Blenheim, for all his Baroque and Roman detail, his dream comes true. The terraces, as they rise from the lake, give this castle a base and a platform, while the undulating Park and the woods give it a most Arcadian setting. Here, in the poetic sense, is a great military monument which – after all – is what Blenheim is all about. But here also, a century before its time, is a romantic scene, a Claude Lorrain or a Turner, made to come true by Vanbrugh's genius. Blenheim Palace may be just one more stately home, but in its groves one might hear the tramp of ghostly armies.

We must not concern ourselves too much with that long and bitter quarrel between the Duchess and her architect – the quarrel as to whether he was building a monument or a house. If he was the prototype of all extravagant and imprac-

tical architects, she was that of all clients' wives. Nevertheless – in fairness to Vanbrugh – given innumerable servitors to carry in the dishes and to remove the commodes, Blenheim was a good house to live in – even a home. The joinery, for instance, was superb so that even on winter nights when the gales were blowing across the Cotswolds, not a candle flame was seen to flicker in those corridors. Of course Vanbrugh put Splendour before comfort. It was what he was being asked to do. It was the Age of Splendour – of Grandeur. Alas, it was also the Age of Satire, and Vanbrugh – like all upstarts – could hardly escape the poison pen. It was Abel Evans who wrote the famous rhyme:

See, sir, here's the grand approach,
This way is for His Grace's coach;
There lies the Bridge and here's the clock,
Observe the lion and the cock,
The spacious court, the colonnade,
And mark how wide the hall is made!
The chimneys are so well design'd
They never smoke in any wind.
The window's to retire and talk in;
The council chamber for debate,
And all the rest are rooms of state!'

'Thanks, sir,' cried I, 'tis very fine,
But where d'ye sleep, or where d'ye dine?
I find by all you have been telling,
That tis a house, but not a dwelling.'

1 Blenheim Palace, an engraving of the north front. 2 The kitchen court – kitchen and stable wings embrace the main forecourt.

This kind of thing was irrelevant to the monumental purpose for which Blenheim was built, but it must inevitably find an echo in many minds today – so obsessed with domestic economy, so incapable of understanding the whole ethos behind an Age of Grandeur. Moreover, I think we must admit that inside these palaces Vanbrugh sometimes fails us. His rooms may occasionally soar to dim heights, may often be gloriously adorned, but are often only a few paces across. Most of them simply line the corridors, like so many hotel bedrooms, to be cut off in lengths according to their purpose. Of course

there are the superb moments – at Blenheim, for instance, there is the dining saloon, its dim painted walls a foil to the crisp black and white marble of the doorheads; and there is the Great Library. Nevertheless we have to ask – was Vanbrugh a great decorator?

I think he was not – not by his own criteria of grandeur and splendour. His fecund imagination worked best when he was arranging towers and pavilions among the woods or upon the gentle hills. It was William Kent, almost a generation later, who would design fine furniture, and it was Robert

3 *The entrance hall, Castle Howard, and 4, the Hall, Blenheim – 'a slice of Saint Paul's domesticated', two of Vanbrugh's greatest interiors.*

Adam who was to be, *par excellence*, the great decorator. Even if we look back to an earlier day, it is difficult to find many Vanbrugh interiors to match, say, the Double Cube Room at Wilton or the Presence Chamber at Hatfield. To these strictures there is at least one exception, the Great Hall at Castle Howard – one of the finest rooms in all English architecture, certainly the finest of its century.

This Hall is something of a miracle in that it is both monumental *and* domestic. It is, in effect, a slice of St Paul's, and yet its Pauline size and gran-

deur are somehow made to be part of a house. This involves something of that subtle business of 'scale', of which Vanbrugh was such a master. The Hall at Castle Howard is very big – some eighty feet high – and yet there is no grand or ornate furniture – only little stools which, like the human figure itself, give us the measure of the thing, telling the eye that this place is big because they, the stools and the humans, seem so small. In the midst of all this Roman Baroque grandeur there is a fireplace, elegant but very domestic. One can sit beside it but, lest it should seem crushed by the architecture, there is a remark-

1

Vanbrugh's Seaton Delaval on the Northumbrian moors, now a ruin. 1 The main front and 3 a detail of the interior.

able overmantle leading up, first, to a fascinating oval painting and then linking to the architecture itself. And above the overmantle is the landing balcony, halfway up the stairs, again introducing the human figure but at a different level. And then, above that – arch within arch – it soars to the painted ceiling. Vanbrugh, as a decorator in the narrow, boudoir décor sense, may never have achieved very much, but as an architect he could create, now and again, a remarkable interior.

So many of Vanbrugh's years were absorbed by Castle Howard and Blenheim that the list of his buildings is not long. One must remember, however, Her Majesty's Theatre in the Haymarket – the present theatre is the fourth on the site where Vanbrugh built the first. He must, in his martial mood, have enjoyed remodelling two ancient castles, at Kimbolton near Huntingdon and at Lumley in County Durham. The strong rustications of Grimsthorpe in Lincolnshire also have an air of fortification about them. Eastbury in Dorset is a smaller but sufficiently fantastic house where, denied the felicity of tower building, he made towers out of the chimneys, a theme which he took

2 *Grimsthorpe, in Lincolnshire, heavily rusticated with fortress-like projecting corner towers, shows Vanbrugh in a military vein.*

to bizarre lengths at King's Weston near Bristol. But perhaps it is in that gem of a ruin, Seaton Delaval, that he at last achieved real ripeness. Seaton Delaval, by Vanbrugh standards, is not a big house, but here, in this house for the Delavals – all mad, bad and beautiful – he gives us the realisation of a vision – macabre and lonely on the Northumbrian moors.

And what, meanwhile, of Vanbrugh's loyal amanuensis – Nicholas Hawksmoor? Well, an Age never expresses itself so clearly, because so unwittingly, as in the trappings of death. And those trap-

pings, too, can be part of an Age of Grandeur. The Mausoleum of the Howards had to maintain above their coffins all the grandeur, all the pomp and bravery of Earldom. These Howards would surely arrive in Heaven in their laced coats and their full-bottomed wigs, there to be presented to Almighty God, to kiss his ring as if at some vast levee – and all this must be proclaimed by their Mausoleum.

The Mausoleum at Castle Howard was based by Hawksmoor upon Bramante's little circular church in Rome, S. Pietro in Montorio. It stands, a mile from the mansion, in solitary splendour upon an

The architecture of High Toryism. 1 James Gibbs's Senate House, Cambridge, and 2, his church of Saint Mary-le-Strand, London.

eminence in the Park. Seventy-six feet high, the handling of all the detail is masterly. Inside the sarcophagi are dwarfed by the architecture but, somehow, lose no dignity thereby. It has been spoken of as Hawksmoor's last great effort, the final affirmation of his own personal and romantic loyalty to the Rome which he never saw. It was also a last tribute to his master, John Vanbrugh, and to the man who is buried there – that Earl of Carlisle for whom Vanbrugh and Hawksmoor had built one of the greatest houses in England. And still, beneath that lonely dome, as the years pass, the corpses of the Howards are gathered together to moulder with those of their predecessors.

In the sheer excitement of Vanbrugh and the whole Baroque fever, one must not forget James Gibbs. If Wren hobnobbed with Church and Crown, and Vanbrugh with the Whig lords, then James Gibbs did much the same with High Tories and with Jacobites in the dark panelled rooms of old Catholic houses. At the Scots College in Rome he narrowly escaped the priesthood, but was so enchanted with the real Baroque being built all around him that back in England – with St Paul's, Castle Howard and Blenheim all rising from the ground – he became an architect. Thereupon he toadied to such men as Harley, Cavendish, Chandos, Vere and Mortimer, the Welbecks and Wim-

poles – the names of their estates still recalled in those streets which Gibbs helped to plan and build.

It was Lord Harley who introduced Gibbs to Cambridge. The Cambridge Senate House is a Gibbs masterpiece – excelled in Cambridge as a classic building only by Wren's Library at Trinity. Note how Gibbs's Corinthian columns, running through two storeys, give both size and dignity – Michelangelo's old dodge of the 'giant order'. Nearby, at King's College, Gibbs designed a new Fellows' Building, an amazingly successful foil to the great Gothic Chapel. It is a pretty compliment to Gibbs that, after two hundred and fifty years, it is still called 'Gibbs's Building'.

His final masterpiece, however, is the Radcliff Camera at Oxford. He won it from Hawksmoor in some kind of informal competition. An earlier plan recalls Wren's Library in Cambridge, but a circular one was finally accepted, with the bookcases radiating from the perimeter of the room. Externally the merit of the Radcliff lies in the subordination of the plain base to the rich columns of the upper storey, and of course in Gibbs's emphasis upon the essential roundness of it all.

One of his London buildings, only a little less known to millions of tourists than St Paul's itself, is St Martin-in-the-Fields. St Martin's may lack the pristine charm of Gibbs's own St Mary-le-Strand –

they called that church 'Gibbs's Fair Daughter in the Strand' – but it is impressive, superbly so today when, freed from an earlier clutter of buildings, it stands high on its steps dominating that confusion which we call Trafalgar Square. It also became a kind of insignia of Anglicanism – there are versions of St Martin's as far away as Massachusetts and Connecticut.

Can we ever really be at one with these men of another age? We have seen my Lord of Carlisle, with his train of forty coaches and wagons, making his way through the mud of the Great North Road, from one country seat to another, until at Castle Howard he pulls in at his own Court of Triumph, and Wren passing his serene old age in the house his sovereign had given him outside the gates of Hampton Court. We can imagine Vanbrugh taking snuff in St James's or strutting on the lawns at Blenheim. We sympathise with Hawksmoor, a lonely hypochondriac and, so one guesses, a frustrated artist, and think of Gibbs, closeted with the Fellows of some college to drink to the King over the Water. But there remains a certain barrier to our good will. Those years after the Restoration seem further away than almost any Age. All these men come to us across the years as snobs, most of them as libertines.

Their science hardly mitigates their superstition, nor religion their sadism. They have lice in their beautiful wigs, and brandy on their breath.

And yet, for all that, a Vanbrugh or a Hawksmoor – each in his own way – could do a very big thing in a very big way. They could even, now and again – and we can ask no more of a man – give real and potent form to a remarkable vision. It was not one which outlasted them.

With the end of the wars in Europe and with some stability at home, there were new generations of architects and patrons – all very aware of their potency and of their taste. They disliked Gibbs's Jacobitism no less than they disliked Vanbrugh's monstrous castles. And even poor old Wren could be dismissed by Lord Burlington as 'a certain Court architect who has served us long enough'. The new generation – the pendulum must always swing – was moving away from the Baroque of Wren or Vanbrugh towards the Palladianism of Kent or Adam; it was moving away from the grossness and the poxy wit of the Kit-cat Club towards elegance, politeness, correctness, good taste and even cleanliness. Away from virility towards connoisseurship. The Age of Grandeur giving way to the Age of Taste, the beating of the drums to the violins.

Palladio's Villa Capra (known as the Rotonda), and (below the title) a detail of a villa from the second of his 'Four Books on Architecture'.

4

JOHN JULIUS NORWICH

....

A SENSE OF PROPORTION

High on a North Italian hill-top, some fifty miles or so from Venice, stands the Villa Capra – better known as the *Rotonda*. It was built in about 1570. Cool, stately, without a trace of pomposity, its four lovely porticoes look down to north, south, east and west on to the olive groves and vineyards of the Veneto, all ripening in the sun. Nothing, one feels, could be more Italian, more suited to the prevailing climate or to its own surroundings; so the surprise is all the greater when one finds it again – or something so like it as to make no difference – no longer on an Italian hill but uprooted, transported and set down, about 150 years later in the 1720s, in a rather humid hollow just outside the village of Mereworth in Kent. How did it get there, and why?

To answer that question, the first thing we have to do is to look at the English social and political scene in about 1720. Queen Anne was dead, and so were all her seventeen children, not one of whom had survived her. George I, an ill-educated and stolid German without a word of English, had accepted the throne a few years before with a delighted *Jawohl*; and the artistic and intellectual leadership, which in the days of Charles II and his successors had centred on the Stuart court, now passed to the Whig aristocracy. They looked on life with new, liberal eyes. They hated autocracy, the Stuarts, Roman Catholicism and indeed anything that reminded them of Rome – which included Baroque architecture and its greatest English exponent, Sir Christopher Wren. As their oracle, the third earl of Shaftesbury, wrote:

Through several reigns we have patiently seen the noblest publick buildings perish under the hand of one single Court-

The title page of the 'Quattro Libri' of 1570. Leoni's edition of the books in English was a landmark in English Palladianism.

Architect; who, if he had been able to profit by experience, would long since at our expense have proved the greatest Master in the world. But I question whether our Patience is like to hold out much longer.

Wren was dead and discredited; dying, too, was the majestic, grandiloquent baroque of his two brilliant followers, Vanbrugh and Hawksmoor. On the continent, in France and Italy and Spain, in Germany and Austria, this baroque was to develop still further, becoming more and more extravagant and exuberant until it was to burst out into the riot of rococo. But not in England. Here, men were conscious of the dawn of a new age – the age of reason, of a quiet, logical order in which there was no place for these vain, unmanly, continental fripperies. And so, suddenly, English men of taste stopped dead in

Palladianism in England. Mereworth Castle in Kent, by Colen Campbell, modelled on Palladian villas like those on pages 104 and 105.

their tracks, looked around, shuddered, and executed a sharp about turn. They turned first to their own great compatriot Inigo Jones, who had tried, already a hundred years before, to give architecture just that cool, classical perfection they were looking for; he had designed the Queen's House at Greenwich as early as 1616, but outside court circles his austere style had never really caught on. Then,

through Inigo, they looked back further still – to antiquity and the writings of Vitruvius, and to antiquity's most brilliant sixteenth-century interpreter, Andrea Palladio.

It was not his real name. To start with he was simply Andrea, son of Pietro, a member of the stonemasons' and bricklayers' guild in the city of Vicenza. But around 1536, when he was still in his

1 William Kent and 6 Lord Burlington. 2 Chiswick House interior. 3 The Entrance front of Chiswick and 4 the gardens, looking north.

twenties, he was spotted by a local nobleman whose villa he was helping to build. This man, Giangiorgio Trissino, more or less adopted him, taught him everything he knew, gave him his classical nickname – which stuck – and took him off to Rome for serious study. Over the next forty years – he died in 1580 when he was 72 – Palladio was responsible for perhaps 40 villas and public buildings – not really very many, particularly since most of the villas were never finished. He lived in Vicenza and, with one or two insignificant exceptions, never built anything more than 60 miles away from it. And yet he was

arguably the most influential architect the world has ever known.

What was his secret? He had two of them. The first was that although he did not in any sense invent the classical Renaissance he understood, better than anybody had understood before him, how to adapt the classical idiom to the needs of his time: how to turn a temple into a church, for example, or into a villa that would be equally practicable for gracious living and for practical farming. His second secret was that he was a superb publicist: what he called his *Four Books of Architecture*, published in 1570 after

6

5

5 An engraving of Burlington House fronted by Colen Campbell's gateway which was to appear in Hogarth's satirical prints (see p. 112).

twenty years' hard work, set out briefly and lucidly, with superb illustrations and detailed drawings, all the theories and conclusions reached by Renaissance architects over the previous hundred years.

Now these *Four Books* were not entirely unknown in England. Inigo Jones had a copy of the Italian edition, and various so-called 'translations' had appeared by the end of the seventeenth century. But in 1715 there were published, only a few weeks apart, two works which, among those who cared for such things, were to make Palladio a household name. The first, in gigantic and magnificent folio,

was entitled *Vitruvius Britannicus*, and was the work of the Scottish architect Colen Campbell – he who ten years later was to build Mereworth. The plates in his book provide engravings of the principal English Renaissance buildings to date, including a good many of the author's own; but in his introduction Campbell nails his colours still more firmly to the mast:

... above all the great Palladio, who has exceeded all that were gone before him, and surpassed his contemporaries; whose ingenious labours will eclipse many, and rival most, of the Ancients ... How affected and licentious are the works of Bernini and Fontana? How wildly extravagant are the designs of Borromini, who has endeavoured to debauch mankind with his odd and chimerical beauties where the parts are without proportion, solids without their true bearing, heaps of materials without strength, excessive ornaments without grace, and the whole without symmetry?

The second publication was the most lavish edition of Palladio's own work ever to appear in this country. It was produced by a Venetian architect, Giacomo Leoni, who had settled in London only a year or two earlier to join his friend and compatriot Sebastiano Ricci, now England's most fashionable and distinguished painter. It was dedicated to King George I; and Ricci's frontispiece, with Britannia presiding while Father Time unveils a bust of the Master illuminated, as if from a spotlight, by the Garter Star, makes Leoni's message clear: the genius of Palladio is revealed anew in England, under the patronage of its King.

Whether George I cared a rap about Palladio one way or the other is questionable; but his wealthier subjects did, and before long the library of every cultivated Whig boasted its copy of Campbell or Leoni, or both. No English nobleman, however, embraced the new gospel with more enthusiasm than did Richard Boyle, third Earl of Burlington.

Burlington had succeeded to his title – and to untold wealth – in 1703 at the age of nine. Within a decade he had become England's leading patron; when he was still only twenty-one one of Handel's librettists was writing to him:

The particular encouragement you have given to the liberal arts not only shows the delicacy of your taste but will be a means to establish them in this climate; and Italy will no longer boast of being the seat of Politeness, whilst the Sons of Art flourish under your Patronage.

But for Burlington, patronage was not enough. He was determined to be, himself, a practising architect; and two years later he had created his first building – a little garden pavilion in the grounds of his house in Chiswick. Meanwhile he had commissioned Colen Campbell to redesign his London mansion, Burlington House in Piccadilly, giving it the first Palladian façade in London. Under Campbell's influence, Burlington came to look on Palladio, if not actually as a god, then at least as a prophet of a very high order, a law-giver to whom the sublime truth had somehow been revealed. During his first Grand Tour he had barely halted at Vicenza; but in 1719 he set off again for Italy, determined to study the Master's work at first hand. This he did, and was back just before Christmas,

bringing with him a collection of Palladio's drawings, an Italian edition of the *Four Books* – and William Kent.

They must have seemed an ill-assorted couple: Burlington aloof, exquisite, an aristocrat to his fingertips; Kent a bluff, barely-literate Yorkshireman who – thanks to other more modest patrons – had spent ten years in Rome studying painting in the high baroque manner of seventeenth-century painters like Guido Reni or Guercino. Unfortunately he was never very good at it; but his flair for decoration and design was unmistakable, and Burlington sensed, rightly, that Kent possessed all the ideas and imagination that he himself lacked. On their arrival in London Kent was installed at Burlington House, where he was to live for twenty-nine years until his death.

Kent was not the only recipient of Burlington's hospitality. Others, who stayed for months, sometimes years, at a time were Campbell, by now the Palladian architect *par excellence*, the Italian sculptor, Giovanni Battista Guelfi, and even George Frederick Handel, a fellow-director with Burlington of the newly-founded Royal Academy of Music. The Academy was dissolved in 1728 after the vogue for Italian music had been destroyed overnight by John Gay's *Beggar's Opera*, but even then Burlington bore no grudge; Gay too became a long-term visitor – though he was later ungratefully to complain that Burlington had not helped him enough after he lost his shirt on the South Sea Bubble – and wrote:

Yet Burlington's fair palace still remains;
Beauty within, without proportion reigns.
Beneath his eye declining art revives,
The wall with animated picture lives;
There Handel strikes the strings, the melting strain
Transports the soul, and thrills through every vein;
There oft I enter (but with cleaner shoes)
For Burlington's beloved by every Muse.

Lord Burlington was, by all accounts, a modest man; but by the middle 1720s he unquestionably saw himself as the leader of a new classical renaissance in English taste; and in 1725 he began to build himself a Palladian villa on his estate at Chiswick. Typically, he designed it not for living in – he had a perfectly good Jacobean house next door – but as a pavilion of the spirit, in which to surround himself with beauty – books and paintings and sculpture, all in a setting of immaculate Palladian proportions. Like Colen Campbell's Mereworth, it was based

The gallery, Chiswick House. The house has a typically Palladian plan of interconnecting rooms. The rich embellishments are Kent's.

1 Hogarth's satire on masquerades. 2 His parody of Kent's Saint Clement Danes altarpiece. COLOUR *James Paine's chapel at Gibside.*

loosely on the Villa Rotonda, except that it was a good deal smaller, and had only one portico instead of four.

At this early stage, Burlington's Palladian style was not yet faultless. I suspect, for example, that Palladio would have been horrified by the staircase leading up to that portico. It was far too complicated and fussy for his taste. But this, and other features, were almost certainly due to the influence of Kent, who after ten years of steeping himself in Roman baroque, was probably finding the austerities of pure classicism a little hard to swallow.

Inside the building, however, he was allowed a considerably freer hand. The octagonal Domed Saloon, to be sure, with its classical busts and segmental windows, maintains all the Burlingtonian dignity and grandeur, as does the gallery which runs the entire length of the west front and – thanks to its subtle subdivision into three parts affording a broken vista, through two arches, from one end to the other – looks even longer. But elsewhere, notably in the three so-called Velvet Rooms (Blue, Red and Green) the elaborate carved chimney-pieces, the profusion of swags and garlands, of gilded and painted beams and gambolling cherubs, Kent's decorative imagination has run riot.

It was inevitable that Lord Burlington's villa,

when completed, caused something of a sensation in fashionable London society; opinions on it, however, were mixed. Horace Walpole – who, heaven knows, was never over-lavish with his praise – complained that the villa suffered from 'too strict adherence to the rules of symmetry', but on the whole he approved:

A model of taste – more worth seeing than many fragments of ancient grandeur, which our travellers visit under all the dangers attendant on long voyages.

Others, however, were less kind. Lord Hervey observed that the villa was 'too small to live in and too large to hang to a watch'; Lord Chesterfield, who had anyway objected on principle to noblemen practising architecture – 'the minute and mechanical parts of it – leave them to masons, bricklayers and Lord Burlington' – now broke into verse:

Possessed of one great house for state
Without one room to sleep or eat,
How well you build, let flattery tell,
And all mankind, how ill you dwell.

That, I suspect, was the trouble about Lord Burlington – he took himself too seriously; and it was his misfortune to live at a time when English satire was at its most deadly. A further problem was that his star protégé, Kent, was still working primarily as a historical painter in the grand manner and, despite a

dazzling talent in other respects, in this particular field was rapidly proving himself, as Walpole put it, 'below mediocrity'. When he was working for Burlington, as at Chiswick or at Burlington House, he escaped with a little gentle mockery; but in 1721, through Burlington's influence, he had received the commission to paint and decorate Kensington Palace in preference to Sir James Thornhill, Sergeant-Painter to the King. The older artistic establishment was scandalised, and feelings ran higher still when an independent committee reported on Kent's work in the Cupola Room:

'Tis our opinion, that the perspective is not just; that the Principle of the Work, which consists of Ornaments and Architectures, is not done as such a place requires. Mr. Nesbot adds that the Boys, Masks, Mouldings, etc., far from being well, he has seen very few worse for such a place; and Mr. Ramber affirms that the said work, far from being done in the best manner, is not so much as tolerably well performed.

As for Queen Caroline's drawing-room: 'The general effect, *if you do not look at it*, is rich.'

It was probably the Kensington Palace affair that made for the new Palladians their deadliest enemy of all; William Hogarth, who in 1729 was to marry Thornhill's daughter Jane. Hogarth was the most English of English painters, and the most earthy; the Olympian élitism of Burlington and the Italianate allegories of Kent represented everything he most hated. In 1724 he published his first attack on them – an engraving which satirised the splendid Palladian porch that Campbell had erected at the entrance to Burlington House, crowned by a statue of Kent with Raphael and Michelangelo modestly supporting him, giving aristocratic sanction to the popular taste – which causes everyone to flock to Italian pantomimes and masquerades while Shakespeare, Dryden, Congreve and the rest are carted off to the scrapheap.

The next year there followed a still more withering blast. Kent had been commissioned to paint an altarpiece for the church of St Clement Danes. From the beginning it had been a failure, the more so because the principal female figure bore a disconcerting resemblance to Princess Sobieski, the wife of the Old Pretender. After his ten years in Rome, Kent was often suspected by his enemies of being a secret Catholic and Stuart sympathiser; this painting seemed to confirm it. Kent, who was the most easy-going of men and took no interest in politics, protested his innocence in vain; the parish council were outraged and had it removed. Natur-

ally, for Hogarth, the opportunity was too good to miss. He immediately published a burlesque of the altarpiece, with sarcastic notes underneath it.

But Lord Burlington remained loyal. By now he had realised that Kent would never be much of a painter; but that his inventiveness and flair for any other branch of the visual arts made him indispensable. As for the attacks on himself – Burlington simply ignored them. As another of his protégés, Alexander Pope, wrote:

You too proceed! Make falling Arts your care,
Erect new wonders, and the old repair,
Jones and Palladio to themselves restore,
And be whate'er Vitruvius was before . . .

And so he did. His self-confidence was absolute. The great Palladian principles to which he had consecrated his life were not, for him, a matter of fashion but of Right and Wrong, of an Eternal Truth, which it was his mission to disseminate.

Perhaps, at this point, we ought to investigate those principles rather more closely. And there is nowhere better to do so than at the Villa Foscari, called the Malcontenta, just outside Venice. It looks rather sad nowadays; the open country that Palladio knew has degenerated into a shapeless suburban sprawl. But the villa itself remains virtually unchanged from when he built it in the late 1550s, and illustrates perfectly the basic theories that he developed into a whole philosophy of architecture.

These theories sprang from two sources: classical antiquity and the laws of nature. The classical influences are not very hard to see: Palladio was the first architect, anyway for 1500 years, to graft a Roman temple façade to the wall of a house. It caused quite a stir at the time, but he saw nothing wrong in it because he believed that classical temples had evolved from private dwellings; the frescoes at Pompeii – in his day still undiscovered – have subsequently proved him right.

As for the laws of nature, there were three main ones as far as Palladio was concerned: symmetry, harmony and proportion. All his nineteen villas are built with an absolutely rigid left-right symmetry: fold any of the plans down the middle and the two halves will coincide, even to the wall partitions, the doors and the staircases – which, incidentally, he always liked to tuck away into dark corners, unlike his English followers, who tended to make them an important architectural feature.

COLOUR *One of Veronese's frescoes at Maser. They bring the countryside into the villa itself, painted horizons carrying on real horizons.*

1 Britannia sees Palladio's bust unveiled by Time: frontispiece to Leoni's translation of the 'Four Books'. 2 The villa Malcontenta.

Proportion was equally important, and was based – incredible as it may seem – on the laws of musical harmony. The purest form of harmony is the octave; when a vibrating string is stopped halfway along its length, the sounding half vibrates twice as fast and sounds, consequently, an octave higher; so the ratio of an octave is 2:1. Similarly a ratio of 2:3 will give a perfect fifth, of 4:5 a major third, and so on; and just as these harmonies are pleasant to the ear, so, Palladio claimed, when their ratios were applied to architecture, would the resulting proportions beguile the eye – they too being consonant with the laws of nature.

The trouble is that any analysis of Palladio's methods and techniques makes him sound cold and pompous. In fact, you have only to enter any of his country villas to be struck by the extraordinary informality which he achieves within the stately framework. At Malcontenta, for example, there is not even a vestibule; you walk through the huge doors, made of rough wooden planks – no ostentation here – straight into the main room of the house, that marvellous vaulted cruciform hall which extends right through the building to the garden front. This was, as it is today, the focus of the life of the house. Of the six other rooms that surround it, all interconnecting – Palladio had a hatred of corridors or passages – all have curved and vaulted ceilings, all are painted in lovely faded fresco, and all have heights precisely calculated to harmonise

3 The villa Barbaro at Maser by Palladio. 4 The frescoes by Veronese in the villa Barbaro. 5 A grotto in the gardens at Maser.

with their horizontal dimensions. The furniture is sparse and simple, as it always was; with a house such as this, elaborate furnishing or interior decoration is unnecessary – the architecture itself says all that needs to be said.

Quite apart from the inherent beauty of these perfect proportions, they must have made life much easier when the fresco-painters arrived – as they generally did – to decorate the interiors. Palladio was not invariably lucky with these artists; the frescoes inside the Villa Rotonda are so ludicrous that one almost feels they must have been intended as a deliberate joke. At Maser, however, the best-frescoed of all the villas, he had one of the greatest of Venetian painters – Paolo Veronese. Better,

perhaps, than anywhere else, Maser shows that there is nothing forbidding about Palladio; all is light, and graceful, and airy.

Maser was built around 1560 for two brothers named Barbaro – one of whom, Marcantonio, was for two years Venetian Ambassador to London, where he wrote the first detailed report on England and the English for his fellow-countrymen. But little of it seems to have rubbed off on him or on his villa; certainly nothing could be further in style from the great houses that were being built in England at roughly the same time – Longleat, for example, or Burghley. Maser is Italian through and through, a celebration of light and sunshine and the wooded hills of the countryside near Treviso, which

1 *An engraving from Palladio's 'Four Books' of an 'Egyptian Hall'. It was the basis for 2, Lord Burlington's Assembly Rooms at York.*

Veronese contrives to bring into the villa itself: painted horizons extend to the window openings, where their line is carried on by the real horizon till the other side of the window where the paint takes over again.

The other delight of Maser is the little church a stone's throw across the way. It was built some twenty years after the villa and is Palladio's last religious building. By this time he was an old man; but unlike most people he seems to have become more frivolous, rather than more austere, in his old age. With the wealth of stucco plasterwork inside and out, and the classically indefensible but wholly enchanting garlands swooping from capital to capital across the façade, the building seems to murmur of rococo, a hundred years or more before its time. A modern authority has called it 'the irreverent child of the Pantheon'; but although, as a circular, domed construction with a temple front it is obviously a direct descendant of its ancient Roman prototype, it is as different from it in character as a ballerina is from a High Court judge.

But the Palladian villas were by no means purely decorative; many of them were designed as working farms. At Maser the two side wings and their linking colonnades were expressly designed for agricultural storage; indeed, had it not been for the dictates of agriculture, this villa and several of its fellows – like the Villa Emo – would probably never have been built. Now this is important, because it explains not only why so many rich Venetians commissioned Palladio to build them villas but also why, two centuries later, the English adopted his style so enthusiastically. In a curious way, they were both very much the same sort of people. The Venetians who turned to agriculture in the mid-sixteenth century did so because, since Vasco da Gama had discovered the Cape Route to the Indies in 1498, their immense commercial Empire was rapidly declining and they were looking for a safer alternative to trade. But they were still rich, highly educated, and, essentially, still citizens of the world's most beautiful, civilised and sophisticated city; and they insisted that their farmhouses, though practical,

3 *The Assembly Rooms today. In the eighteenth century the close spacing of columns led to the seating being put in front of them (see 2).*

should yet breathe an air of cultivated grandeur.

And so did the English Palladians of the eighteenth century. They were not always aristocrats like Lord Burlington; Henry Hoare, for whom Campbell completed Stourhead in 1725, was a banker. But they were the same sort of people, economically and socially, as Palladio's patrons – they too had strong ties with their capital city as well as with the land; and they too had had a good sound classical education. Finally, they lived in the Age of Reason. They had read their Locke and Newton, and when Palladio, or his mouthpiece Burlington, started talking about harmony and natural laws, they instinctively responded.

Thus, from 1720 for the next half-century, the cult of Palladio dominated English architecture. Admittedly, as more and more social climbers tried to jump on to the Palladian bandwagon, some attempts were more successful than others. Pope continued his epistle to Burlington:

> You show us, Rome was glorious, not profuse,
> And pompous buildings once were things of use.

Yet shall (my Lord) your just, your noble rules
Fill half the land with imitating fools;
Who random drawings from your sheets shall take
And of one beauty many blunders make;
Load some vain Church with old Theatric state,
Turn Arcs of Triumph to a Garden Gate;
Reverse your Ornaments, and hang them all
On some patched dog-hole eked with ends of wall,
Then clap four slices of pilaster on't
That, laced with bits of rustic, makes a Front;
Or call the winds through long arcades to roar,
Proud to catch cold at a Venetian door;
Conscious they act a true Palladian part
And, if they starve, they starve by rules of Art.

Of these rules, though Burlington continued to be the chief interpreter, he was by no means the best. He was too unimaginative, too inflexible, as in the house he built for General Wade in what is now Old Burlington Street, London. Horace Walpole wrote to a friend:

It is worse contrived in the inside than is conceivable, all to humour the beauty of the front.

while Lord Chesterfield remarked, even more acidulously:

Holkham Hall, Norfolk. There are hardly two adjacent openings in the same style. Unity comes from symmetry and proportion.

As the General cannot live in it to his ease, he had better take a house ever against it, and look at it.

This inflexibility was shown with unfortunate clarity when Burlington – 'the Maecenas of our Age' – was invited in 1730 to build a suite of Assembly Rooms in York. Immediately he turned to Palladio, and found his version of a design by Vitruvius for what he called – heaven knows why – an 'Egyptian Hall', and described as being 'particularly suited for festivals and entertainments'. It never seems to have struck him that sixteenth-century Venetians – let alone first-century Romans – should have taken their pleasures somewhat differently than did the citizens of York in his own day; or that the latter should be rather more cumbersomely dressed. The result was the most severely classical building of the early eighteenth century in all Europe – but it was hardly festive, and very far from practical. The side aisles were too narrow to sit out in; the distance between the columns was fixed, with Palladian precision, to just double their diameter, so that couples sitting behind them either felt caged in or else invisible, which at times proved still more embarrassing. As the Duchess of Marlborough pointed out:

The columns stand close as a row of ninepins; nobody with a hooped petticoat can pass through them. . . . It exceeds all the nonsense and madness that I ever saw of the kind, and that is saying a great deal.

Holkham Hall. The entrance hall. The motif of a staircase rising within an apse, and the screen of four columns, is, again, from Palladio.

In an effort to remedy this unsatisfactory state of affairs the seats were brought forward in front of the columns, with the result that the already narrow room was made yet narrower and all Lord Burlington's carefully calculated proportions were ruined. Later still, the walls running behind the colonnades were removed altogether, so that the Assembly Rooms today are even less like what their noble architect had in mind when he designed them.

But they remain unquestionably grand, and whatever the drawbacks of the 'Egyptian Hall' itself the shapes and groupings of the subsidiary rooms had an immense influence both in England and throughout Europe. Before Burlington, virtually all rooms in England were square or rectangular; he it was who first introduced the idea of square, absidal and circular rooms all opening out of each other – an idea that was to be developed still further by his old friend William Kent.

Kent was already in his mid-40s when he started to design Holkham, his first major work of architecture, for Thomas Coke, first Earl of Leicester. Clearly, Burlington's influence is still very strong. His hall-marks are everywhere – the three-light Venetian windows, for example, which Palladio hardly ever used in this way but which Burlington made a feature of his Chiswick villa, and the charac-

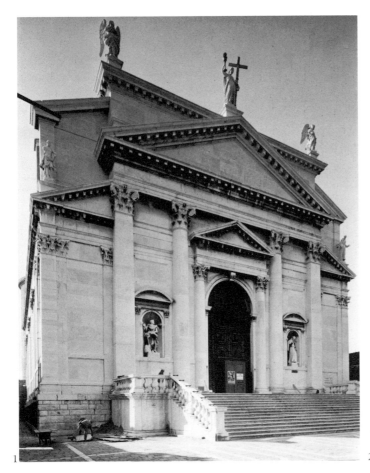

Palladio's Venetian churches: 1 The Redentore and 2 S. Giorgio Maggiore. In both, the English Palladians found inspiration.

teristically Burlingtonian *staccato* treatment: as with all his work, the individual units are what count; there are hardly ever two adjacent openings of the same design. The unity comes from two things only – symmetry and proportion. Even then, there is little immediately attractive about that almost aggressively plain façade of yellowish brick, or the ruthlessness with which all superfluous decoration has been eliminated. The result is formal and stately – there is no doubt about that – but it is strangely lacking in warmth. The easy-going, pleasure-loving Kent, one feels, would never have shown such restraint had he not had his unbending aristocratic mentor at his elbow, sternly insisting that a gentleman's house must eschew vanity and reflect only the old stoic virtues of reason, moderation and robust common sense. But the planning of the interior, together with the detail and the skill in which all the different ideas and features are combined – all that is Kent's, and Kent's alone.

Lord Hervey described how in a great Palladian house the 'base or rustic storey was given over to hunters, hospitality, noise, dirt and business', while the *piano nobile* was dedicated to 'taste, expense, state and parade'. At Holkham the real *tour de force* is the transition between the two: a colonnaded Egyptian hall, with two purely Palladian embellishments. The first, an apse with ascending staircase, appears in Palladio's design for a classical basilica; the second – a group of four columns used as a screen within the apse, comes from a new source we have not yet looked at – Palladio's churches in Venice.

I suppose everybody's favourite Palladian church is S. Giorgio Maggiore, above all because the island on which it stands is so superbly placed across the basin of St Mark's from the Piazzetta. It was his first church – that in which he solved the problem of adapting the classical temple front to a church with nave and lower side-aisles, by the simple expedient of superimposing a tall narrow front on another broader and squatter one. John Ruskin hated Renaissance architecture; even so, his reaction to S. Giorgio comes as a surprise:

It is impossible to conceive of a design more gross, more barbarous, more childish in conception, more servile in

3 *James Paine's chapel at Gibside is a rare, but perfect example of an English Palladian church. See also colour, facing page 112.*

plagiarism, more contemptible under every regard. But few people even in Ruskin's day, and even fewer now, would share his view.

Palladio's later, greater masterpiece is less well known and less well loved – except perhaps on its annual feastday when a bridge of boats connects it with central Venice across the broad Giudecca Canal. This is the Church of the Redeemer – the *Redentore*. Here the harmonic proportions of the façade have all the ingenious complexity of a Bach fugue; it would take a whole chapter of this book to do them justice or even describe them in detail. But that is not our purpose here. Inside the building, we can form a far clearer picture of the way Palladio applied to church architecture the same principles he used for his villas – the principles on which his English followers so enthusiastically fell when their turn came. Here, for example, are his inter-communicating rooms: now they are side-chapels, but as all their dividing walls have doorways, together they constitute the side-aisles which the church otherwise lacks. Here too is the equivalent of the central hall in the villas: the short transepts

and crossing merge together to form what the Italians call a tribune – a vast open space, subtly separated by projecting piers from the nave proper, in which the doge and other dignitaries could attend the annual feastday celebrations in a style appropriate to their state. And here, behind the altar, are the four columns forming a screen across the apse: the columns that William Kent transposed to Holkham. What a pity, one feels, that the English Palladians did not do more church-building of their own: James Paine's exquisite little chapel at Gibside, near Newcastle, is one of the few entirely successful examples of the *genre*.

After Holkham, Kent was established as one of the country's leading architects. It was a great disappointment to him that his drawings for the new Houses of Parliament were not accepted; he did, however, build the new Treasury around 1735 – and also, ten years later, designed the Horse Guards building itself. This last was built only after his death, but that did not prevent Hogarth's mockery. The Palladians were still being accused of sacrificing utility to elegance; and in his painting 'Canvassing

Stowe. The view from the house: 'a world stretching out before you with its obelisks, rotundas, its River Styx and its Elysian fields'.

for Votes' – one of the 'Election' series – Hogarth shows, on an inn-sign, a picture of the Royal Coach driving under the Horse Guards arch – which unfortunately proves rather too low and knocks off the coachman's head.

Lord Burlington, the Apollo of Arts, found a proper priest in Mr. Kent. . . . He was a painter, an architect, and the father of modern gardening. In the first character he was below mediocrity; in the second, he was a restorer of the science; in the last, an original, and the inventor of an art that realises painting, and improves nature. Mahomet imagined an Elysium, but Kent created many.

Horace Walpole was right. Kent's greatest con-

tribution was not in painting, architecture or interior decoration; it was in gardens and landscape. At Chiswick and Claremont, at Rousham and Stowe, he set about 'educating' Nature. The days of formal planting in the French style, of pastures and quincunxes, topiary-work and knot-gardens, were gone for good. Pope, himself a passionate gardener, described them best:

No pleasing intricacies intervene,
No artful wildness to perplex the scene,
Grove nods at grove, each alley has a brother,
And half the platform just reflects the other;
The suff'ring eye inverted Nature sees,
Trees cut to statues, statues thick as trees,

Nature made to be as she ought to be: 'Nature shall join you, Time shall make it grow | A work to wonder at – perhaps a STOW'.

With here a fountain, never to be played,
And there a summerhouse, that knows no shade . . .

The new idea was very different – to make a landscape look natural, but in the way that Nature ought to be rather than in the way she actually was, so that the final effect should be similar to that of a painting by Poussin or Claude. Kent was the first man to do it: as Walpole said, 'He leaped the fence and saw all Nature was a garden.' And Pope explained the technique:

To build, to plant, whatever you intend,
To rear the Column, or the Arch to bend,
To swell the Terras, or to sink the Grot,

In all let Nature never be forgot . . .
Consult the Genius of the Place in all,
That tells the waters or to rise, or fall,
Or helps th'ambitious Hill the heavens to scale,
Or scoops in circling Theatres the Vale,
Calls in the Country, catches opening glades,
Joins willing woods, and varies shades from shades,
Now breaks, or now directs, th'intending Lines,
Paints as you plant, and, as you work, designs . . .
Nature shall join you, Time shall make it grow
A work to wonder at – perhaps a STOW.

To anyone who has ever visited Stowe, the fact that it owes its present form to one said to have been the richest man in England comes as no surprise. Richard, Earl Temple, inherited three major for-

1 *The gardens at Rousham, in Oxfordshire, by Kent. Brown and Repton followed him in 'educating' nature to imitate Claude and Poussin.*

tunes, married a fourth and – particularly after his sister's marriage to the elder William Pitt – had no difficulty in making a fifth out of politics; and when he died in 1779 he left the house and gardens much as they are today.

But the splendour of Stowe lies neither in its size nor in its magnificence – there are many houses in England far larger and more ornate; nor yet in its beauty, though to me at least there are few more beautiful. What really sets it apart is the grandeur of the overall conception, and the triumphant success with which this conception has been realised. For Temple – and his uncle Lord Cobham, who began the work – sought to create not just a house, but a world to enclose it: an ideal Palladian world in which the ancient virtues were revered, the ancient philosophic truths illustrated. You have only to stand beneath the south portico of the house and look out across the park, to find that world stretching out before you, with its obelisks and rotundas, its River Styx and its Elysian Fields, all seemingly artless and yet in fact so rigidly conceived that the fourteenth-century village had to be eliminated, and the church – in which, incidentally, Capability Brown was married – rendered invisible by a dense and deliberate screen of trees.

Of Temple's own temples – the pun may be forgiven, since he incorporated it in his family crest – over thirty still remain in the settings for which they

were intended. Most perfect is the Palladian bridge, copied (with improvements) from that at Wilton; most enjoyable, the Temple of British Worthies – kings, soldiers, statesmen, poets, scientists and philosophers – the sixteen leading heroes of the Age of Reason. All these temples repay the effort of seeking them out; all contribute to the Grand Design. That is what counts. Through it, Stowe tells us more about the eighteenth century, its tastes and values and its underlying philosophies, than any other house in England.

Now just how much of a paradox was it that, at the very moment when architecture was at its most formal and symmetrical, gardens went the other way? Not as much as might be thought. These new gardens, though more natural than their predecessors, followed an inner logic of their own; Kent and his followers, Capability Brown and Repton, were seeking laws in nature just as Palladio and Burlington had sought them in the buildings of antiquity.

Then *Rules* of old discovered, not devised,
Are Nature still, but Nature methodized;
Nature, like Liberty, is but restrained
By the same laws which first herself ordained.

Those lines sum up, better than any others, the Spirit of the Age; and they are applicable equally to the architects and to the gardeners of the mid-eighteenth century. And notice that word 'Liberty'. Englishmen prided themselves on the new political

2 *Scamozzi's false perspectives in the Teatro Olimpico, Vicenza.* 3 *The circus, Bath, started by John Wood the elder and completed by his son.*

freedom they had enjoyed since the Glorious Revolution of 1688, contrasting it smugly with French autocracy and absolutism. And of that freedom, the new art of landscape gardening – perhaps the most valuable and certainly the most English of all our contributions to the visual arts – was a conscious and deliberate reflection.

So much, then, for villas and churches, public buildings, and gardens; now what about towns? Palladio himself, though he was responsible for much of the civic centre of Vicenza, never thought of town planning on the grand scale; and there are only two instances I know of Palladian towns worthy of the name. One is ideal, in Italy, and one is real, in England.

The ideal Italian one exists on the stage of the so-called Teatro Olimpico – the Olympian Theatre – of Vicenza, designed by Palladio when he was in his 70s. It is made entirely of wood, and though the superb false perspectives were in fact the work of his star pupil Scamozzi, the proscenium is entirely his, and the whole ensemble shows Palladianism at its most brilliant and assured.

The real, English, one is Bath.

Bath is a city of superlatives. First of all, it is the most beautiful in Britain. Next, it is the most appropriately named; had it not been for those extraordinary springs which, every day since the world began, have hurled forth a quarter of a mill-

ion gallons of water heated to a constant 120 degrees, the Romans would never have adopted it as they did or adorned it with buildings of which enough have survived to constitute the most important classical remains we possess. Nine centuries after them, Bath saw the coronation of the first King of all England. Finally, and most gloriously of all, it is the one city in this country where fine building and inspired town planning go hand in hand, together creating an atmosphere of Palladian elegance and civilised refinement without equal anywhere.

It was an astonishing achievement, the more so when one remembers that at the beginning of the century it was still an unassuming little town, quite unremarkable except for its hot springs. Then Queen Anne went to take the waters. High society followed, and with it five architects, who together span the century – the two John Woods, father and son, Thomas Baldwin, John Eveleigh and John Palmer. All, however, owed their inspiration to one man, the presiding genius of eighteenth-century Bath – a professional gambler called Richard 'Beau' Nash. Arriving penniless from London in 1703, he soon became Master of Ceremonies and within a few years had given his adopted home a social *cachet* that no other English provincial city has ever enjoyed before or since. Distinguished visitors were welcomed by peals from the abbey bells, and

1 Bath: The Royal Crescent; the first crescent in English architecture, and the grandest of the linked ranges of houses that make up the city.

soon found that Bath society during the high season, while marginally – and refreshingly – less exclusive than that of the capital, yielded nothing to it in brilliance of sophistication. The price they had to pay was discipline. The Beau was a martinet, and for half a century he ruled the city with a rod of iron. Clothes to be worn in all the public rooms were precisely regulated by his decree; offenders were asked to leave and did so. He even laid down the pattern of daily life, always beginning with the required three glasses of spring water in the Pump Room.

The first Pump Room opened in 1706, the joint brain-child of Nash and his doctor William Oliver, inventor of the Bath Oliver biscuit. By the end of the century, however, it could no longer contain the number of visitors and a new one was designed by Baldwin, the City Architect. Today, as one sits in prim gentility over coffee and tea-cakes while a three-piece orchestra plays selections from *Rose Marie*, the fashionable world described by Jane Austen seems far away; but the room itself has lost nothing of its splendour, with its Corinthian columns, *oeil-de-boeuf* windows, and the lovely little arched recess from which, gazing down on the Roman Bath while sipping the water, one scarcely notices that it tastes, as Sam Weller pointed out, of luke-warm flat-irons.

At noon, in Nash's day, one crossed the square for a short service in the Abbey. (Begun in 1499,

this was the last church of its size and importance to be built in England until Wren tackled St Paul's nearly 200 years later.) Then came dinner, a rest, drives and visits; to be followed by an evening at a concert, the twice-weekly ball or – most popular of all in the first half of the century – the card-tables. Now the focus shifted to the Assembly Rooms. These, too, had to be replaced to cope with Bath's increasing popularity. The present ones were built by the younger Wood in 1770; gutted by a bomb in 1942, they have been marvellously restored by the National Trust.

John Wood the Elder settled in Bath in 1727 and two years later started work on his first important composition – Queen Square. He never saw the great Roman Baths – they had not yet been excavated – but he knew that the city was originally Roman and, good Palladian that he was, he was determined to recreate the classical spirit. He therefore planned a Forum, a Circus and what he called an 'Imperial Gymnasium' for 'medicinal exercises'. We do not know what this last would have been, because it never materialised; and the Forum fared very little better. But the Circus, with its three splendid superimposed arcades loosely based on the Roman Colosseum, is a triumph. Still unfinished when John Wood died in 1754, it was completed by his son, who went on to create an even grander concept – the Royal Crescent, the first crescent in English architecture.

2 *Prior Park. The view up the hill, past the Palladian bridge to 'the most complete recreation of a Palladian Villa on English soil'.*

In the work of both Woods we can see the principles of Palladian landscaping being followed just as
much as those of Palladian proportions. In the Circus, the streets leading in are carefully arranged *not*
to bisect it; in the same way the Royal Crescent,
though less than 300 yards away from the Circus
down a dead straight street, is actually invisible
from it – which makes the surprise of its sudden
discovery one of the great dramatic moments of
European architecture.

Yet the beauty of Bath, and its uniqueness, lie
less in these individual triumphs than in the *ensemble*
– in the Squares and Crescents and Parades, ranging
from the Circus to many a secluded, unpretentious
little street behind. It is the quantity of fine houses
that impresses, almost as much as their quality. The
life they were built to sustain was vacuous, vapid
and, one suspects, quite shatteringly dull; but
they themselves embody very different values –
strength, reason, humanity, permanence. This is the
paradox of Bath. When the guide-books call it 'a
monument to bygone elegance' they are wrong.
Only the perishable has perished. The elegance
remains.

The second of Bath's luminaries, after Nash himself, was Ralph Allen who, as owner of the nearby
quarries at Combe, popularised that marvellous
stone that adds so much to the beauty of the city;
and for whom in 1734 the elder Wood built Prior
Park – a house which Dr Pevsner has described as

'the most ambitious and the most complete recreation of a Palladian villa on English soil'. The bridge
was taken direct from one of Palladio's designs and
is consequently an almost exact replica of those at
Wilton and Stowe.

Of all the cities of England, and despite the indig-
nities it has suffered over the past decade, Bath
remains not just the most beautiful but the most
civilised. But then, the Palladian was the most
civilised of styles. Unlike the baroque which it followed, it was never pompous or grandiose; unlike
the neo-classical which it preceded, it was never
over-delicate or effete. It spanned them like that
bridge, elegant and graceful, yet always firm, masculine, and four-square. And it also bridged what
we might nowadays call the two cultures –
mathematics and the natural sciences on the one
hand, the classical heritage on the other. It carried
nothing to excess, for it recognised that man was the
measure of all things and it sought to place him in
the most perfect setting that the laws of nature
could devise. That, surely, is what civilisation
means, and humanism, and those magnificent lines
that John Dryden had written on St Cecilia's Day,
1687:

> From harmony, from heavenly harmony
> This universal frame began;
> From harmony to harmony
> Thro' all the compass of the notes it ran,
> The diapason closing full in man.

Antiquities in Sir John Soane's Museum, London and (below title) one of Soane's studies for the mausoleum at Dulwich College Art Gallery.

JOHN SUMMERSON

LANDSCAPE WITH BUILDINGS

In Sir John Soane's Museum in London hangs the portrait of a young man with dark, penetrating eyes who holds rather ostentatiously in his left hand the symbol of his profession – a pair of architect's dividers. The portrait is of John Soane himself, but it was painted long before he had reached a condition of life in which creating a museum was remotely possible. The portrait was painted in Rome in 1779. Soane, a country builder's son, found himself there because he had won the Royal Academy's gold medal for architecture and been chosen as the King's travelling student. He was a nervous, brittle young man of twenty-six, with ten years of slogging professional life behind him, now consumed with ambition to be a great and original architect. When the portrait was painted he had seen and studied Rome, gazed at the temples and theatres he knew so well from the books and made drawings of many things not in the books. He had explored the ruins of Hadrian's villa and the temple at Tivoli. And he had been south to Naples, had visited Herculaneum and prowled with his sketch-book by moonlight on a forbidden site at Pompeii. More enthralling still, he had seen what very few Englishmen had then set eyes on – the temples at Paestum.

Paestum was the profoundest of the young architect's experiences in Italy. Centuries older than anything he had seen in Rome, these temples built by colonial Greeks in the sixth century BC were for him, in a strange way, modern. They were a revelation of what lay behind Rome, far behind and much nearer to the beginning of things. They possessed a primitive power, almost like a force of

1 John Soane, in Rome in 1779. 2 Temples at Paestum, which Soane visited when travelling on a studentship from the Royal Academy.

nature, and it was this that gave them a certain exciting relevance – a modernity. In addition, of course, they had the charm of having been for centuries overgrown and forgotten, rarely illustrated, rarely visited, still less imitated. How could such things be imitated? They could be dismissed, as some academicians at home would dismiss them, as the crude antecedents of the pure architecture of Rome and thus not to be taken as serious architecture. But was that right? In the presence of these things one could hardly believe so. But imitation was not the point. It was the pure spirit of architecture which Soane experienced; the upward rush of the fluted columns, the sense of weight triumphantly carried, the grand rhythms. Here, in this wild desert landscape, was architecture at the source, and the impression of that was indelible. It remained always with him.

As we look about the museum in Lincolns Inn Fields we can quickly see what future lay ahead for young Soane: a great career as an architect and wealth enough to build round himself a rich collection of books, antiquities and works of art, in a house designed for the purpose. When he died here

in 1837, he left it all as a national collection, having endowed it on the specific condition that it should never be altered. It never has been, and here, if anywhere, we can feel ourselves in the ambience of the age of a man who, born under George II, died on the eve of Victoria's accession.

But we must not fix our attention exclusively on Soane, the man. We shall return to him and his house but first let us try to see through his eyes the London of his youth. The brown brick monster sprawled everywhere into the fields, still, however, with a skyline of memorable variety and beauty – the dome and steeples of Wren and, round the bend of the river, Westminster's double-towered abbey. Of public monuments, apart from what Wren had built, there were not many: the churches of Hawksmoor and Gibbs, the Horse Guards and the Royal Mews, Westminster Bridge, a few splendid houses and, more recent, the works of George Dance, Soane's master. Of these last Newgate Gaol, with its massive walls and chain-hung entries, was the latest and greatest. But there was a public building more recent still and this was the Strand block of the new Somerset House, just finished when Soane

3 *Somerset House, by Sir William Chambers (from an engraving). 4 Newgate Gaol by Dance. 5 Royal Academy exhibition in Somerset House.*

came back from Italy in the early part of 1780.

Somerset House was designed by Sir William Chambers, the nation's premier architect, the King's Surveyor General, Treasurer of the Royal Academy and the social model to which every young architect aspired. Somerset House, now beautifully restored, stands as the conspicuous symbol of the 'establishment' culture of its time. It looks backwards with refined and selective learning and faces the future with absolute complacency. Its architecture is appropriate for the government departments for whose occupation it was built and by which it is still partly occupied. Specially appropriate was the allocation of the Strand block, with its columned façade and vaulted entry, to the three learned societies under royal patronage: the Royal Society, the Society of Antiquaries and the Royal Academy of Art – the last of these being the youngest and the one with which Chambers himself had, from the beginning, been associated.

In 1780, Sir Joshua Reynolds, the Academy's first president, was preparing to celebrate the building's completion. The annual exhibition was held in it for the first time in October and Soane will hardly have missed hearing the president's inaugural address. Like the building it was elegantly complacent:

We have already the happiness of seeing the Arts in a state to which they never before arrived in this nation. This building, in which we are now assembled, will remain to many future ages, an illustrious specimen of the Architect's abilities. It is our duty to endeavour that those who gaze with wonder on the structure may not be disappointed when they visit the apartments.

The apartments on this occasion were indeed handsomely lined. Among the 489 exhibits were seven portraits by Reynolds, sixteen paintings (portraits and landscapes) by Gainsborough, majestic history paintings by West, horses and heifers by Stubbs – a noble harvest from a great generation. For Soane, as for most men of his age, Somerset House and the Academy radiated authority and glamour. Reynolds was one of the facts of English life. Chambers, too, was unassailable – the model architect, the perfect professional. His *Treatise on Civil Architecture*, published and republished over the years, carried a prestige not unlike that of Reynolds' *Discourses*. Somerset House was beyond criticism, a final statement of the classical position to which the Augustan age had led.

1 Robert and James Adam's Adelphi, with the unfinished Somerset House and Saint Paul's beyond. From an engraving by T. W. Edy.

And yet in that same generation there were other men and other ways. There were, in architecture, Robert and James Adam, the Scottish brothers who never exhibited at the Royal Academy but who, for twenty years, had enthralled the great families of England with their new fashions in design. Like Chambers, they had studied in Italy but their researches had been of a more restless sort, stressing the decorative remains of imperial palaces and of interiors adorned in the antique spirit by Renaissance masters. With these as his inspiration, Robert Adam claimed a freedom of design which was antipathetic to Chambers. He invented details, used new proportions and borrowed freely from the published engravings of the great travellers – Robert Wood in Palmyra and Le Roy in Greece. His opportunities lay mostly in the installation of grand new sets of rooms in the substantial shells of older country houses. But he built also in London.

The Adelphi, upstream from Somerset House, had been created by the Adams in 1768, before Chambers' building had been begun. It was their own speculation. They embanked the Thames and built above it an ordered arrangement of brick streets; no columns and entablatures in fine masonry here, but delicate strips of honeysuckle ornament in a patent composition, sharp and clean. Here, a new taste with a new, free, linear elegance

Robert Adam's interiors at Syon House: 2 The ante-room. 3 The great hall. 4 The library – a Jacobean long gallery transformed.

was proposed for London's street architecture.

Further up the Thames, where the river bends round Kew, is Syon House. The walls of Syon are old, plain and battlemented but inside them Adam built a Roman palace of his imagination. He shows himself as learned in the ancient sources as Chambers but he has more movement and invention. There is more invitation to explore and to experience differences of space and mood. The great hall has in it something of a Roman basilica, with its beamed ceiling and the judicial niche where, instead of a magistrate, the Apollo Belvedere presides. From the gravity of all this, white marble steps lead behind doric columns into another room, the ante-room – as different from the last as trumpets from muffled drums. The scale of the ante-room is smaller but the brilliance tremendous. The grey marble columns, brought from Italy, are drawn up in fours like those of a triumphal arch; there is triumph in the gesturing figures and again in the trophies on the walls. Hard and metallic, this is not a room for living in but an episode in a house of many rooms, as changeful in shape and character as the movements of a sonata.

We come to the library, a room of a kind never dreamed of in Rome and, in fact, truly English because it is a Jacobean 'long gallery' transformed. Here Adam is at his wittiest, playing the Roman

Symond's Yat, an aquatint from the 1778 edition of William Gilpin's 'Observations on the River Wye and several parts of Wales'.

game in a room of un-Roman size and shape and intended for shelving and showing books. How does he do it? The books are the clue. With their tooled bindings, they propose a miniature scale. They are enclosed by diminutive architecture – a very real architecture and complicated, but tiny. Tiny, panelled pilasters slide up to little gold capitals; architrave, frieze and cornice are all there in appropriately diminished scale. Then comes the ceiling, Adam's geometrical equivalent of those crazy fretted ceilings of which Jacobean builders were so fond. There is freedom and fun in Adam's designing and, of course, it was infectious. Not in architecture only but in all the crafts, in furniture, pottery, silver, textiles, even in such trifles as fire-grates and door-handles, the Adams' elongated lines and delicate profiles found an echo. Soane, years later, recalled the 'electric' effect of the Adam revolution in the arts of design.

Soane was only a boy when the Syon library was new. As he grew up, the age to which it belonged, with all its complacency and all its gaiety of invention, was slowly and gracefully fading. By the time he was forty, in 1793 (the year after Robert Adam died), it had vanished. The giants had left the scene.

Soane's world was different – grimmer in some ways. The shadows of the French revolution were lengthening across the channel. There were haunting new ideas about the rational, the primitive; about things seen behind and beyond Roman civilisation, things as severely questioning as the Paestum temples; about nature and natural beauty. In England, isolated by war, inward-looking, people began to scan the commonplace with new eyes, observing the familiar English landscape with new wonder. A movement started. From the very beginning it grew round one word – 'Picturesque'. The word sounds almost trivial to us now, but in the 1790s it was not trivial. It conveyed new insight into the beauty of landscape, a romantic, ideal penetration.

Adam, of course, had known about the Picturesque; so, indeed, had Gainsborough. Adam once described himself as 'a picturesque hero' and in his later years he let his fancy play in drawings of wild mountain landscapes and ferocious castles – nothing if not picturesque. Gainsborough, without having any more theories about picturesqueness than did Adam, painted the very soul of it in his cottage scenes. But to understand how the con-

Tintern Abbey. The quality Gilpin discovered in the Wye Valley – picturesqueness – is what millions now recognise without thinking.

scious thread of the Picturesque wove itself into the new century we must attend to somebody of the same generation as Adam and Gainsborough but not exactly an artist.

He was a Hampshire clergyman: the reverend William Gilpin. We know Gilpin as he was most widely known in his day, through his books of *Observations*. These are slim, oblong volumes containing sketches reproduced in lithograph, and short explanatory texts. The first of these books, compiled in 1772, was about the Wye Valley, and its purpose was to persuade the visitor to look at the river landscape and its effects as a connoisseur would look at a work of art. Here, almost at random, is an extract. It describes a part of the valley which he calls New Weir:

The river is wider, than usual, in this part; and takes a sweep round a towering promontory of rock; which forms a side-screen on the left; and is the grand feature of the view. It is not a broad, fractured face of rock; but rather a woody hill, from which large projections, in two or three places burst out; rudely hung with twisting branches and shaggy furniture; which, like mane round the lion's head, give a more savage air to these wild exhibitions of nature.

His view is still recognisable – we call it Symonds Yat. It is rather more thickly wooded now and a

good deal more populous. Gilpin's description may strike us today as quaint and stilted: he was no great stylist. The point is his *observation*. The quality he discovered and dissected here in the Wye valley – the quality of picturesqueness – is what millions now recognise without thinking. In Gilpin's time it still had to be thought.

Gilpin gave the word 'Picturesque', for the first time, a categorical meaning. Edmund Burke, before him, had two ways of classifying scenery. It could be 'beautiful'; or it could be 'sublime'. Gilpin saw that the kind of thing a painter would want to paint was not necessarily either beautiful or sublime. It could be either, but what it must be was 'picturesque'. So his books aimed at teaching the ordinary cultivated person to look at scenery as if it were nature offered as a work of art.

This was Gilpin's contribution to the Spirit of the Age and a very remarkable one it was, for all its seeming amateurishness. His books were published long after he had completed them and it was not his own but the next generation of tourists whose eyes were opened to the aesthetics of scenery, and among them were eyes more inwardly penetrating and more romantic than his.

3 Richard Payne Knight. 1 and 2 Illustrations from 'The Landscape' showing an imaginary scene before and after Brown's treatment of it.

Wordsworth knew his Gilpin when he first visited the Wye in 1793 but it was when he returned there five years later that he wrote of it and did so in a way quite inconceivable in the Gilpin context:

> Once again
> Do I behold these steep and lofty cliffs,
> That on a wild secluded scene impress
> Thoughts of more deep seclusion; and connect
> The landscape with the quiet of the sky.
>
>   *   *   *
>
>   And I have felt
> A presence that disturbs me with the joy
> Of elevated thoughts; a sense sublime
> Of something far more deeply interfused,
> Whose dwelling is the light of setting suns.
> And the round ocean and the living air,
> And the blue sky and in the mind of man
> A motion and a spirit that impels
> All thinking things, all objects of all thought,
> And rolls through all things.

Those famous 'Lines written above Tintern Abbey' are a long way from Gilpin. They are quite a long way from the notion of the Picturesque which possessed most people at the time the lines were written. Wordsworth, indeed, was soon to turn his back on the Picturesque; he was set on a course with a remoter goal and it is not for us to follow him.

What bearing had the Picturesque and these new feelings about natural scenery upon architecture? This is not altogether an easy question and the best way to answer it is by introducing some of the personalities who answered it in their own way, which soon became the way of many.

In the west of England lived two intellectual squires whose names will always be associated with the Picturesque – Uvedale Price of Foxley in Herefordshire and Richard Payne Knight of Down-

4 *Downton Castle.* 5 *The Claude, owned by Payne Knight, shows the same irregular grouping of buildings he achieved at Downton.*

ton in Shropshire. Uvedale Price, like Soane, had visited the Paestum temples and been deeply moved by their primitive eloquence. But also he was a friend of Gainsborough and valued the cottage simplicities of the English scene. Early in life he inherited the estate at Foxley and there dedicated himself to the exposition of the Picturesque both in writing and in the manipulation of landscape. His friend, Payne Knight, shared the same experiences and interests. He, too, had inherited an estate while still very young so that his developing ideas, backed by considerable wealth, were able to be realised over the years. He was the more intellectually brilliant of the two and, in fact, a considerable scholar. He was a student of some of the more esoteric aspects of classical archaeology and his frankness in dealing with erotic symbolism was once found

rather alarming. His attitude to landscape started, as did Price's, with a revulsion against the landscaping so widely practised by an older generation – in other words, the art of the celebrated Capability Brown. Brown, in the course of his enormous practice as a landscape-gardener, had evolved certain formulas which he applied, perhaps somewhat ruthlessly, to every landscaping project which came his way. Knight thought that Brown, in trying to 'improve' Nature, had made her unnatural – destroyed her. His poem, *The Landscape*, is all about this and with the poem, published in 1794, are two engravings which drive the message home. They show an imaginary house and its surroundings before and after Brown's treatment of them.

First, we have the house, a grand old Elizabethan derelict, in a setting which seems just to have grown round it, a setting full of natural accidents, which might have attracted Claude Lorrain, greatest of seventeenth-century landscape-painters; while in the foreground is the kind of raffish growth which the Dutchman, Ruysdael, would have handled with affection. Then we have the same scene 'improved', so to say, by Brown with his characteristic swards, clumps, serpentine water and so on; and with the old house refaced in the crudest mid-Georgian. This is grossly unfair to Brown but anybody with an eye for the Picturesque would see exactly what Knight meant.

Obviously, at Downton there would be no 'improvements' of the Capability sort. If anything had to be done, Knight would consult his prime authorities – the great landscape painters, especially Claude and Nicholas and Gaspar Poussin. But Knight had another problem. He found it necessary to build himself a house. The question at once arose, what sort of a house should it be? About the interior arrangements there could be no doubt: they must provide a convenient and rationally elegant home for a man of standing in the county who was also a classical scholar. But what of the outside?

Knight laid it down in one of his books that a house in a picturesque landscape should be in 'that mixed style which characterises the buildings of Claude and the Poussins'. What 'mixed style' means here we can easily ascertain by looking at the pictures Knight had in mind. Both Claude and Nicholas Poussin often show in their landscapes buildings of the purest classicism. But they also show (Claude especially) buildings which have grown through different uses into irregular groups – villas which are also farms, or little castles which have perhaps been modernised as villas. It so happens that Knight possessed a painting by Claude in which a group of this kind is charmingly conspicuous. It hangs still on a wall at Downton and the building is suggestive of Downton Castle itself.

So Downton was built with a perfectly classical interior – to the extent that the dining-room is a plausible miniature of the domed Pantheon at Rome; while the exterior is more or less like a Gothic castle, with a strongly irregular silhouette, and a crenellated tower that reminds one of War-wick. But it is less the style than the irregularity which counts, and this calculated irregularity was a great discovery, much greater than was realised at the time.

This irregularity did not immediately become a general taste. When Downton was new it will have seemed an amusing experiment, but twenty years later the old assumptions about symmetry began to give way. Not far from Downton is a little house called Cronkhill which, even more than Downton, seems lifted out of a Claude landscape. It makes no pretence of being an English castle; the circular tower with the conical roof is as Italian as can be. The irregularity is nicely balanced – the static vertical tower against the strong horizontal rhythm of the loggia. Built in 1802, it was one of the first of its kind. The architect was John Nash.

Nash is the central figure of the Picturesque in architecture. He was a witty, provocative character, with a genius for the quick manipulation of ideas. He started humbly in London, tried his hand at speculative building but went bankrupt, retreated to Wales and then re-emerged as a fashionable country-house architect. He worked for Uvedale Price and certainly knew Payne Knight to whom, and to Downton, his work owes much. He formed a partnership with another great figure in the world of the Picturesque, Humphry Repton. Repton was a genteel but extremely business-like character who built up, in the course of very few years, a wonderful practice as a landscape-gardener in the new natural style which emerged from the dialogues of Price and Knight and the reaction against Brown. Repton, the landscape-gardener (he was the first to call himself so), and Nash, the architect, operated together, Repton proposing 'improvements' in the scenery of country estates and Nash providing such architectural accessories as were required – a lodge, a dairy, a conservatory, the refronting of an old house or even the projection of a new one.

Repton had a special way of presenting his proposals to those who came to him for advice. He prepared what are called his 'red books' (because mostly bound in red morocco), oblong albums of watercolour views, accompanied by an obsequious and neatly hand-written text. The views show the estate as 'improved', but over each view is a 'flier' showing the scene as existing. Ingenious and persuasive, these little books enshrine, collectively, Repton's theory and practice of landscape-gardening and, indeed, were used by him as the substance of a printed and richly illustrated work (fliers and all) under that title. In the red books are found, from time to time, architectural proposals by 'my friend Mr Nash', but in due course these references cease and there are dark hints of a separation. The ambitious architect developed his own reputation as an innovator in the country-house sphere

1 *John Nash. Two of his buildings: 2 A small country house, Cronkhill. 3 Cottages built in 1811 at Blaise Hamlet, near Bristol.*

John Nash's designs for the Regent's Park. 1 The ideal proposals of 1811 with 2, the first plan. 3 Cumberland Terrace, 1827.

and the partnership broke up. Of Nash's work as a country-house architect little now survives. There were Italian villa-type houses like Cronkhill, craggy castles inspired by Downton, houses in the older formal tradition and occasional excursions into Gothic or even Jacobean. And there were the cottages. An important element in the Picturesque was the rehabilitation of the English cottage. It came about through the spread of Rousseauesque sentiment, through Gainsborough, perhaps, and the pervasive lure of the primitive. In any case, Nash

was the first architect to treat cottage design as a serious study. Time has been ruthless with most of the results but at Blaise, near Bristol, is a beautifully preserved group which seems to be in the nature of an anthology of his creations in this mode. Built in 1811, they were intended as a more humane, as well as a more picturesque, version of the usual bleak row of almshouses which some landowners provided for their pensioners.

It was in the year that Blaise Hamlet was built that Nash started to bring the Picturesque to town. It

4 *Detail from one of the panoramas in the Public Record Office showing Nash's idea of the Park as a harmony of buildings in landscape.*

was the year in which the leasehold of Marylebone Park – the Regent's Park to be – reverted to the Crown. Plans by various architects were considered and Nash's, certainly the most inventive, was chosen. In the Public Record Office in London are the original drawings. The lay-out looks very much like what we see on the map today, but with it are two panoramas, each over 15 feet long which show something rather different. What we see as we unroll them is a beautifully planted garden city, with villas sheltering in woody groves and crescents and ter-

races in the background – an ingenious urbanisation of the Picturesque. Regent's Park was never quite like this. Few of the villas materialised. The terraces did, however, and they are still there, circuiting two-thirds of the park and presenting a wonderful variety of classical compositions, all done in stucco at the front and common brickwork at the back. The façades are pure scenery, for behind them the houses are ordinary and narrow, all very much alike. Most of the park is now open grass-land with not many trees but here and there we can still discover

The Grange, modelled by William Wilkins on the Theseum at Athens. 'Nothing can be finer, more classical or like the finest Poussins.'

vignettes of trees, water and classical architecture which remind us that Regent's Park was the brain-child of a country-house architect filled with the spirit of the Picturesque.

Architecture like this, designed for picturesque viewing in consciously contrived landscape, can always be accused of pretence and shallowness, of being a kind of suburban mimicry of the splendours belonging to ducal seats in county parks. Supposing this kind of thing to be typical of London after Waterloo we may well ask what had become of the venerable spirit of classical architecture of which Sir William Chambers had been the admired custodian and expositor. Had it vanished? Not exactly; but it had taken a new direction, towards the cool refinement and grand solidity of ancient Greece.

What we now rather quaintly call the 'Greek Revival' (presumably to counter-weight the 'Gothic Revival' in which *revival* has a more plausible mean-ing) was a movement towards the use of Greek rather than Roman elements in an already developed architectural system. Its first important realisation came soon after 1800. As the Greek genius for architecture expressed itself almost ex-clusively in temple building, the urge to construct Greek temple porticoes on every possible occasion was great. In Hampshire is a temple-like house, now half ruined, called the Grange which, at a fair distance, at certain angles and in the right light can look absolutely like the real thing. 'Nothing can be finer', said C. R. Cockerell when he visited the Grange soon after it was built, 'more classical or like the finest Poussins' (an echo here of Payne Knight's enthusiasms); 'there is nothing like it on this side of Arcadia'.

It was nearly thirty years since young Soane had marvelled at the sight of Paestum. The Grange is not an imitation of Paestum, nor was its architect Soane, but a much younger man, William Wilkins, and his model was the Theseum at Athens. Yet the Grange brings down to earth the image which had haunted Soane and which haunted the age – the image of a primitive purity of form, near to nature. The Grange marks a thrilling moment in the realisa-tion of an ideal. But moments pass and ideals become tarnished. It was not long before Greece, from being a dream became a fashion, and like the Adam fashion before it, ranged through all the arts.

The leader of the Greek fashion was the immensely rich and no less talented Thomas Hope

The Elgin marbles: Beside the Theseus of Phidias (above), according to Flaxman, the Apollo Belvedere was 'a mere dancing master'.

of Deepdene. He had explored the Middle East and come home with the conviction that ancient Greece was the sacred source of all magnificence and elegance in the arts. In London, he built himself, near Cavendish Square, a house which was (as Soane's was later to be) at the same time a museum and picture gallery. The house had a sadly short life but we can see from the line engravings of Henry Moses what it was like – how Greek it was in almost everything: Greek architecture, Greek furniture, Greek silverware. And if Henry Moses is to be believed the ladies of Thomas Hope's parties wore something like Greek costumes. Hope's patronage encouraged the Greek twist in painting and sculpture. We see it in Flaxman's monuments and in his illustrations of Homer, and what added momentum to the movement was the arrival, in 1803, of giant fragments of real Greek sculpture, hacked out of the Parthenon and the Erectheum for Lord Elgin. The sculptors were taken by storm. Beside the Theseus of Phidias, said Flaxman, the Apollo Belvedere is 'a mere dancing master'.

In architecture Greek styles soon became the established convention. In London, the new Covent Garden theatre of 1809 had a colossal Athenian portico. In no time at all there was one in Newcastle, another in Glasgow. After 1815 no public building anywhere was complete without Greek columns – either the severe Doric or the gracious Ionic. Courts of justice, council houses, town halls, exchanges, hospitals, colleges and custom houses – all were Greek. Even churches deserted the heritage of Sir Christopher Wren and went Athenian. At St Pancras, in London, much of the fabric was copied, line for line, from the Erectheum at Athens. Here, conscientiously reproduced, is the famous 'tribune' with, instead of columns, captive women, interpreted as mourning figures guarding the subterranean vaults. Strange acolytes, surely, these pagan figures, in a Christian church; but that was a thought which disturbed few people at the time.

In every great city of the kingdom rose these Grecian piles. But there was one city above all whose dedication to the Greek was so conspicuous and so noble that it nicely matched the title the city had earned for itself – the Modern Athens. This was Edinburgh.

If we take our stand on the Castle Rock at Edinburgh, with our backs to the afternoon sun, we see before us all urban design from Adam and Cham-

Greek style became the convention. 1 Saint Pancras church. Courthouses at 2 Glasgow and 3 Newcastle. 4 Covent Garden Theatre.

bers to the Picturesque and the Greek, telescoped into a matter of fifty or sixty years of building. It started with the creation of the New Town, across the valley from the old, in 1767. This was begun prosaically enough, in the London style, with two squares joined by a main street. There is nothing picturesque here, except, indeed, the view of the old town from the new (it would have occurred to nobody to think of the old town, tumbling down from the castle to Holyrood-house, as picturesque before the new town existed). The orthodox lines are enriched by some noble monuments – Chambers' house for Lord Dundas in St Andrew's Square, Robert Adam's façades and Reid's domed

Turner water colours, of the crypt of Kirkstall Abbey and a mountain landscape, both from Sir John Soane's collection.

1

COLOR *Soane's drawings for two interiors of the Bank. 1 A detail of the exterior of the Bank of England.*

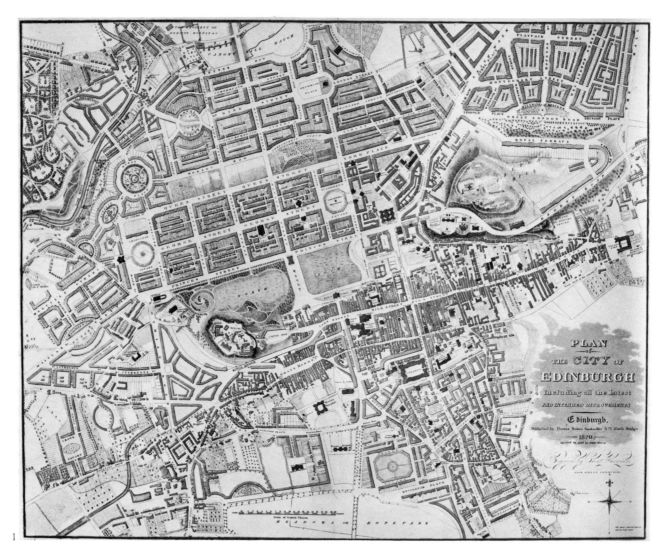

1 Edinburgh – a plan of the city in 1820. 2 Saint Bernard's Well, a view by the water of Leith. 4 Moray Place in the New Town.

church in Charlotte Square. All is regular and in the grand tradition.

But at the east end of this classical half-mile is a natural feature which invited something different. This is Calton Hill. Rough and rocky, the hill seemed to call for a Gothic silhouette, answering the ancient castle across to the south-west. The first buildings on it must, it was felt, have battlements. The old observatory, the two prisons on the lower slopes and, after Trafalgar, the cylindrical Nelson tower, were all rude, castellated and in the most conventional sense, picturesque. Then the mood changed. Princes Street was driven towards the hill and roads built round it. The rough old hill was to be

3 *The Edinburgh acropolis as it was foreseen – a Parthenon (5 shows the fragment that was built) fronted by the Royal High School.*

civilised and there was talk of landscaping in terms of Claude and Poussin. A new image, still picturesque but immensely grander, emerged. Calton Hill could be the *Greek* counterpart of the *Gothic* castle – an acropolis.

The notion proved so acceptable that a facsimile of the Parthenon was seriously proposed, and even

begun, as a memorial of the Napoleonic wars. Twelve lonely columns stand there, sad witnesses of too rash ambition, but more evocative perhaps than the mass of a reproduced Parthenon could ever have been. After that, everything on the hill was to be in a Grecian Spirit. On the lower slopes stands a truly original and scenically magnificent interpreta-

1 Sir John Soane's museum. 2 His portrait in old age by Lawrence. 3 The Breakfast Room exemplifies Soane's 'poetry of architecture'.

tion of the Greek – Thomas Hamilton's Royal High School. Had the mock Parthenon been finished, the High School would have played, visually, the supporting role of the Propylaea at Athens. But in isolation it is still an impressive piece. By some miracle of ingenuity Hamilton managed to accommodate the school with hardly a single window showing in the grand front. We read the building simply as a poem in praise of Greece.

Edinburgh after Waterloo, grew fast. The architects of the New Town, versed in all that had been achieved beyond the border – in Bath by John Wood and his son, in London by Nash – invented within the outlying estates a composite labyrinth of streets, circuses and crescents. You can lose yourself in the cool monumentality of the scene: cool and hard with the veined hardness of Craigleith stone. With such stone at hand, how exciting to be truly and precisely Greek! And as you move into the fringes of the town and go down by the Water of Leith, wrought stone and nature meet in a delicious suburban Picturesque. Nowhere in this island do you feel nearer to the Spirit of the Age.

'Landscape with Buildings', the title chosen for

this journey into the past, seems, so far, to have justified itself, even in the perimeters of great cities like London and Edinburgh. How much further can we go? Does the spirit of the Picturesque extinguish itself in suburbia? Is it exclusively a property of nature and the open air? We can try these questions by going to the heart of the greatest urban agglomeration of the age, the City of London, and considering a building totally withdrawn, windowless and concentrated inwardly on one purpose only – the protection and management of a great hoard of bullion – the Bank of England.

No London building, except perhaps Newgate Prison, fenced itself so positively from intrusion – and, one would suppose, from the Picturesque. But that is to take the exterior only and too literally, at face value. Unhappily, the bank as it stands today, its interiors rebuilt and an arrogant superstructure raised above the old walls, can tell us little. The old building we must visit in imagination, helped by the many drawings still preserved in the place from which we set out – Lincolns Inn Fields, No. 13, Soane's house and museum. For Soane was the architect of the Bank.

Soane's Bank was not one building but many. Within those disciplined walls was a mystifying system of halls, court-yards, residences, offices and dwellings, built over a long period. Of those buildings the chief were the domed or vaulted halls where the Bank's business was conducted and it is in these that we would have found irresistible evidence of the picturesque spirit. The halls had to be lit from the top or high up at the sides. They could not be conventional architecture and Soane did not try to make them so. He had to draw on the spirit of the primitive, the 'natural', that spirit which he had absorbed as a young man in the dawn light of Paestum. Severe and cavernous, the bank halls were decorated only with such ridges and grooves and flutings as would catch the light and fortify the geometry of the forms. The play of light was all.

This submission to nature and the sheer excellence of light was not unique to Soane or, indeed, to architecture. We find it in the painters, and in one painter especially – Turner. Turner and Soane, as it happens, were friends. Soon after Soane had finished the first group of halls, in 1803, Mrs Soane bought two watercolours from the painter and presented them to her husband. They are still in the Museum. One is of the vaulted crypt of Kirkstall Abbey, a dark interior, gently disturbed by sunlight from two sources, one seen, the other unseen. The other has only distant buildings; it is an explosion of cloud and light in a mountain landscape. Light in landscape, light in an ancient ruin, light in vaulted halls in the City of London – an unspoken community of feeling between architect and painter.

In Soane's Museum we can see in miniature this play of light and space. Soane called it the 'poetry of architecture' when he described his little Breakfast Room, a room where a shallow dome hangs between two hidden sources of light while at the top of the dome is a tiny lantern filled with old stained glass. Walls and dome are grained like oak and among the few enrichments is a scroll ornament borrowed from Mycenae – another reminder of Soane's reverence for the primitive roots of his art.

We began our excursion by looking at a portrait of Soane at twenty-six. We may end it under Sir Thomas Lawrence's portrait of the same man fifty years later, in 1829, eight years before his death. Soane survived to the very border-line of the age to which his ideas belonged. Turner and Wordsworth, younger than he, moved forward, transmuting the spirit of that world into something different, something which lived on. Soane, old and honoured, professionally as grand as Sir William Chambers had been in his time, died and took his fame with him.

He was buried under the monument he had built, twenty years before, for his wife. It stands in a public garden, once a parish graveyard, in the railway hinterland of St Pancras. All the headstones have been shifted; they are huddled round a tree. But the Soane monument survives, standing alone, to puzzle the rare visitor by its extraordinary form. It is a sort of dolmen, a primitive chamber-tomb, wrought and domed by a Georgian hand. Within the 'dolmen' is a more refined monument of white marble with miniature Greek columns: civilisation, as it were, lodged within the vault of eternity. Eternity is the theme for, wrapped round the pinnacle of the tomb is that ancient symbol, a snake devouring its tail. Stranded where it is, in a little urban park, the monument is a melancholy thing. Soane imagined it in a different scene. Among the many studies he made for it is one which shows it alone and radiant in an English landscape, with woods, a stream and a background of distant hills – the world of the Picturesque: a world where death is less odious, where bleak eternity becomes the everlastingness of Nature.

Soane's tomb.

6

MARK GIROUARD

ALL THAT MONEY COULD BUY

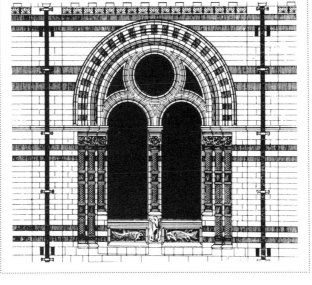

Fifteen years or so ago, when I was first getting really hooked on Victorian architecture, St Pancras Station, and especially what used to be the St Pancras Hotel, were favourite resorts of mine. Security wasn't so tight in those days. On Sundays or late in the evenings there was an unattended back door through which one could slip into the hotel and have the whole building to oneself. When I first came onto the extraordinary staircase I could scarcely believe it was possible. Almost nobody knew about it; it lay unvisited and inaccessible. Although it was in the centre of a great city, one felt like an explorer stumbling on a deserted temple in the jungle.

But it wasn't only the staircase which was extraordinary. I think it was on a winter Sunday morning that I first penetrated to the very top storeys of the building and came upon an iron ladder scaling the wall and vanishing through a trap door. It was irresistible. I went straight up to it, and found myself in the eerie spaces of the main roof, crisscrossed by a web of rafters. It felt like being inside an immense skeleton. I climbed rather gingerly up the long quivering ladders and finally came to what I knew must be the last trap door. One push, and I was through it, on a little platform perched on top of the world, with the huge balloon-like roof of the train shed immediately beneath me, and all London spread around me.

It was a memorable moment, and has left me with an especially warm feeling for St Pancras. It's not a feeling shared by everybody. It used to be considered one of the biggest jokes in London. Writers on architecture had a stock sermon, in which Kings

Cross and its neighbour St Pancras featured as the good and bad sisters – honest functionalism as opposed to pretentious historicism. Tastes have changed, but most people still think of it as an amazing, and even slightly sinister, oddity. And yet so much of its age is summed up in it. It's worth using it as the base for a circular trip through the past, and coming back with, perhaps, better informed eyes; because the more one understands St Pancras, the more one understands Victorian architecture, and the society which lay behind it. The trip can start, naturally enough, with the railways, and especially the Midland Railway, of which St Pancras was the terminus.

We tend to take the railways for granted nowadays, but in the nineteenth century they were dynamite – quite literally – millions of tons of rock and hill were blown up as they thrust their way across the British Isles, and so was a way of life that had lasted for centuries. When it took four hours to get from London to York instead of four days everything was bound to be different. It wasn't only people that could move faster and more cheaply but materials and ideas as well.

In the old way of life people lived in small communities and off the local countryside: for the most part never moved outside them. They built out of the local countryside as well, using local materials, because it was impossible to get anything else, and local styles – only very slowly modified as a new idea trickled through – because they didn't know any others. The railway changed all that. They produced cities, monstrous conglomerations of humanity crowded together in a few square miles, sucking in people, food and materials by rail from all over the country and spewing them out again. The materials were changed by the marvels of mass production into goods of every kind; far cheaper, more plentiful and easier to come by than ever before. The people were primed with new ideas, new knowledge and new techniques. The old small communities survived to a large extent alongside the new cities, but their old isolation was gone for ever. The cities themselves were joined to other cities by the railways, while steamships forged across the oceans to yet more cities joined by more railways (the latter mostly financed by British money and built by British firms). The world had shrunk.

One result of all this was money. Money distributed with gross unevenness and unpredictable in its behaviour – but nonetheless great glorious gol-

den piles of it for those who were tough or lucky. Money for merchants and manufacturers, lawyers and property developers, builders and bankers. Money which poured into the pockets of those who had property already, as it doubled and redoubled its value. Money which those without had to fight for but which, once won, was theirs to do what they liked with. For it was an age which believed in low taxation and unbridled competition. Money to build not only bigger and better houses but all the new types of building which the new cities produced. Money for hotels and railway stations, for office and government buildings, for factories and hospitals. Money for the new town halls with which each new city armed itself to demonstrate it was richer than its neighbour. Money for libraries, colleges and schools, to teach more and more facts and techniques to more and more people. Money to build all those buildings so solidly that they could last for centuries and to cover them with unlimited quantities of ornament.

All this money didn't, of course, only produce enormous buildings. It produced hundreds of thousands of small buildings, many of them equally fanciful, on their more modest scale. None were more so than typical Victorian country railway stations and of these Cromford Station, in Derbyshire, is perhaps the best to survive. It too is a product of the Midland Railway, but at the other end of the scale, and of the line from St Pancras. When one first sees it, it is impossible to take seriously. One expects an Emmet train of the most whimsical variety to come puffing out of the tunnel, and a globular station master with curling moustaches to emerge from his office and sing an aria about his love for a gas inspector's daughter. But in fact, like all these wayside stations, it was a little stick of dynamite, disguised as a box of chocolates to make it seem harmless to the natives.

The explanation for its fanciful appearance is that it acted as a kind of railway entrance lodge for the family that lived at Willersley Castle up the hill. But these weren't old-established country gentry. They were the Arkwrights, descendants of the man who invented the spinning jenny. He settled in the Cromford valley in the late eighteenth century because the River Derwent provided power for his cotton mills. A string of other families built mills along the valley after him. A canal was built to take away their products, and also the lead and iron mined up in the hills. Then the railway came and threw the whole world open to them, and you can

The railway station at Cromford in Derbyshire. Built by the Midland Railway, it served as a kind of entrance lodge for Willersley Castle.

watch how their mills swelled and soared as a result.

The line ran from Derby to Manchester; the idea behind it was to link the Midland towns and mills to the Manchester warehouses, and beyond them to the Liverpool docks and to America. To do so the engineers had to blast through the Pennines, building viaducts, and cutting tunnels, and in the view of conservationists of the time, raping some of the most beautiful scenery of the British Isles in the pursuit of wealth. In passing, the railway lifted up the little town of Matlock from a very minor eighteenth-century spa to a booming tourist and health resort. In 1857 John Smedley, whose father owned a stocking factory up above the valley, founded there what was to become the world-famous Smedley's hydro, to which rich industrialists, gorged with a year's overeating, flocked from all over the British Isles to be flushed out with

his hydropathic water treatment. Smedley did so well out of it that he built himself a mock castle up above Matlock, from which he could survey the town he had created like a feudal baron above his fief.

It wasn't only the middle classes who benefited from the railway line. If one follows the River Derwent upstream past Matlock, past Darley Dale where the great Manchester armaments manufacturer, Whitworth, made a little settlement, it will take one into a dream landscape of an Arcadian beauty famous all over the world: Chatsworth, the home of the Cavendishes, Dukes of Devonshire. It seems a long way from the cotton mills, railways, stations and hydros around Matlock. But it isn't, and I'm not only talking about geography. Much of the immense wealth of the Cavendish family in the nineteenth century was derived from the intelligent

Paxton's Crystal Palace of 1850 was a model for later prefabrications. Cast iron and glass technology found another use in train sheds.

development of their estates, so that they benefited to the full from the railways and the industrial revolution.

The link between the Duke of Devonshire and the world of commerce and industry, Joseph Paxton, was a clever young gardener who had caught the eye of the bachelor Duke when he was working next door to one of the Duke's many houses. He was made head gardener at Chatsworth, and after that never looked back. He became an extraordinary combination of pupil, friend, business adviser, companion, governess, counsellor and protector to the Duke. He made the garden at Chatsworth the most famous in the British Isles, but he soon became much more than a gardener. Among other things, he introduced the Duke to the railways, and especially to the Midland Railway Company – who

were ultimately to build St Pancras. In 1844 when the Duke was short of money, Paxton negotiated, on very profitable terms, the sale of one of his properties to George Hudson, chairman of the Midland Railway. The Duke got the money he needed, Hudson got a fine country house and a large estate which effectively blocked the route of a proposed railway line financed by another company. So everyone was happy.

In 1845 Paxton thought up the idea of a line from Derbyshire to Manchester. He got the Cavendish family, and the business men from Birmingham, Derby, and Leicester, who ran the Midland Railway, to join together to finance it. One advantage to the Duke was that the line went by way of Buxton, a spa and holiday resort which had grown up on land belonging to him – the moment the railway got to it

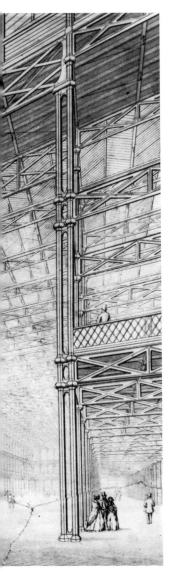

A London terminal for the Midland Railway. By 1868 the arch of Barlow's great-train shed for Saint Pancras Station was taking shape.

it rapidly doubled in size. Another was that the Duke got his own semiprivate railway station at Rowsley, near, but not too near, Chatsworth.

The line from Manchester to Matlock has been closed, Rowsley Station is empty and abandoned, and it's hard, now, to think back to the days of its glory – the day for instance in 1851 when the Duke of Devonshire set out from here for the opening of the Great Exhibition in the Crystal Palace in London.

The Crystal Palace was very much a combined product of Chatsworth and the railways. Paxton had built a series of bigger and yet bigger glasshouses at Chatsworth – culminating in the so-called Great Stove, in its day the biggest glasshouse in the world. He had no practical training – he just had a brilliant practical intelligence. In 1850 he applied his glass-house expertise to an even bigger fish – a new building for the International Exhibition proposed to be held in Hyde Park in London in 1851. A special committee had been appointed to design a building for it, and had finally come up with something so expensive and so ludicrous that there was a universal howl of protest.

Meanwhile time was running short. It was at a board meeting at the Midland Railway office in Derby that Paxton first doodled his solution on a piece of blotting paper. Everyone knows the ultimate result – it was the culmination of his Chatsworth glasshouses, the first large-scale piece of prefabrication in the world, made up of hundreds of standardised parts which were assembled at such miraculous speed that the building was designed, accepted and completed within eight months of the

1 *Thoresby Hall, Nottinghamshire, a great Victorian country house. Domestic offices and courtyards proliferate to the right of main entrance.*

blotting paper sketch. But it was the railways that made it possible. It was the Midland Railway engineer, W. H. Barlow, the man who finally pushed the High Peak rail through to Manchester, who checked the structure and made sure it would work. It was the railways which carried the standardised girders and columns down from the factory in Staffordshire and brought the glass from Birmingham. And it was the railways which finally brought visitors in hundreds of thousands from all over the British Isles and from all over the world to see the handiwork of all nations in the completed building. The situation is typical of the period – the railways as the solvent, the middle-class businessmen col-

laborating with the aristocrat, the aristocrat backing the inspired amateur, the amateur collaborating with the clever professional.

Having seen the upper layers of the Victorian social cake in action in one valley, it's time to examine them at home, work and play over a wider area. Everywhere, the railways changed the quality of life. A familiar trophy, for instance, in country houses all over the British Isles is an elaborately decorated wheelbarrow and silver spade, equipped with which a local landowner would cut the first sod for a new stretch of railway line. There's a set at Thoresby Hall in Nottinghamshire, complete with an inscription recording their use by the third Earl

The visitor to Thoresby, met by butler and footman at the front door (2), made an organised progress to meet his hostess in her drawing-room (3).

Manvers, the owner of Thoresby, to inaugurate the Sheffield-Lincoln stretch of the Manchester, Sheffield and Lincoln Railway in 1890.

The line crossed his land three miles to the south of Thoresby Hall where he lived. It was a late arrival on the Victorian scene because Lord Manvers, like many Victorian landowners, began by being extremely suspicious of these newfangled railways. Up till 1890 they came no nearer to Thoresby than the Great Northern line at Retford, six miles away. But like all his fellows he came to terms with it in the end, because there was so much in it for him.

It wasn't only that the railways whisked him and his guests to and from Kings Cross, taking him up for a quick visit to London or smoothly conveying twenty or thirty guests down for a weekend. Less socially, but more remuneratively, they carried away the coal from the mines which were springing up on his estate (suitably out of sight of his house of course). By the 1860s coal was appreciably swelling his already large income. The first Thoresby had been built in 1671 and accidentally burnt in 1745. The second Thoresby had been built in 1762, on a reduced scale because the family finances were embarrassed at the time. The third Thoresby replaced it in 1868 and was much the biggest of the three.

The first visit to a great Victorian house like

Thoresby Hall. All over Thoresby inconspicuous doors linked the world of the grand staircase (1) to another completely utilitarian world.

Thoresby always made a deep impression – especially if the visitor was a foreigner, who didn't know what to expect. The curtseying lodge-keeper's wife who opened the gates, the long drive through a richly rolling park, the deer grazing under the trees, the first view of the great house with its towers and turrets, the front door which swung open as they arrived to disgorge butlers and footmen, the stately progress to their welcoming hostess sitting in her drawing-room or dispensing tea under the cedar on the lawn, the thickly car-peted and luxuriously furnished bedrooms, the effortless and almost invisible care with which they were looked after, made up an inimitable mixture of informality and grandeur – which was, nonetheless, imitated and admired by other upper classes all over the world.

It all must have seemed wonderfully feudal at the time. And so, in one way, it was. But Victorian country houses – older houses adapted for the Victorian way of life and especially brand-new houses like Thoresby – were in their way pieces of Vic-

3 *The Hall, at Thoresby.* 4 *The two-storey conservatory of Flintham Hall, near Newark, an evergreen world overlooked by a balcony.*

torian machinery as elaborate as Victorian steam trains or beam engines. They worked just as smoothly, to designs worked out just as carefully, by Victorian professionals – in this case architects rather than engineers. All over Thoresby inconspicuous doors linked the world of the grand staircases, halls and corridors to another quite different completely utilitarian world, threaded underneath and in between the grand part of the house, a world of back passages and back stairs up which footmen and housemaids hurried and scurried carrying their trays, buckets, jugs and scuttles.

The front door opened to disgorge its reception committee so magically when a guest arrived because the butler, in his pantry in the tower over the porte-cochère, had a panoramic view of the park and drive and could, the moment a carriage came in view, slip with his minions down a backstair and along a short passage to a back door which took them straight into the entrance vestibule. And as the guest was being ushered with pomp and ceremony first to his welcoming hostess, and then up the grand staircase to his bedroom, his luggage, which had vanished inconspicuously through a little entrance just by the front door, was ascending to the bedroom floor in a gurgling hydraulic lift by the backstairs. By the time the guest made his or her bedroom everything was neatly unpacked. Another backstairs took the tea tray up from the still room, where the housekeeper and the still room maids made and kept cakes, tarts, scones and jam. Another hidden route conveyed Lord Manver's dinner invisibly for the fifty yards or so from the kitchen through basement passages and up yet another backstairs to a serving room next to the great dining-room, where it was heated up again.

All over the house, up and down these concealed bolt-holes, servants were hurrying all day long – taking dirty boots to the boot room, muddy coats to the brushing room, dirty linen to the enormous and cumbrous sinks and boilers of the laundry, and dirty paraffin lamps to the lamproom, or answering the jangling bells that summoned them to every quarter of the house – each bell connected to its bell pull by a system of wires threaded through pipes that wound and snaked behind walls and under floor boards all over the building.

On three sides of the exterior of Thoresby there's nothing to show that all this secret life was going on. But on the fourth side the bland world of carriage sweeps, lawns and flower-beds give place to something very different. An inconspicuous semi-underground road to the right of the entrance court-yard leads to a warren of back yards, service yards and kitchen yards, of bakehouses, washhouses and laundries, of dry larders, wet larders and game larders, of storerooms and sculleries. An arch over the sunken road connects the laundry to the walled yard where clothes were hung out to dry. Beyond it is the stable yard with its long rows of stalls, looseboxes and coachhouses and the harness room once festooned with polished and glistening tackle.

The social centre of all this busy life was the immense servants' hall. There were fifty indoor servants at Thoresby in its prime. The senior servants, it's true, ate in semi-aristocratic seclusion in their own room, but the outdoor servants ate in the servants' hall along with the junior servants, so there was no problem about filling it.

And at the end of their long day the servants filed up yet more backstairs to the bedrooms in the attics. They weren't bad little rooms, each with its own fireplace and a view out over the park or the roofs of the house. But they were certainly a long way removed from the comfort and spaciousness of the principal bedrooms. In wandering through them it's impossible not to ruminate on how unevenly the cake was sliced in Victorian days, and how the Victorian way of life and the buildings that went with it were only made possible by an endless supply of, in our terms, outrageously underpaid labour.

Thoresby, of course, is almost as grand as you could get – a home for an earl with an income big enough to support a duke. But one can follow the Thoresby formula right the way down the social scale, for everyone in Victorian England who could anywhere near afford it, wanted to live like a lord – or at least like a gentleman.

Flintham Hall, near Newark (and only about twenty miles from Thoresby) was built – or to be exact remodelled – by a country gentleman called Mr Hildyard in about 1850. It's on a smaller scale than Thoresby, but still imposing enough. It's got a porte-cochère, like Thoresby, and one tower instead of three, a very much smaller park and less extensive gardens. Its servants' quarters aren't as interminable as those at Thoresby, but they go on for long enough. And it is actually one up on Thoresby in that it has a conservatory – a very splendid one two storeys high, tacked onto its enormous drawing-room (also two storeys high with a gallery round it at first-floor level). Even in the depths of winter you can gaze out of the drawing-room windows into lush greenery and imagine you're in Italy: there is even a little semi-Italian balcony window off the gallery for a Romeo and Juliet balcony scene up above the geraniums. Conservatories attached to the house were a late Georgian invention, but under the Victorians they proliferated, and advances in glass and iron technology enabled them to become bigger and more elaborate. A passage in the *Daisy Chain* (1856) by the novelist Charlotte M. Yonge nicely evokes the feelings of wonder which these exotic appendages inspired at the time. In it the local doctor's son describes how Meta Rivers, the graceful young daughter of the squire, goes from the drawing-room into the conservatory to 'cut sprays of beautiful geraniums, delicious heliotrope, fragrant calyanthus, deep blue tree-violet and exquisite hothouse ferns . . . It is a real bower for a maiden of

The staircase, St Pancras Station. For Scott the station demonstrated that Gothic could be made to work in a complicated modern building.

COLOUR *A painted ceiling at Castell Coch.* 1 *A perspective of the Norham Manor estate, prepared in 1860 for Saint John's, Oxford.*

romance, with its rich green fragrance in the midst of winter. It is like a picture in a dream. One could imagine it a fairyland, where no cares, or grief, or weariness could come.'

If Thoresby is Mark I and Flintham Mark II, Marks III, IV and V are all the hundreds of rectories and villas and desirable seaside residences which the Victorian age brought to birth like mayflies in summer. In them the porte-cochère has vanished and the park shrunk to a shrubbery, but there is still often a tower and almost always a conservatory and a backstairs and a servant wing at the back opening onto a back yard. Some of these villas and rectories can be pretty imposing, with a billiard room and a servants hall, ten bedrooms and a platoon of monkey puzzles. But even the smallest cling to their turret and conservatory and carriage sweep that twists as much as it can to make the most of the fifteen yards from the road to the front door. And inside there's still a ladder-like backstairs for the two servants and a back door opening out onto a minute yard for the coalshed and the toolshed. And never, never, is it possible for the servants to direct their vulgar gaze out of the kitchen window and watch the gentry – the vicar's daughter or the bank manager's daughter, or whoever it might be – playing croquet on the lawn.

By shrinking the country house it was possible to accommodate every layer of the middle classes. Don't be misled into underrating them by the fact that their houses are less grand than the great country mansions of the upper classes. As a body they were a formidable force. It was they who had largely created and developed the industrial revolution and as the cities and the factories and the railways grew the middle classes grew with them. Early on in the nineteenth century they discovered that, although they might be small fry compared with the great aristocrats individually, if they banded together they could become the most powerful force in the country. Perhaps their first triumph was the Reform Bill of 1830, which forced the upper classes to take them into partnership in governing the country. Another victory was the repeal of the Corn Laws in 1846 which brought cheap bread to the cities at the expense of the profits of the country landowners. Repeal was the result of agitation by the Corn Law League, an exclusively middle-class pressure group. All over the country groups of solid prosperous middle-class men dominating city and town councils, hospital and school boards, committees to run railways or joint stock banks, were commissioning buildings which are, in the aggregate, far more impressive than anything built by the upper classes.

Villas or houses, like this one in Hampstead, which were scaled down versions of Victorian country houses, sprang up everywhere.

Middle-class houses and villas also have to be seen in the aggregate. The whole becomes greater than the sum of the parts. Any individual villa is one of a set of twenty or fifty or a hundred others, discreetly spaced along leafy roads, bastions of influence and respectability, with a church in the middle where the neighbourhood can come and express its communal solidarity on Sunday morning.

Sometimes a group, by forming together in a more organised way, managed to get something that approached the amenities of a country house, with lodge gates and a lodge keeper to keep out undesirables, a winding drive and a little park, or at least a spacious communal garden, with villas in a circle round it. The first of them, Calverley Park at Tunbridge Wells, was designed by Decimus Burton in the 1830s and 40s. But you find them all over the British Isles – often on the high ground of a city, out of sight (and mind) of the back-to-back houses crammed in the valley below.

If the middle classes could get something of the

The middle classes made palaces collectively. The central saloon of the Reform Club, Barry's version of a Renaissance palazzo courtyard.

amenities of a country house by joining together in the suburbs, they could enjoy even more of the amenities of a palace by joining together in the City centres. Fifty years ago Pall Mall, in London, was a street of palaces – and a good many of them still survive. The palaces are the great clubs, put up mainly by the middle classes in the nineteenth century – the upper classes tended to congregate round the corner in much smaller eighteenth-century clubhouses in St James's Street.

The Reform Club is not the earliest of the Pall Mall clubs, but architecturally it is the most influential. Its name indicates its nature. It stood for Reform, which at the time really just meant more power for the middle classes. It had a sprinkling of aristocrats among its members, but essentially it was for the cream of the middle classes – from merchant princes to the Editor of *The Times*. A good few of the directors of the Midland Railway belonged to it.

The Club started because Brooks's Club in St James's Street – the club for Whig aristocrats and gentlemen – refused to admit this class of member.

Scarborough: The view is dominated by the distant Grand Hotel: a typical Victorian seaside resort at the height of its splendour.

So they went off on their own and the result, if not as select, was a great deal more magnificent than Brooks's. The Club was built between 1839 and 1841 to the designs of Charles Barry, the architect of the Houses of Parliament. He had the brilliant idea of making it like a Renaissance palazzo – brilliant because many of those palazzi were built for the merchant princes of the Renaissance and this was to be for the merchant princes of the Victorian age.

The Reform had the best food in London, and the building went with the food. It was an architectural banquet with each course different from, but as sumptuous as, the last. The culmination was the great central saloon, the result of another brilliant stroke by Barry. Most palazzi have an open central courtyard, with arcades round them – very suitable for a Mediterranean climate. Barry simply roofed the courtyard in and the result was a glorious room – where the members can sit in their leather armchairs up in the galleries sipping their coffee and commenting on how old Jones is showing his age as he shuffles across the floor below.

The palazzo – merchant prince idea caught on

The pattern was for the upper classes to make a place fashionable and the middle classes, who flocked to it, to make it large.

with the middle classes. Innumerable other palazzo clubs sprung up in cities all over the British Isles. And the palazzo type was adapted for the banks where the middle classes stored their money and even for the warehouses where they stored the goods which produced the money. There's scarcely a main street in Britain which doesn't show the influence of the type.

The combined purchasing power of the middle classes was formidable in the suburbs, formidable in the cities and equally formidable when they went on holiday. Holiday resorts were largely an eighteenth-century invention but in the nineteenth century the railways and the middle classes immensely increased their size and numbers. The normal pattern was for the upper classes to make a place fashionable and the middle class to make it large. A Victorian merchant liked to think he was as good as any lord. But he also rather liked to meet a lord on the promenade when he was on holiday.

Scarborough is a typical Victorian seaside resort. It started as a spa frequented by the Yorkshire gentry in the eighteenth century. The railways arrived in the 1840s. About 1860 a very rich and

1 In Scarborough's Grand Hotel men could live like lords, their wives like ladies. 2 The staircase of the Royal Hotel, Scarborough.

smart Yorkshire peer, Lord Londesborough, bought a big villa at Scarborough as a holiday residence. He used to have the Prince of Wales – the future Edward VII – to stay, which set the seal on the town's reputation as a place frequented by a nice type of person. It grew and grew in the nineteenth century and then, like a lot of English resorts, stopped growing in the twentieth when people discovered that the Mediterranean was warmer.

So it survives today as an almost untouched Victorian resort. Everything is there. The classical railway station, where the trains disgorged their cargoes of nice solid Midland families, very well capable of paying their bills. The plentiful sprinkling of good expensive churches, all Gothic. An equal sprinkling of good expensive non-conformist chapels – mostly classical, to show they were different. A spa building, with ballrooms and concert rooms attached, rather French. A town hall, neo-Jacobean. Mile after mile of terraces, crescents and villas, all solidly built of good Yorkshire stone, and nearly all letting rooms. And finally, endless hotels

– small hotels, medium-sized hotels, large hotels, and one monster – the Grand Hotel.

The giant hotels, another joint product of the railways and the middle classes, appeared wherever the Victorians gathered in large numbers, for business or pleasure, away from their homes and clubs. The first to be built in London in the 1850s were mostly attached to the railway terminals, but they were soon to be found in holiday resorts as well. Like clubs they needed a distinctive image and they found it in a mixture of German schloss and French château. The great mansart roofs that were recognisable from half a mile away also provided useful accommodation for the servants.

The Grand Hotel was designed in 1863. The money to build it came from Leeds, as did the architect and, I suspect, a large slice of the clientele. The architect was Cuthbert Broderick, who had made his name with Leeds town hall. The town hall still dominates Leeds, in spite of later tower blocks; the Grand Hotel dominates Scarborough even more effectively. With typical Victorian self-

confidence, not to say brashness, it enters into competition with the great Norman castle which, even in ruin, had lorded it over Scarborough for centuries – and comes off with at least equal honours.

The clientele could live like lords – even more lavishly, if less selectly, than in a club – moreover their wives, who were not allowed into the club, could live like ladies. They could stand on the top of the great staircase and walk down it to the music of a string band and feel like Lady Manvers walking down the great stairs at Thoresby to open a ball. Now, of course, everyone goes up and down by lift – but there wasn't a lift when the Grand Hotel was built, and in a big Victorian hotel a grand staircase was an essential.

It's time to turn to a character upon whom much of this chapter hinges – the future architect of St Pancras, who was destined to out-trump the Grand Hotel and make its great staircase look like the Third Division. Scarborough is a suitable place in which to introduce him, because he spent two months there at a moment of crisis in his career. In 1859 the Grand was not yet thought of, and he probably stayed in what was then Scarborough's best hotel, the Royal. It was a much smaller concern than the Grand, but also had a very splendid main staircase weaving and curving up a pillared central hall. He must have been a distinctive figure as he walked up and down the promenade with his wife and four sons. His massive brow – for he was what the Victorians liked to call 'nobly bald' – bulged out between scanty but ill-combed side locks above a set of handsome features. His clothes were very untidy, but, as someone put it at the time, 'his negligent dress and ill-brushed hat were counter-balanced by a certain unconscious dignity in his manner'. One might have taken him for a distinguished but ineffective don, had it not been for an occasional exceedingly sharp glance which shot out from under his thick eye-brows – and for his astonishing ability to collar the best seats in the lounge. The hotel servants if asked would have told one that he was Mr Gilbert Scott, the great architect, that he was a thoroughly nice gentleman who put on no airs, and that he was in Scarborough to recover from his shocking treatment by the government in the matter of the new government offices.

It's worth lingering a bit over Scott. Up till now we've been looking at Victorian buildings, mostly in terms of who lived in them and how they were used – it's time to try and look through the eyes of the

architects who designed them. And no eyes were more typically Victorian than those of Scott. He was – ignoring the snide remarks of some of his fellow architects – the pride of his profession and the epitome of the successful professional man. Born in Buckinghamshire in 1811, he was the son and grandson of evangelical clergymen, and spent his youth in a succession of country rectories. In his autobiography – a fascinating and revealing document – he takes pains to make it clear that he was also distantly related to several very good families and that his mother was a 'particularly ladylike person'. As a boy he spent so much time wandering round the local churches and antiquities that his father decided he should become an architect. He entered an architect's office at the age of fifteen, with his head stuffed full of visions of noble Gothic churches – it came as an unpleasant shock when he found himself set to drawing up two-storey brownbrick suburban villas. Later on he graduated to the office of Henry Roberts, the architect of the Fishmongers Hall, at the end of London Bridge, and he made most of the working drawings for that delicate and distinguished classical building.

In 1834, at the age of twenty-three, he decided to set up his own practice, in partnership with a young Cornishman called Moffat, who had worked in the same offices as he had. That year the famous or infamous Poor Law had been passed, which required workhouses to be built in immense numbers all over the country. Scott and Moffat spent the next five years travelling furiously up and down the country selling themselves to Poor Law Guardians and working night and day producing designs for workhouses. They did well, and although the work brought them little if any prestige it brought in enough money to enable them to branch out into more reputable fields.

It didn't really matter very much what style the workhouses were built in as long as they were cheap. But once he started to become more ambitious, Scott, like all architects of his generation, had to decide the burning question of the day: what were his buildings to look like? This was a relatively new question for architects. Limitation of money and materials, of knowledge and technology had limited the options open to architects and pushed the history of architecture along a relatively narrow course – or, to be exact, a series of narrow courses. But during the nineteenth century these limitations disappeared. The architect who sat at his drawing board in the 1840s knew too much. A series of handsome folios in his library provided him with illustrations of the architecture of all the world and all the ages. New technologies enabled him to make his spans wider, his buildings taller and his panes of glass bigger than ever before. New machinery was mass producing ornament. New means of transport immensely increased the range of materials available to him. And new money was bubbling and gushing out of his clients' pockets to pay for it.

As a result of all this knowledge, and of the changing attitudes of mind which it produced, the classical tradition which had dominated European architecture since the sixteenth century lost its hold. Architects had dug back into the English past to revive old styles, whether Norman, Gothic or Elizabethan, or old types like the country cottage or the feudal castle. They went abroad for ideas, and had a go at the Egyptian, Indian, Moorish and Swiss styles. Even within the classical tradition all sorts of old styles were revived, from Greek to Rococo.

On the whole, by the 1830s architects were taking this all for granted. An architect's job was to choose the style which suited the commission. Gothic was suitable for churches, Egyptian for cemeteries, castles for the aristocracy, country cottages for their mistresses, Greek for learned bodies, Italian Renaissance for clubs, Indian for retired nabobs, and so on. Most architects kept to one style for one building, but a few were more adventurous and experimented with mixing styles together.

Gilbert Scott started as an eclectic architect. In the 1830s he produced buildings that were classical, Gothic and Elizabethan. He might have gone on doing this sort of thing for the rest of his career. Many architects did so, but others were less happy – especially architects from serious religious middle-class backgrounds like Scott. All these styles and all this money and all this opulence worried them. Shouldn't the Victorian age have a style of its own, like every other age? They were ready for a prophet, and the prophet came. He spread a new gospel by means of a series of slim cheap books bound in green cloth and stamped in gold with his initials, AWP – Augustus Welby Pugin.

What Pugin had to say was a revelation to young men in a muddle – it was so utterly and refreshingly simple. Everything that had been done in the last three hundred years was trash. The only hope for architecture was to go back to the middle ages and start again where they left off. Everything must be Gothic. He backed his thesis up with a lively battery of arguments. In the first place Gothic was 'English'.

'Another objection to Italian architecture is this: we are not Italians we are Englishmen.' This went down very well at a time when England was rapidly engaged in making itself top nation. And then Gothic architecture was Christian – the architecture of faith and the architecture of charity. This went down with all the people, and there were a lot of them, who thought that a set of cold-hearted intellectuals were destroying the fabric of English society. Pugin's great hate was the Poor Law. To him it was the ultimate symbol of reason instead of heart, the State grinding down the faces of the poor, as opposed to the church looking after them.

Finally Gothic architecture was truthful, based on true principles. According to Pugin there were three main principles behind Gothic architecture and his statement of them was to be enormously influential in the nineteenth century. Firstly, Gothic was truthful in its use of materials. Stone looked like stone and wood looked like wood – in contrast for instance to the Nash Terraces around Regent's Park all built of stucco to imitate Bath stone, or the plaster painted to imitate marble, or the cheap wood grained to imitate expensive wood so often found in the interiors of buildings of that time. Secondly, one could tell from the outside of a Gothic building what was going on inside it. In a Gothic college for instance you could see at a glance where the hall was and where the chapel was, where the warden's lodgings were, where the students lived, where the tower was, and where the bells hung. A modern college was usually just one great solid block. Finally, Gothic decorated its construction instead of constructing its decoration. You could see at a glance how it stood up – the buttresses, flying buttresses and the pinnacles that weighed them down expressed its construction, and these constructive elements were ornamented to make them decorative features. Pugin supported his thesis with lively illustrations, glowing passages of purple prose and slashing attacks on all the buildings of his own time. 'No one can look on Buckingham Palace, National Gallery, Board of Trade, buildings at the British Museum or any of the principal buildings lately erected, but must feel the very existence of such public monuments a national disgrace. . . . In the new Royal Exchange we have another stale dish of ill-adapted classicisms. . . . A man who remains any length of time in a modern Gothic room and escapes without being wounded by some of its minutiae may consider himself extremely fortunate'.

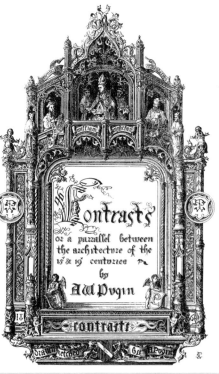

1 The title page of Pugin's 'Contrasts'. 2 A plate from the book contrasting Soane's house ('The Professor's own house') with one in Rouen.

In contrast with all this he covered page after page with glowing and euphoric illustrations of what Gothic buildings in the nineteenth century could be.

All Victorians with a religious background tended to think in terms of conversion, of the moment of truth that changed their lives. They tended to experience conversion not only in a religious sense. Some were converted in a blinding flash to teetotalism, others to Gothic architecture. Scott was one of the latter. As he put it himself: 'Pugin's articles excited me almost to fury. I suddenly found myself like a person who has been awakened from a long feverish dream which had

Pugin's Saint Giles, Cheadle (3), and 4, Alton Castle: a proof that Gothic was not just for churches, but could be the setting for a way of life.

rendered him unconscious of what was going on about him. Being thus morally awakened my physical dreams followed the subject of my waking thoughts. I used suddenly to dream of making Pugin's acquaintance and to wake once while on a night journey in high excitement at the imagined interview.' The interview finally came and was not a

total success. 'He was tremendously jolly, but had almost too much bonhomie to accord with my romantic expectations. I very rarely saw him again, but I became a devoted reader of his written and visitor of his erected works and a greedy recipient of every tale about him.'

During the 1840s Scott had a lot of work on in

Scott's Foreign Office from Saint James's Park (classic, despite his protests). His brother Gothicists thought he had betrayed the cause.

Staffordshire, and one can be just about certain that he went to see Pugin's masterpiece, the church of St Giles at Cheadle. Here Pugin had the backing of the richest and most pious of his patrons, the millionaire Earl of Shrewsbury. St Giles was a three-dimensional expression of everything he had written. Its immense spire, soaring out of the rather dingy little town, shouted out that Christianity was still important in an increasingly agnostic world. Everything was solidly built of rich red local stone or the solidest oak timber, but it was the interior that really sold Pugin's message. His enthusiasm,

his warmth and his excitement washed all over it in glorious waves of pattern and colour. There was colour everywhere, colour in the tiles, colour in the windows, nets and waves of colour and gold rippling and washing up and down the walls and columns. The local people who came crowding in when it was first opened thought it was like going into fairyland.

But Cheadle wasn't the only building put up by Lord Shrewsbury and Pugin in that neighbourhood. The Earl lived a few miles away at Alton. There his father had built a crazy house in an immense extravagant garden which stood for everything that

The richly carved and decorated top of George Gilbert Scott's Albert Memorial, erected on the site of the Great Exhibition in Hyde Park.

Pugin hated. The garden was crowded like a junk shop with buildings of every style, from a scaled down model of the Choragic monument to Lysicrates in Athens to a Chinese pagoda in the middle of a pond. But on the other side of the deep ravine which ran beneath the village Pugin put up a little Gothic settlement. There was a school and a chapel, a convent and an alms house for poor men. Perched on a crag at the edge of the ravine was a house for the Earl himself. It all went to show that Gothic wasn't just for churches but could be the setting for a way of life.

So Scott, as a result of reading Pugin's books and seeing his buildings, was converted to Gothic, thought Gothic, dreamt Gothic and built Gothic. He sat on committees, led deputations, wrote letters to the paper and pamphlets – all for what he liked to call the Cause with a capital C. He wasn't by any means the only Gothic revival architect, and a good many of his fellow Gothicists thought that he was too much of a populariser, but he was much the most successful of them. To begin with he designed mostly churches, and had a special line in restoring cathedrals, but then in 1856 came his great chance

1 *The Natural History Museum at Oxford, as it appeared in 'The Building News' of 1859, by Woodward, but influenced by John Ruskin.*

of showing that Gothic was just as adaptable for a great secular building. A competition was held for new government offices in Whitehall, including the new Foreign Office. Scott went in for it with a set of Gothic designs. The competition was divided into two parts, Scott came third in one of them, but didn't get a mention in the other. 'I did not fret myself at the disappointment', he wrote. 'But when it was found a few months later that Lord Palmerston had coolly set aside the entire results of the competition, and was about to appoint Penne-thorne, a non-competitor, I thought myself at liberty to stir.'

The results of his stirring were typical of his career. A new government had come in, and although Scott had only been third in the competition for one of the buildings, he somehow managed to get himself appointed architect for both of them. It seemed a moment of triumph had come both for him and for the Cause.

But then the government changed again and Lord Palmerston was back. Like the majority of educated men of the time he was an eclectic, and he thought Gothic was perfectly all right for churches, but that a big public building in Whitehall should be classical like all the other buildings there. 'Lord Palmerston

3 The interior of the Natural History Museum. Iron capitals support the main ribs of the roof. 2 Stone ones from the surrounding arcades.

sent for me and told me in a jaunty way that he could have nothing to do with this Gothic style. And that though he did not want to disturb my appointment, he must insist on my making a design in the Italian style which he felt sure I could do quite as well as the other.'

Poor old Scott was in a predicament. For two years he wriggled and protested. At one time he tried out a compromise, and made a design in what he called 'Byzantine turned into a more modern and usable form'. He thought that the result was both original and pleasing in effect, but Lord Palmerston didn't. He described it as 'a regular mongrel affair,

neither one thing nor t'other', and would have nothing to do with it. In the end Scott gave in. He bought, as he put it, 'some costly books on Italian architecture', and designed the building that stands in Whitehall today. He defended himself with vigour: 'To resign would be to give up a sort of property which Providence had placed in the hands of my family, and be simply rewarding my professional opponents for their unprecedented attempt to wrest the work from the hands of a brother architect'. But most of his brother Gothicists thought that he had betrayed the Cause. It was during this unfortunate episode that Scott retired to

Scarborough for a couple of months to recuperate.

In spite of the Whitehall setback his career as a Gothicist continued to flourish. In the 1850s he designed a group of great Gothic country houses. In 1862 he won the commission for the Albert Memorial, which was to become much the most familiar, and also, at one time, the most derided of his buildings. But at the time it was much admired especially by the most important person of all. 'August 9th, 1872, I have been to stay at Osborne to be knighted. I have had a very agreeable day. Having made my bows the sword was handed to the Queen, she touched both my shoulders with it and said in a familiar gentle way, "Sir Gilbert". I thank God for the honour.'

But all the time Scott was coming under new influences. In the 1850s and 60s the Gothic Revival was in a ferment. The theory behind it had always been that it wasn't just going to copy or even to adapt Medieval Gothic, it was going to develop it into something Victorian. But how was this going to happen?

One way was to go back to Nature for ideas. Going back to Nature is something people are always doing, and what they mean by Nature is usually completely different in different centuries, and even in different generations. Around 1800 nature was thought of in terms of picturesque landscape. As long as vegetation or rocks formed picturesque contrasts of light and shade, people didn't care very much what species of vegetation or rocks they were – they could have been made of cheese for all they cared. But by 1850 people were looking at nature with the microscopic eyes of ants crawling over its surface – ants with a scientific training. Nicely brought up young girls picked and brought home bunches of wild flowers, drew each one with minute accuracy, and then pressed and kept them in slim leather-bound volumes. Their brothers crawled up and down cliffs and rocks tapping with their little hammers and bringing back sacks of geological specimens to clutter the shelves of their bedrooms. Painters – and especially pre-Raphaelite painters – painted rocks and leaves and flowers in a kind of fury of excitement, as though every vein in a petal or rock, every dewdrop on a leaf, was a matter of life and death to them.

In the Natural History Museum at Oxford the specimens have spilt over into architecture. Each capital on each of the pillars has a different plant carved on it. Some are rough and spiky with thistles, some are covered with waving ears of corn, others

with the delicate ferns that the Victorians loved to grow in their conservatories. A look up into the roof reveals a whole lot more vegetation (in wrought iron instead of stone), sprouting round the framework that holds the glass – and that iron framework is a kind of architectural version of the ribs of the skeletons underneath it. And every column is made of a different marble. Even the arches are made of stones of two different kinds.

The museum was designed in 1854 by a shy young Irish architect called Benjamin Woodward. But a dominant personality behind its appearance was John Ruskin, the greatest and most influential writer on art and architecture of his day. Ruskin was hypersensitively conscious of the beauty and the structure of rocks and trees. He too saw with that microscopic, ant-like vision. He had the ability to put his feeling across, both in exquisitely sensitive water-colours – which few people saw except himself – and in books which were read by hundreds of thousands.

Inspired by Ruskin and others, mid-Victorian architects became more and more aware of the materials of which their buildings were made. They were really turned on by the stoniness of stone, the brickiness of brick, and the flintiness of flint. To see the kind of effect this had, one only has to go up the road from the Oxford Museum, to St Philip and James in the Woodstock Road.

St Philip and James was built in 1859–60 to the designs of George Edmund Street. Street had been one of the first pupils of Gilbert Scott, but I suspect in later life he didn't think all that much of his old master. His buildings are tougher than Scott's and don't rely so much on quotations from English cathedrals or Venetian palaces. St Philip and James is all about the stoniness and heaviness of stone. Street used two sorts of stone in horizontal layers; their alternation gives one a feeling of how the wall is built up, each layer pressing heavily on the next one. The spire is a great heavy chunky stone thing, and the windows are made up of heavy slabs of stone with holes punched through them. Inside, the church is a huge broad cave of rough stone. The arches don't have any mouldings to soften them, they are cut square to make as obvious as possible the thickness and weight of the wall they're carrying. And the columns are almost absurdly squat and wide, as though they'd been squashed by the heavy wall above them.

The nave is much wider than one might have expected, and the aisles much narrower. If the

St Philip and James, Oxford, by Street. 1 and 4 as it is today, and 2 and 3 as it was seen in 1861 by readers of 'Building News'.

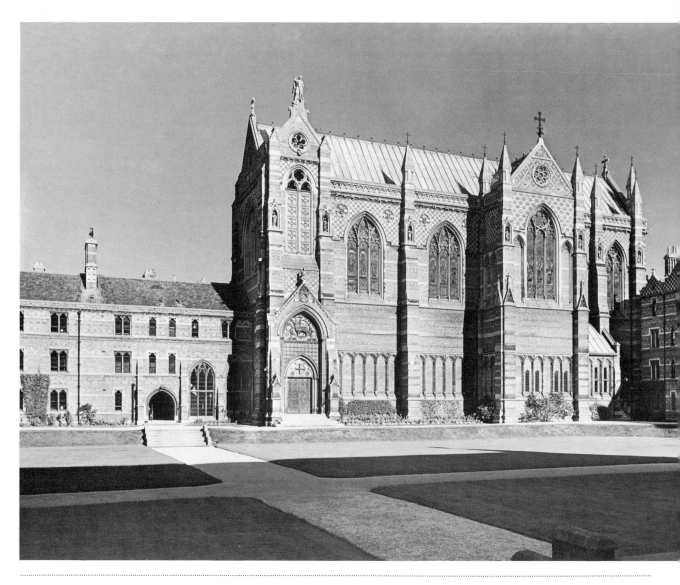

Keble College, Oxford. The mid-Victorians wanted things tough and solid and masculine: muscular buildings for muscular Christians.

church was imitation medieval Gothic this would be all wrong, but it isn't an imitation, it's a development. In the middle ages naves were narrow, and as a result the pillars got in the way of the view, because the builders couldn't manage a wide roof. Street, with improved techniques, could, and so he made very narrow aisles, really just to act as passages. The nave narrows when it gets near the altar, and width isn't needed any more. It narrows in the most casual way; it just bends in and runs smack into the cross wall. It isn't pretty, nothing about the church is pretty, but the mid-Victorians didn't want things pretty, they wanted them tough and solid and masculine. The slang word for this kind of architecture at the time was 'muscular'. It went with the hairy mid-Victorian man with huge beard, going round the world, bossing people and showing that England was on top.

At much the same time as St Philip and James, Street designed St James the Less in Pimlico which is a kind of half-brother in brick to his stone church in Oxford. It has the same tough strong shapes, but Street used the more manoeuvrable material to produce much more complicated and smaller scale patterns in two colours. The church is shaped and spotted like some glorious red and black zebra. The most virtuoso Victorian performance in this line, however, is back at Oxford, just across the road from Woodward's Natural History Museum. It is Keble College, designed in 1867 by William Butterfield.

Keble was intended for the children of clergymen, and was largely paid for by a rich and pious family called Gibbs, who had made a fortune from guano. At Keble, Butterfield mixed two colours of brick and one of stone to cover the whole building

Keble chapel – a detail of the decoration. Every surface covered with chequer boards, zigzags and diapers, in two colours of brick, one of stone.

with chequer boards, zigzags and diapers. It may seem a long way from nature, but it isn't really, it's just a different kind of nature. The patterns are no more exotic than those to be found on the shells, the feathers on the breasts of birds, or the fur of animals on display in the museum across the road.

One can find this kind of decoration scaled down (just as one can find a country house scaled down to the proportions of a villa), until one ends up with a gay little non-conformist chapel, patterned in two colours, with spires like candle snuffers, or back-street terraces where the houses have patterned tiles in the front porches and carvings of ferns, and tiles, to either side of the bay windows. Sometimes one can find a whole hierarchy of materials in one place. At Shadwell in Norfolk it neatly follows the social hierarchy. This complex was built in the 1850s by an architect called S. S. Teulon for the local squire, Sir Robert Buxton. One starts with labourers' cottages, very nice simple buildings in brick or flint. This is the lemonade or ginger beer level. With the vicarage we're on to the sherry – everything is just a bit more elaborate. But the fun really starts up at the hall, which is a kind of manic cocktail party. There are two colours of brick, flint either rough and knotty or split smooth, and stone either straight or elaborately carved. Sometimes these ingredients are served individually, but usually they're mixed in every imaginable combination and spread over buildings of strange and wonderful shapes.

Structural polychromy was all very well, but, except in remote country districts, it had to fight against another typically Victorian element. In spite of all Ruskin's efforts, the dominant colour of the Victorian age was black. Black soot belched out of

Victorian fortunes like the Marquis of Bute's were built in thriving, squalid cities. 1 A Cardiff courtyard in 1891. 2 Warehouses by Doré.

thousands of factory chimneys and produced black banks and black town halls. Black filth poured into black rivers and black canals sluggishly moved between black warehouses. Black smoke gushed from the funnels of the railway trains that were carrying all those gaily coloured materials over the country, and settled on black back-to-back houses crouching under black viaducts.

The Victorian age was the first great age of pollution, of cities spreading over the green countryside like a black growth. The underside of Victorian architecture is squalor, slums, poverty, filth and noise. If you were rich, you got out. At the beginning of the nineteenth century the mouth of the River Taff in South Wales was little more than a swamp. By the end of the century it was Cardiff docks. Eight million tons of coal a year rumbled and smashed down the shutes into the holds of the coal

boats that crowded there. Thousands of dockers lived in rows of little houses by the dock gates. Beyond the little houses was a big, thriving, filthy city created out of the coal which passed through it.

And at the edge of the city lived the man whose family had created it all – the Marquis of Bute. When he came of age he inherited an income of about £150,000 a year. He was a curious, clever, remote man – uneasily poised between two worlds – at one moment managing Cardiff and his other immense properties, playing the role of a public figure, but then escaping with relief to the delights of scholarship, of travel, of archaeology and of building.

His house at Cardiff had been a castle, and he turned it back into one – with formidably fortified walls and towers to keep the city and the nineteenth century at bay. His architect was William Burges, a

William Burges's medievalist fantasy, Castell Coch, only five miles from the centre of Cardiff. 3 The gateway. 4 Lord Bute's bedroom.

man obsessed with the Middle Ages. In the 1870s and 80s Burges built him an even more secure retreat a few miles up the river. It's called Castell Coch. It has a draw-bridge and portcullis that work, holes from which to pour boiling oil on unwanted callers, and even a fireplace in which to boil the oil. Inside everything is very dark, and very solid, and very unreal. It's a strange, brooding Gothic world of vaulted rooms and rich colour, fluttering butterflies and mysterious carved figures, mirrors and crystal balls glowing in the dim light. Even the everyday business of washing one's face becomes mysterious and exotic when the washstand is like a little castle.

If you look through the Gothic windows the view looks for a moment like something in a medieval illumination – a clean river in a green valley. But if you lift your eyes up you see something else – in the far distance the cranes and towers and smoke of

Cardiff. There's a funny feeling of tension in the room. Perhaps it's because this brooding quietness up here is living off all that noise and dirt down there.

At Castell Coch medievalist fantasy and nineteenth-century reality are separated by a five-mile gap. At St Pancras they're on top of each other. It's time to go back to that extraordinary building and look at it again, perhaps better prepared to understand its size, its flamboyance, its architecture and its architect – who was, of course, Sir Gilbert Scott.

In 1865, a few years before Castell Coch was started, Scott heard a bit of news which seems to have sent him into a fever of excitement. For many years the Midland Railway had been chewing up more and more of England, but it had never had its own line to London. Now it had acquired one.

1 William Barlow's train shed for the Midland Railway at St Pancras, completed 1869, had the greatest span of any building in existence.

William Barlow, who had constructed the Peak railway line, and advised Paxton about the Crystal Palace, was celebrating its arrival with a gigantic railway shed at St Pancras which would have the biggest span of any building then in existence in the world. But in addition the railway directors were holding a competition for a gigantic new station hotel. A hotel admittedly wasn't as prestigious as a great government office, but here was another chance for Scott to design an enormous secular building in the middle of London. He retired to a little hotel near Portsmouth and set to work.

By then the Grand Hotel at Scarborough was going up, and Scott must have seen the designs even if he hadn't seen the building itself: it was the most magnificent hotel of its kind in Europe. Scott set out to design something even more magnificent, and something Gothic. When the elephantine rolls of drawings were carried in before the directors they weren't in any doubt. Scott was their man. What a slap in the eye for their old enemies, the Great Northern at Kings Cross on one side, and the London and North-Western at Euston on the other. A giant hotel was the great new status symbol of the time, and neither of their rivals had anything to compete with it. A Gothic hotel was, it is true,

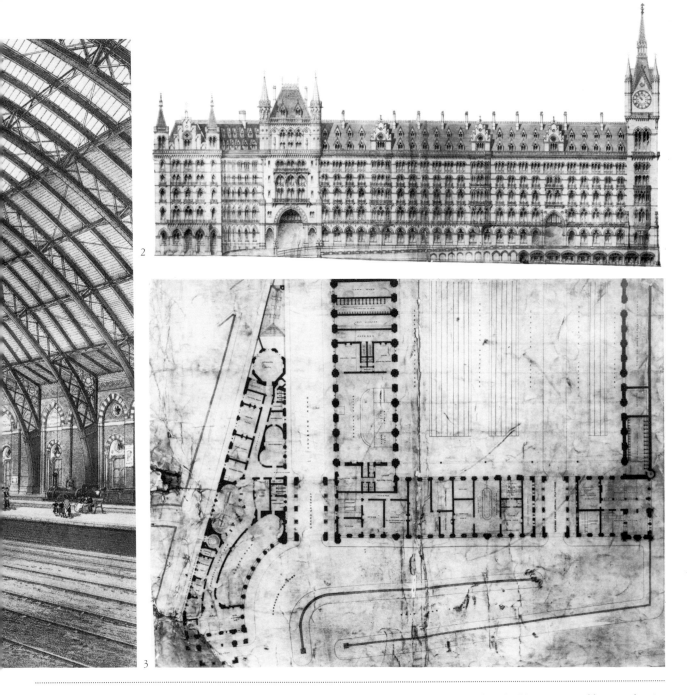

The Saint Pancras Hotel. 2 The Euston Road elevation, with curving ramp. 3 The plan. Scott fitted his building onto an odd triangular site.

unusual, but then it was different, and something different was what they wanted. Something different from the great doric portico at Euston, and from the enormous station arches at Kings Cross which looked as though they had been built on the cheap, as indeed they had. Scott was given the commission.

So he added his hotel onto the front of Barlow's train shed, and one can go through the combination checking off all the typically Victorian elements which it contains. To begin with, Barlow's immense leaping roof of glass and iron is a triumph of Victorian engineering, a descendant of the more modest greenhouses of Paxton. Scott was delighted to

find that for purely engineering reasons, Barlow had made his roof in the form of a Gothic arch.

Then there is the Victorian gift for turning difficulties to advantage; Paxton showed it when he solved problems of time and expense by prefabricating the glass and iron cobwebs of the Crystal Palace. At St Pancras one of the problems was that the railway had to cross over the Regent's Canal further up the line and therefore arrived at Euston Road about twenty feet above ground level. Barlow made capital out of this by raising his train shed and building an immense basement below it, with shops all round the outside and storage space, which could

The Saint Pancras Hotel: 1 Scott's design for the dining-room. 2 One of the bridges that carry the first-floor corridors across the entrance arches.

be let at a good profit, in the middle. Scott made capital out of it by building a curving ramp to bring traffic up from street level and joining the two angles of the ramp with splendid swooping flights of steps. He made capital out of the fact that he was landed with a very odd triangular site between the station shed and the road by bringing the façade of his hotel round in a glorious curving sweep.

And St Pancras is tied up with the economics of its time in a typically Victorian way. It isn't just that it's a piece of competitive advertising for the Midland Railways. It was also an advertisement, and a

3 Saint Pancras Hotel – the train shed is just visible to the left, and the altogether simpler silhouette of Kings Cross Station to the right.

reward, for the Midland firms who used the Railway to carry their goods. Wherever possible contracts went out to customers of the Midland Railways. The stone comes from Ketton in Rutland, the bricks – Grippers patent bricks – from Nottingham. The slates come from Leicestershire. The great trusses of the shed roof were made by the famous Butterley Iron Works near Derby, and proudly carry their name. The wrought ironwork was all supplied by Skidmore of Coventry, and the interminable miles of vaults under the station were all designed to the module of barrels of beer from

Burton-on-Trent. The Burton brewers were at the time mounting a campaign to poach the markets of London brewers. One of their methods was to lend money to London pubs on condition that they sold Burton beer, and a lot of the more gloriously vulgar of late Victorian pubs are built with the Burton-on-Trent brewers' money.

St Pancras represents Scott's great moment of glory. It is commonly believed that he just took the rejected design for the Gothic Foreign Office out of a drawer and with a few strokes of the pen transformed it into a Gothic hotel. This is completely untrue, but it *is* true that all the frustration and guilt that had been building up as a result of the fiasco of the Foreign Office erupted as a result of this commission, and St Pancras came boiling out as a vindication. It's the most ebullient, the most original and the most enjoyable of his buildings.

He himself modestly said that it was perhaps too good for its purpose, but the Midland Railway directors didn't regret it and nor do we. For him it was a demonstration that Gothic could be made to work in a great complicated modern building. All Pugin's doctrines are expressed in it. It's wonderfully solidly built, with the very best materials, the best stone, and the best brick, and the best mahogany curving down the rails of the sweeping grand staircase. You can tell, or at any rate, guess, from the outside what's going on inside. The huge mansard roof with a little platform on top, above the big tower, was by now the recognised hallmark of a hotel. The grand reception rooms on the lower storeys have got very elaborate Gothic windows. The windows get less elaborate as the floors go up and the bedrooms get cheaper, until finally you are up in the roof with the humble dormer windows where the servants are sleeping. The jutting out bay windows mark the sitting-rooms in the more luxurious suites and what, in one case, was intended to be the Board Room of the Midland Railway, although in the end the company never had its offices there. It's perfectly obvious from the outside where the staircases are because the windows run all the way up the façade. It's equally obvious where the main entrances to the station are because of those huge arches like the west doors leading into a cathedral. But here again Scott showed the Victorian ability to deal with difficulties. If the archways had gone right the way through the hotel, the first floor would have been cut into independent segments. And so Scott ingeniously carried the first-floor corridors across the arches in cast-iron

bridges of delicate design. These look very decorative from down below, and when you're actually walking along the corridors you suddenly catch unexpected glimpses down into the station, with cabs driving underneath.

There's no monotonous skyline, such as Pugin hated; the skyline is full of excitement, but it's all got some kind of practical purpose. One tower contains the water tank, the other a clock. Inside on the great staircase, Gothicism is triumphant, but also adaptable and, in the terms of Pugin, truthful. The curving and flying flights of the stone stairs are supported on cast-iron girders, but these are prominently exposed and elaborately ornamented. 'Ornament your construction don't construct your ornament.'

St Pancras also shows signs of the mid-Victorian enthusiasm for 'muscularity' and combinations of materials of different colours. The great archways of the entrance front are rather like caves, dug into a looming cliff face. But they are caves of the kind that excite archaeologists, in which one can see layers of strata in different colours, like a neapolitan ice. The vaults too are striped, and brick and stone alternate in the voussoirs of the arches. Also in evidence are Victorian ideas about bringing nature into buildings, and making the function of a building show in its ornament. Carved vegetation and the heraldic monsters which support the coat of arms of the Midland railway are to be found everywhere. In the booking office the capitals are carved with members of the railway staff – a porter, a signalman, an engine driver and an engineer.

Besides being an exercise in Gothic, the staircase is an exercise in oneupmanship on the staircase of the Grand Hotel and all the other great hotels of the world. It was the most magnificent of them all, and was to remain the most magnificent; for the days of the great staircase were now about to go into a gradual decline. The rival that was to beat them appears, for perhaps the very first time in a big hotel, at St Pancras; a passenger lift, described on the plans as 'an ascending room', is inconspicuously tucked to one side of the stairs. For the time being Midland business men and their wives cautious of new gadgets, could still sweep regally up and down these stairs. And on their way St Pancras could supply them with a castle, as it could supply almost everything else – even if it was only in two dimensions. On the first-floor landing, hotel guests on their way up to bed could regale themselves with a painting entitled the 'Garden of Deduit', which filled an entire apse, railed off from the landing. Here, beneath a castle even more elaborate and fanciful than Castell Coch, medieval lovers dallied with their mistresses in a garden of lush trees, fountains, and fluttering doves. It was a nice piece of escapism for the middle classes.

In fact, the whole hotel could be described as an exercise in escapism. Modern Movement purists have always been shocked by the contrast between the shed at St Pancras and the hotel. They found the straightforward engineering of the shed exhilarating, and the Gothic fantasies of the hotel pretentious. Most Victorians had no such feelings, and who is to say which was right. In their view the shed was a triumph of science, and the hotel a triumph of art. The functions of the two parts were absolutely different. The shed, however sensational because of its scale, was purely utilitarian; it wasn't designed to live in but it was a place you hurried through to catch or leave a train. The hotel was designed to stay in and to linger in. It was designed to make splendidly evident to the people of London the existence of the Midland Railways. It was designed to give provincials up on a visit to London a feeling of glamour and excitement, and in both aims it abundantly succeeded.

It was also intensely class conscious and ostenta-tious to the point of vulgarity. There are some Victorian buildings which are completely free from snobbery and which manage to be impressive as architecture with the minimum fuss and elaboration. They are exciting and moving buildings, but they are not typical. St Pancras is extraordinarily representative of its age both in its virtues and its vices, which is why this chapter hinges upon it. It was an age which had more money and knowledge than it could digest, but in which both had to be fought for except by the small class to which they came by inheritance. So much wealth and knowledge brought problems, but they also brought power and the vitality that comes with the knowledge of power. So much inequality brought more problems, but it also brought the drama of contrast; every clever boy in the slums could dream of becoming a millionaire. In most Victorian architecture one has to stomach the snobbery and the ostentation along with the drama and the vitality. It would be hypocritical to deny that they can be extremely enjoyable. There is an endless fascination in unravelling the social gradation which the buildings expressed so accurately; and it is difficult not to feel envious of an age which could show off with such panache, confident in the knowledge that England was the centre of the world.

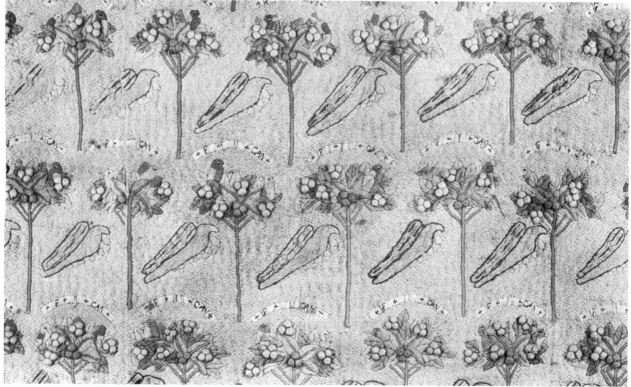

Two William Morris tapestries from Kelmscott Manor. Below the title is C. A. Voysey's elevation of Broadleys near Lake Windermere.

7

PATRICK NUTTGENS

A FULL LIFE AND AN HONEST PLACE

In 1859 the architect Philip Webb was commissioned to build a new house at Bexley Heath. The Red House was a landmark in the history of modern architecture. Not so much because of its style, which was fairly straightforward, based on the work of Butterfield and Street, but because of the furnishings and organisation of its interior, the ideology that lay behind it, and the personality of the man for whom it was built, William Morris.

Morris is generally accepted as the major figure in the birth of what came to be known as the Arts and Crafts Movement. The inheritor of a private income of £900 a year, a substantial sum in the 1860s, Morris went to Oxford University intending to join the Church, changed his mind and decided to become an artist instead.

He was in every way a full-blooded character. A man of ferocious turns of phrase and drastic condemnations – 'the swinish luxury of the rich', 'no slobbering and messing about' – he had furious tempers when he would beat his head with his fists; he was said on one occasion to have bitten his teeth into the rim of a table at which he was dining. He also had a great sense of humour, and was given to shouting, fencing, and having battles with soda-water syphons.

But all the time he was drawing and designing; breaking off the drawing to write poems and then return to designing again; writing poems into the early hours, impatient, bursting with nervous energy, pacing up and down at meals, twisting a fork with his teeth, breaking the occasional chair-back to emphasise a point. Accounts of life in the Red

The Red House by Philip Webb. The five years that William and Jane Morris lived there were crucial to the Arts and Crafts Movement.

House, full of young people at the weekends, with games and fights, with Morris 'coming up from the cellar before dinner, beaming with joy, his arms full of bottles of wine and others tucked under his arm', are of a life that was carefree, full, funny and content. 'We laughed', said a visitor, 'because we were happy'.

The Morrises – William and his stunningly beautiful wife, Jane, the subject of Rossetti's best portraits and model for some of the most characteristic Pre-Raphaelite paintings – lived in the Red House for only five years before returning to London. But it was in many ways a turning point for the arts.

The identification of the worth-while arts with the need to earn a living from them, to design only what you can yourself execute and to teach by doing rather than talking – all of these are central to the Arts and Crafts Movement. It was at its peak between roughly 1880 and the Great War, and continued well beyond that. Its ideas spread wider than the movement itself, forming a philosophy of life as well as a theory of art, a set of ideas that I have called

'A Full Life and an Honest Place'. This essay is an attempt to trace those ideas and to understand them both as history and as a still living tradition.

The basic theory on which the architectural work of the movement rested came from Augustus Welby Northmore Pugin. In *The True Principles of Pointed or Christian Architecture* he had stated the 'two great rules of design': that 'there should be no features about a building which are not necessary for convenience, construction or propriety', and, secondly, that 'all ornament should consist of enrichment of the essential construction of the building'. Of those principles the Red House was a good exemplar. It was Gothic in feeling, but exceedingly simple in its planning and its elevations – unpretentious, denuded of any unnecessary ornament or purely stylistic sophistication. Finished plainly inside, with plain plaster and wood and stone, hung with tapestries, its walls decorated with murals, and furnished with simple settles and benches and kitchen furniture, it was inspired by traditional English craftsmanship.

2 An interior at Kelmscott Manor, 'the house of a working man with a mission'. 3 The young William Morris (right) and Burne-Jones.

To get an impression of the total effect of an interior designed by Morris or influenced by his approach to design, it is best to look at the room in the Victoria and Albert Museum – richly coloured, almost oppressive but resounding with the revival of skills in the decorative arts. Or at some of his stained glass – the figures designed by Burne-Jones, the work carried out by Morris, who was responsible for the decorative backgrounds and the craftsmanship that went into them.

Such windows, and much of the decorative work and furniture, were made by his firm. In 1861 he had founded the firm of Morris, Marshall, Faulkner and Company (in 1875 it became Morris and Company) to design and make decorative work, wall paintings, stained glass, metal work, sculpture, embroidery and furniture for houses or for churches, 'all at the smallest possible expense'.

In fact its products could not be cheap, even if they were original, for he was deliberately fighting against the Industrial Revolution, which he saw as responsible for the degradation of man as well as the ruination of the crafts. The mass-produced goods of the world of mechanisation were contemptible compared with his; but they were, of course, cheaper. He had founded a firm, but he was inspired by a dream:

'Forget six counties overhung with smoke,
Forget the snorting steam and piston stroke,
Forget the spreading of the hideous town;
Think rather of the pack-horse on the down,
And dream of London, small, and white, and clean,
The clear Thames bordered by its gardens green.'

In 1871 Morris acquired the lease of Kelmscott Manor in the Cotswolds, and used it as a summer residence for many months each year.

The house was a traditional vernacular one, built about 1600 and extended about a hundred years later. The Morrises accepted it as it was. Morris furnished it with simple strong massive chairs and tables designed by him and by Ford Maddox Brown, with tapestries and murals, carpets, and, increasingly, wallpapers. There were one or two weirder pieces of furniture, like those designed by

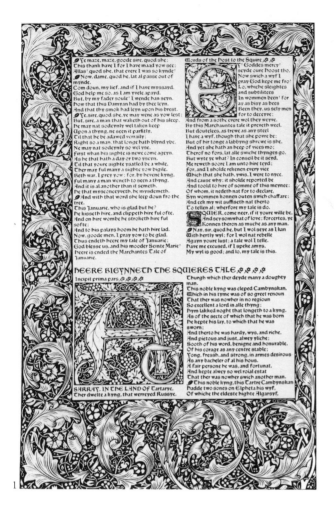

Designs of an astonishing range and quality flowed from Morris's hand. 1 A page of the Kelmscott Chaucer. 2 A chintz design.

Rossetti. But Morris's own designs were simple and straightforward. It was the furniture of the house of a working man with a mission. 'Have nothing in your houses', he said, 'that you do not know to be useful or believe to be beautiful'.

With that doctrine he became the leading theorist of the Arts and Crafts movement. And Kelmscott seemed to represent exactly what he wanted, in his strange, confused world of reality and romanticism. It was, in the title of his poem quoted above, *The Earthly Paradise*, a dream that haunted him as it has haunted the imagination of people since the earliest times. For him it was an earthly paradise of love and work. 'Love and work, yes, work and love! That's the life of a man!' he shouted one day. For that life,

for Morris and his spectacularly beautiful wife, Kelmscott was an ideal setting.

His output was phenomenal. By the time he was sixty he had, as Paul Thompson records in *The Work of William Morris*, 'published seven volumes of important original poetry, four of prose romances, six of prose and verse translation and two of lectures. His designs for patterns for repeated production in wallpapers, textiles, carpets and tapestry numbered over five hundred. In addition there were many individual designs for embroidery, tapestry, carpets and stained glass. He had started a private press which in eight years issued fifty-three books, requiring over six hundred separate designs for initials, borders, title pages and other orna-

3

The Morris Room in the Victoria and Albert Museum – almost oppressive, but resounding with the revival of skills in the decorative arts.

ments. He had supervised the production of more than five hundred stained glass windows, for which he had supplied another two hundred or more figure and pattern designs. He had mastered and revived the largely forgotten techniques of dyeing and tapestry, as well as several other less neglected processes. He had made a financial success of a difficult manufacturing business. He had made a lasting impact on English politics and became one of the few major English political thinkers. In the six years before 1890 he had delivered over two hundred and fifty public lectures. To both art and socialism he had in his prolific years contributed more than any other living man.'

For he was one of the pioneers of socialism. Echo-

ing Ruskin, he declared that 'Art is the expression of man's pleasure in labour'. Life and work and art were one. It was Morris's aim to make for the workman, whether he was a craftsman or any other kind of workman, a full life and one of dignity, in which he would be responsible for what he did and for the part he played in the creation of the environment. 'I do not want art for a few, any more than education for a few, or freedom for a few'. It was to be for everyman, both artist and worker. 'I have tried', he said to Wilde, 'to make each of my workers an artist, and when I say an artist, I mean a man.'

And in addition to all that he had founded in 1877 the Society for the Protection of Ancient Buildings. It was provoked by Gilbert Scott's scheme for the

A dish, designed by C. R. Ashbee for the Guild of Handicrafts in 1902 – the year they took over the old silk factory in Chipping Campden.

restoration of Tewkesbury Abbey, and it established the principles upon which most major restoration of old buildings has been carried on since – a policy affectionately known as 'Anti-Scrape'.

Ironically, such principles do not seem to have informed the restoration of Kelmscott itself. Because of the serious condition of the building and the need, increasingly revealed as the work proceeded, to carry out a major restoration, Kelmscott now presents a picture which William Morris never saw in his own time. It is clean and neat, somewhat sterilised, and rather bare. A fireplace hidden in Morris's time has been revealed. There is no bric-à-brac or clutter. Perhaps in some way it is a fitting symbol of the irony of Morris's own life.

For it is really one thing to create a full and happy life for the artist, even if he is considered as a workman; it is another to do something about the life of the workman. In the industrial environment of high Victorian Britain, improvement really required political action. Almost in the same year as Morris was founding the Society for the Protection of Ancient Buildings, Disraeli was passing his great Public Health Act, giving local authorities power to enact by-laws for health and for housing – for drains and policemen – as part of a remedy for the evils of the growing industrial cities.

Increasingly, by the second half of the nineteenth century, there were two worlds – the world of life and the world of art. There were also two nations – Disraeli's two nations. For most of the people, life meant the Victorian industrial scene, with its slum housing, its aggressive industry, its poverty, disease and misery. At the opposite end was the fashionable world of Art, with Royal Academicians receiving knighthoods, with more elaborate houses, with Architecture as opposed to Building.

In contrast to that, the Arts and Crafts philosophy, as exemplified by Morris, combined a belief in the importance of art and a belief in social reform. Art, like life, was for everyman. But how could art achieve social reform?

It could happen in two ways. On the one hand, Art could be an expression of social problems, revealed in paintings of industrial scenes and human misery. On the other, Art might itself be an answer to social problems, not withdrawing from them and commenting upon them, but in its own way acting as one of the remedies in a general scene of personal irresponsibility. The key to that was making the artist himself responsible, as a responsible workman.

Morris had created for himself in Kelmscott a world of craft and beauty. But such a world as he sought cannot be contained in only one house, or one carpet or tapestry or piece of wallpaper. It must be a society, preferably a community. And where would you find that society? Perhaps it was to be found in the English village or the small old English town.

In 1902 C. R. Ashbee – architect, teacher, socialist, who had been training people in the crafts in the east end of London and had founded the Guild of Handicraft in 1884 – moved to Chipping

Campden in the Cotswolds, took over the old silk mill and a number of semi-derelict cottages, and established his Guild on a larger scale. There were over one hundred and fifty men, women and children. In the silk mill the craftsmen worked together making furniture and metal work, and doing weaving and other crafts.

But getting away from the industrial city was not really the answer. Chipping Campden proved the death of the Guild of Handicrafts because Ashbee had moved himself from his markets. Although parts of it continued on a smaller scale, the Guild itself came to an end after six years. It was partly the result of an economic depression, more the result of the move to the country. And yet, in making the move, Ashbee had added another dimension to the Arts and Crafts movement. With unconscious but unerring instinct, he had in effect selected Chipping Campden as the scene for the recreation of the earthly paradise on a bigger scale than Kelmscott. In the early years of this century Chipping Campden presented a picture so extraordinarily complete, so native, so natural, so beautiful, so unaffected, and so unpretentious. It was coherent and humane.

For the Guild of Handicraft it was more than a perfect back-drop. It was a world of craftsmanship – of lettering, weaving, pottery, metal work, jewellery, furniture – all the decorative arts; a world of the artist as well as the workman. For Art is not just thinking. Art is not just personal expression. Art is not just establishing one's personality in the eyes of the fashionable world. Art is making things. Making things for all people, for every day. Making – and designing – it yourself.

I myself grew up in that tradition, and lived for much of my childhood in my father's studio, aware – and often reminded – that an artist takes pleasure in his labour, that the true artist-craftsman designs and makes and fixes his windows, that knowledge of the craft, a knowledge in the hands as well as the eye, must be the generator of design. My father worked for a time for a stained-glass artist in Chipping Campden. He made, however, his first stained-glass window before the First World War, and is still making windows as I write this. That insistence, upon the unity of design and making, always seemed to me fundamental. It was also central to the philosophy of the Arts and Crafts Movement, nowhere stated more emphatically than in W. R. Lethaby's introduction to Christopher Whall's book *Stained Glass Work* of 1902, the main reference book of the studio.

With the critical attention given to the crafts by Ruskin and Morris, it came to be seen that it was impossible to detach design from craft, . . . and that, in the widest sense, true design is an inseparable element of good quality, involving as it does the selection of good and suitable material, contrivance for special purpose, expert workmanship, proper finish, and so on . . . Workmanship when separated by too wide a gulf from fresh thought – that is, from design – inevitably decays.

If that unity existed, two things seemed to follow. First, in such a workaday world, an art form was very ordinary. There is really nothing unique about a stained-glass window. If somebody smashes it, it is not a major disaster, but a splendid opportunity to make another one. The crafts exist, after all, for the use and pleasure of everyman. They are works not of special genius but of skill and competence.

Secondly, if the work when finished brought new colour to everyone's life, the workshop in which it was made was also a part of life. It was characteristic of Morris and his followers that they not only thought the products should be enjoyed by as many people as possible, but that the artist in making them should create for himself and for the people working with him a satisfying environment. It might be some kind of community; it certainly meant that work could not be directed entirely with a view to making money.

Always, in the background and often in the foreground, was that basic conviction about the identity of art and craft – that there is a difference, known by the artist and craftsman, if not by every observer, between the object conceived, designed, drawn and made by one person, and one that is designed by one person and handed over to someone else to construct. That of course is the problem of architecture – the divorce of design and construction. On a smaller scale, the two can be united; and perhaps, it was thought, there was here a lesson for architecture to learn.

Chipping Campden was ready-made. Why not *create* a place where artists and like-minded people could live in appropriate surroundings? Such was Bedford Park, a suburb in London where, incidentally, my father worked for a most imaginative stained-glass artist, Martin Travers, before and after the First World War. Its church and inn still have the character of that period. The church is by Norman Shaw – large, spacious, with painted wood panels and pews and some stained glass by Travers. The inn with its generous display of coloured tiles by de Morgan, its plain wood, its slightly dull colours and its internal spaces inviting conversation, is very complete as a period piece.

Norman Shaw as the architect of country houses on a grand scale: the entrance front of Cragside near Rothbury in Northumberland.

Norman Shaw, although his work looks very like the work I have been describing, represents for me a different attitude of mind. Much of his work had superficial resemblances to that of the Arts and Crafts movement. He had the same love for a derivative kind of Gothic style, the same ability to play with details, to modernise and simplify them, to make everything a little more stylish, appropriate and contemporary. He could be a scene-painter on a glorious scale. At Cragside, a romantic site in Northumberland, he piled up a castle with all modern conveniences and wonderfully attractive spaces – a brilliant and witty exercise in the fusion of past and present, wholly suitable for a manufacturer of armaments.

He was the architect of country houses, town houses and vast hotels. He knocked up churches and pubs and houses, discovering a style that nicely reflected the mixture of pomp, cheerfulness and absurdity of Edwardian England. He was what Lethaby called a 'soft' architect as opposed to a 'hard' one – full of invention, gaiety, brilliance and novel ideas, an architect who could be whimsical, play in all styles, and bring them up to date. He was, I suppose, the Basil Spence of the nineteenth century.

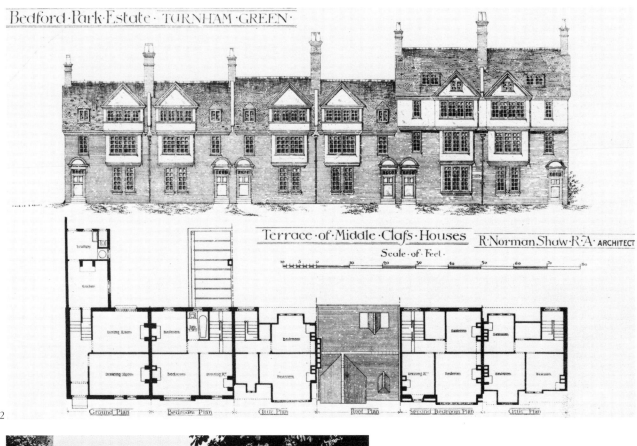

2 Norman Shaw on a domestic scale: drawings for a terrace of middle-class Houses in Bedford Park. 3 Woodstock Road, Bedford Park.

From the stable of Norman Shaw came a succession of architects, working with the same ingenuity, imagination and simplicity. Lethaby was one of them, Walter Crane, the designer, another. The best known in England was probably Charles Annesley Voysey, almost the quintessential architect of what has come to be accepted as the typically English house. His wallpapers were popular in Britain and the Continent. In the eighteen-nineties he became the leading figure in domestic architecture, creating low, homely and obviously comfortable houses, with bare walls and tall chimney stacks, irregular and informal, like a middle-class version of a Tudor manor. They became the prototype for the thousands of houses that lined the roads in the suburbs in the new century. His practice was extensive. He built one of the houses in Bedford Park. Probably his best country house was Broadleys on Lake Windermere, finished in 1898.

Voysey has always been regarded as one of the pioneers of the modern movement of architecture in Britain. In fact he hated it. It just happend that his houses looked simple and white and therefore gave an impression of belonging to the new age. Voysey was as much a romantic as a modern. He was concerned with the design of the house and of all the

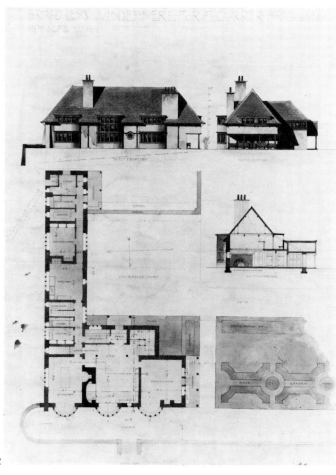

1 C. A. Voysey's 'Broadleys' near Lake Windermere, and 2 his drawings for it. 3 The interior of Voysey's 'The Orchard', Chorley Wood.

things that go inside it, from the furniture and fittings to the knives and forks. He created a delightful, relaxed, civilised and English environment.

But I have always felt that if there was an important quality missing from that school and from those architects, it was that hardness in which buildings are generated, not from appearances or from styles, however purified, however improved, but from the harsh realistic needs which lead to the planning of a building, and from the technological demands which make that building a modern one. To see that approach in one of its most complete expressions, you must go to Glasgow.

For it was in Glasgow in the 1890s that there came into prominence one of the more bizarre and fundamental figures in the development of modern architecture in Britain – a man who to me represents more precisely than anyone else the meaning of architecture at that time. Charles Rennie Mackintosh was born in 1868, the son of a Glasgow policeman. He was a draughtsman, a painter, a

designer, and a poster artist. He had a profound effect upon the artists and craftsmen of the city.

In the eighties and nineties the style of decoration fashionable in London and influential also on the Continent, was Art Nouveau. Mackintosh was able to pick up its themes, to design in them with as much skill as its more famous exponents, and to produce illustrations, lettering, drawings, patterns and artefacts of an equally strange kind. He became the leader of a young group who called themselves *The Four*. They were Mackintosh himself, Herbert McNair, and the Macdonald sisters, Margaret and Frances. Frances married McNair, Margaret married Mackintosh.

The Macdonald sisters were sensitive and gifted artists, of whom I suspect Frances was the more brilliant. It was she who was particularly responsible for the Four being nicknamed 'The Spook School'. Weird elongated figures — like those in Margaret's painting *The Pond*, inspired by Rossetti's sonnet 'O Ye, All Ye that Walk in Willow Wood' – began to

4 'The Pastures', a Voysey house in Leicestershire. The arched porch, buttresses, projecting eaves and leaded casements are Voysey trademarks.

appear in Mackintosh's interiors. Margaret was probably a more brilliant designer than Mackintosh of smaller things – of jewellery, brooches, pendants, knives and forks, all the details of a house.

Mackintosh himself was an unusual person. He had a drooping eye and a deformed foot; he was highly neurotic. He became an alcoholic. He established himself at first as a designer of interiors, simple, clean and white. He was also known as a designer of rather strange, tall and elongated, furniture. In 1896 he met the formidable Miss Cranston, for whom he designed a series of tearooms, which she was establishing in Glasgow. An antidote to gin-drinking, tea-drinking was respectable and artistic.

The tearooms, only parts of which now survive, contained most of the stylistic features of his major work – the use of lily pads, of tapering uprights, of a kind of architectural patternwork inside buildings based upon nature and particularly upon those weirder aspects of nature – ponds and wild woods – so popular with exponents of Art Nouveau. His

furniture, similarly inspired, has sinewy, elongated curves. The chairs are different heights and different types, even in the one room, like the trees and saplings in an enchanted forest: he liked the levels in a room to vary. Some of the chairs may look excruciatingly uncomfortable but underlying the freakishness and fancy was a basic realism – a passionate concern with the function of things. He made a detailed study of the needs of each client: he measured them up to make sure of the dimensions for their furniture, he stayed with them. They in turn paid tribute to his ingenuity and almost obsessive concern with their actual requirements.

He was translating functional needs into abstract patterns: the ultimate generator was always a practical recognition of needs. It is reflected in drawings, like some made on Holy Island (Lindisfarne) between 1901 and 1906. He drew with an unusually exact and sensitive line and the strange, dramatic unrectilinear form of the Castle is conveyed as simply as possible in profile. There is another view of it in which the three-dimensional character of the

1 The 'Willow Tearoom'. 4 The 'Dutch Kitchen'. Mackintosh's Glasgow tearooms contained most of the stylistic features of his work.

building becomes more clear. Those drawings capture the spirit of the place and express his own response to it. But behind that is a more practical Mackintosh. In the drawing of a cobbler's cottage and other studies made on the same island you can see that, essentially, he is an architect, drawing details, sketching out plans, thinking it out in terms of human needs.

The attitude that shaped his drawings, furnishings and interiors shaped his designs for a whole house. Hill House in Helensburgh, down the Clyde from Glasgow, is the best known. (It is now being restored and maintained.) It has a simple, rational plan – more original than the exterior which is fairly traditional Scottish in style. The interior reveals the same use of simple detail, and attention to practicalities. It was, like his furniture, an exercise in thinking things out *de novo*.

It can be seen in a concern for the needs of particular rooms – hall, dining-room or drawing-room – big or small. The sofa, for example, has carefully thought out niches for books. The windows are carefully placed and shaped, whatever effect that might have on the exterior. The best example is the main bedroom. It has three elements: the bed area, the dressing area (with its fittings, chair and washstand) and the sitting space. The room is shaped in such a way that all those uses become meaningful in themselves and have their appropriate place. Yet the whole is a unity – a bedroom that is one of the best known set pieces of the history of twentieth-century architecture.

Hill House was designed in 1902. But already in 1896 Mackintosh had won the competition for a new Glasgow School of Art. The building he set about creating between 1897 and 1899, and in a second phase between 1905 and 1909, was as seminal a public building in the history of the modern movement as Hill House was a private one.

The School of Art stands along a slope on the hill

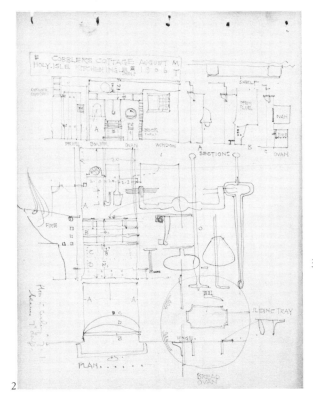

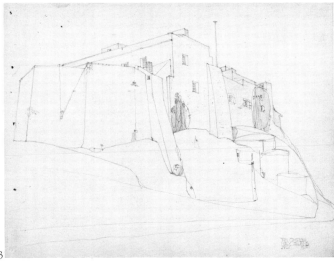

Mackintosh as a draughtsman: 3 The castle on Holy Island – before Lutyens's additions. 2 The kitchen of a cobbler's cottage, Holy Island.

rising northwards above Sauchiehall Street. It is organised in a straightforward functional way. The studios are along the north, the corridors, one above the other, are on the south. The library and lecture room are on the west. It was all very sensible, and capable of being built in stages. He modified things as he went along, adding at the later stage a further storey, linking the whole building together across the top.

The street front is plain and unsensational. But once inside, the magic of the manipulation of space for expressive purposes begins.

From the low entrance hall, the central stair rises up, timber built, dark stained with tapering lily stems with flat pads at the top. Horizontal floor joists project through and overlap, the walls are punctuated by tall vertical balusters with chequers at the top. What starts as a confined dark stair then spills open into the middle of an exhibition space, the corner posts carrying on upwards to join and support the roof truss. A roof light floods the space with unexpected brilliance. The themes are very basic – a movement from horizontal to vertical; from long to square; from close to open; from dark to light. These elemental things inspire his invention more fundamentally than the details that belong to his time.

The basic unit in a School of Art of the time was a studio. The main studios are twenty-six feet tall, splendidly lit by huge windows (originally by roof lights as well). The tall easels were designed by Mackintosh. The walls between the studios had their top halves hung by metal straps from deep iron roof beams, so that the lower halves could be moved and the studios opened up and enlarged. It was, in short, a flexible building.

Beneath the great windows, to their full width, are banks of horizontal pipes. And that reveals another dimension of Mackintosh's practical mind. Glasgow in the nineteenth century was a centre of

1 *The bedroom, Hill House. 2 The Library, Glasgow School of Art – everything is by Mackintosh, even lamps, chairs and periodicals' desk.*

technological innovation. Making use of developing knowledge in a city of shipbuilding and advanced technology, he became a pioneer in the application of systems of heating and lighting to architecture – in the technology of the servicing of buildings.

Below the basement corridor is another one – a man-height horizontal duct that runs the length of the building. Air was sucked in from the front, filtered through a screen sprayed with water to give it the right humidity, blown by a belt-driven machine made in Baltimore across hot pipes to warm it, and then into the duct. When the sliding shutters along the walls were opened, the warm air blew up vertical ducts placed along the internal spine walls of the building and entered the studios and other rooms at high level through grilles and adjustable vents. Such a system was fairly revolutionary in a building of this kind, and it had its faults. As the ducts got dirtier inside, the effect of

turning on the blown air was to deposit layers of dirt in the studios, sometimes on top of people's paintings. But it ran for forty years and was only replaced at the start of the Second World War when a new barbaric tangle of pipes and wires was littered around the building. The innovations did not stop at heating. There is another duct between the ground and first floors, ventilated from louvres on the south side, which took the electric conduits; it was one of the first buildings to be completely planned for electric lighting.

Mackintosh was unusually perceptive in recognising what was happening in building at the end of the nineteenth century. There probably never was a better time for building construction than the period roughly between 1870 and the First World War. It was the time when many new domestic gadgets were invented, when lifts came into use, when window openings became more sophisticated, when radiators began to appear, when the

Glasgow School of Art. 1 Wrought-iron brackets act as buttresses and rests for a cleaner's plank. 2 Studio with easels designed by Mackintosh.

lower levels of a building were ventilated in order to avoid dry rot. All sorts of cast-iron gadgets – shutters, pulleys and levers, stoves and warmers and coolers, and all the other appurtenances that the new age of technology made available – were used.

All the main components of the School of Art demonstrate Mackintosh's flair for making a vivid image out of a practical function. The end stairs, which were added in the second phase, pass through a sequence of strange bare spaces, of brick and plaster, concrete and iron, exposed as materials in their own right. In that manipulation of spaces and curves in three dimensions, you feel that the air has been carved up into solid forms. It is space seen in movement. At the top of the staircase the landing is protected by a wrought-iron grille of square chequers, which is in fact the projected diameter of a flat iron circle fixed to the roof ties – an abstract pattern generated by three planes at right angles.

Along the main corridor the patterns and themes continue. Rough dark boarding lines the walls. Windows are transformed, with unusual concern for

the social needs of students, into snug conversation boxes. At the end of the west wing is the library – perhaps the most distinctive room in architectural history.

Everything in it is by Mackintosh, including the chairs (although they came from one of the tea rooms that he was designing at the same time), the periodical desk (an assembly of eccentric interpenetrating structures) and the lamps. Simple geometric themes are used to create a deceptively elaborate hierarchy of spaces.

The basis of it is rectilinear. Strong vertical posts are met by gallery floor beams which strike them horizontally. A vertical plate at right angles to the beams covers the junction. The gallery front itself is set back, also at right angles to the beams. Its panels project downwards below the angles of the floor and end in Gothic frets, each of them different. At another right angle the gaps between the posts and the gallery are spaced with scalloped and coloured balusters. But if the interpenetrating right angles are the basic theme that creates the space, there is

Glasgow School of Art. 3 The main staircase. 4 The Director's room above the main entrance – the furniture is again by Mackintosh.

also a subtle descant – a rhythm of waving lines. The horizontal strip fixed to the front of the gallery is a wave on its panels. Above, on a different plane, there is a shallow arch along the top. The whole thing begins to swing together. The familiar square chequers darkly compose the ceiling. And across the gallery they are echoed in light by the square window panes. It is an extraordinary piece of virtuosity.

And it makes this fundamental point. To an architect like Mackintosh, architecture is not a matter of style or scholarship, of elevations or exteriors. It is the magical creation of space. Mackintosh is supremely the architect of space. Space is not just volume. Volumes may be big or small. Space is the manipulation of volume and mass, to create what Le Corbusier later called 'the miracle of inexpressible space', to make a meaningful interior in which the human being will feel at home and in scale, able to measure his activities against the three-dimensional reality that he inhabits.

And that seems significant to me, thinking against the background of the Arts and Crafts movement, because, in architecture as in an individual artefact like a stained-glass window, the ultimate realities are the simplest and most basic of all the things you have to deal with. And what does an architect have to deal with? He has to deal with ground and air and the materials he uses. The ultimate meaning of a building is communicated not by history or by style, but by sheer delight and joy in the site, in the space and in the materials themselves: if the space is left as clear as possible, and if the materials are used with their own particular characteristics and in their own natural organic way – where wood is wood, and iron is iron, steel is steel, and copper is as coppery as copper could ever be. The space, the air inside the building, is as real and tangible as anything else. What the stained-glass artist does with light, the architect does with light and space and the movement of people.

There are two features of the Glasgow School of Art that seem to me especially expressive of Mackintosh's attitude to design. If you look up the

The Garden City: Letchworth, a panorama taken in 1912. The town was begun in 1903 with low densities, a rational organisation

windows inside the library, you see on one side the projecting bay windows and on the other a cut-back part of the gallery. They mirror each other. One is dark on light, the other light on dark. Each is the reverse of the other, in shape and pattern, figure and ground – a composition in space of wholly abstract form. Mackintosh's architecture contributed to the development of abstract painting, which in turn came back to inspire modern architecture.

The other feature is the row of wrought-iron brackets on the windows of the north front. At first sight they might be mistaken for merely decorative twists of metal, playing with space and making it look more dramatic. In fact the brackets are structural, buttressing the huge mullions of the studio windows. And more. The bases of the brackets are projected to make iron pads so that boards can be laid across them and window cleaners can rest their ladders on them. Organisation and technology, structure and aesthetics, are united in one meaningful form.

Mackintosh's work had, for a short time, a great influence on the Continent. When he and his wife went to an exhibition of his designs in Vienna, in 1900, they were drawn through the city in a flower-decked carriage by architectural students – as rare an honour as any architect has experienced.

The more general influence of the architecture of Britain on the Continent was stimulated by a significant publication between 1905 and 1911. Hermann Muthesius, secretary at the German Embassy in London, was so inspired by what he saw about him that he published three volumes under the title *Das Englische Haus*. That 'Englische Haus' – the English House – became for a time one of the main influences upon the architecture of the Continent. Muthesius's three large volumes are in effect a history of possibly the most inventive and humane period in the domestic architecture of this country. He studied it not merely as an example of style, picking out the more interesting and evocative examples; he looked at the house in its entirety, at its plans and its details, its electricity, its heating and its plumbing, and also at its gardens and its setting.

For the logic of the Arts and Crafts movement demanded that the full life and the honest place must extend beyond the interior and the house and

of roads and play spaces. It remains a conscious attempt to create an unpretentious background for the growth of a community.

the garden and the village and the public buildings to the town and the city. It was an idea about community. And any idea for a better house must be vitiated if the town it lay in was itself inhuman and degrading.

Lethaby, writing in *Form in Civilisation, 1922,* related this problem to the town of Oldham. 'All England', he said, 'is becoming more and more like Oldham. Until we can heighten the life of such towns and get them to rebuild themselves and put themselves in order and clean themselves, nothing will happen to architects or to anybody else. But in the rebuilding of our towns, if we could set about it, we might find some vitalising principle in our architecture. . . . I remember myself how beautiful were the towns throughout England fifty years ago. In the little town in which I lived no vulgarity had touched it at that time. It was a thing which had grown, a work of art and beauty, a work which Turner would have painted. But now it is wrapped round with railways and exploited and miserified. It is that which conditions our architecture. Until the spring of life bursts out in our towns what does any architecture matter? Nothing at all

until more public work gives us a new tradition.'

A new tradition was in fact already being formed. Its main spokesman was Ebenezer Howard, whose booklet *Tomorrow; a Peaceful Path to Real Reform* was published in 1898 and republished two years later under the title *Garden Cities of Tomorrow.* The planner who took up Howard's ideas and translated them into a practical plan for a community was Raymond Unwin. As a boy he had listened to Ruskin lecture and become a friend of Morris; he was a socialist and a humanitarian. If Howard had an idea for co-operative ownership, Unwin had a vision of the form and function of a garden city. It was to provide, in two phrases that occur separately in his lectures, 'a full life and an honest place'.

Experiments in the building of towns were not new. Model towns for industrial workers had been founded in the 1850s and 60s. In the 80s Bournville and Port Sunlight had been laid out by enlightened manufacturers, to provide a better environment, a more reliable work force and an antidote to squalor and alcohol. They were the cities, no longer of dirt and drink, but of soap and cocoa. What was new was the idea of a garden city, inspired by ideas about

1 *The church of Saint Jude in Hampstead Garden Suburb by Lutyens.* COLOUR *A William Morris bed-curtain from Kelmscott Manor.*

man and society. The garden city was not, however, just an exercise in bringing the garden to the house and the house to the garden; it was an idea for a community.

Unwin's first experiment was the garden village of New Earswick, just north of York, started by Joseph Rowntree in 1902. The next was Letchworth, started in 1903, a more complete expression of the developed idea. The financial structure was devised by Howard and it was more successful than he expected. Letchworth, now preserved, is thickly landscaped, with handsome houses, fairly large, with plenty of space, low densities, a rational organisation of roads and play spaces, schools and communal buildings and shops. It remains a con-

scious attempt at civic unity, an expression of the belief that you cannot live the good life in the wrong kind of town, nor can the right kind of town emerge if the wrong kind of architecture is built. The third experiment was a suburb – Hampstead Garden Suburb, started in 1906. And there, particularly in the church of St Jude, you meet the work of the man who seems to dominate British architecture from the turn of the century almost until the Second World War – Edwin Lutyens.

At Munstead Wood, the 'woodland cottage' of Miss Gertrude Jekyll he had already, in 1896, built in sturdy traditional English style, with oak frames and trusses and long windows. 'Aunt Bumps', as she was affectionately known, was the garden designer

e wold ꞏ and ꞏ the night is ꞏ a cold   and ꞏ thames ꞏ runs ꞏ chill

ill   but ꞏ kind & dear ꞏ is ꞏ the ꞏ old house here

warm ꞏ midst ꞏ winter's ꞏ harm   rest ꞏ then & rest ꞏ and think

COLOUR *The bedroom, Hill House, by Charles Rennie Mackintosh. 1 Lindisfarne Castle, Holy Island, restored by Edwin Lutyens.*

with whom he collaborated on many subsequent projects. In the great English tradition, he understood that the house must be a part of its landscape and the landscape a part of the house.

He had studied and understood building construction and the importance of the technical services in a house. He understood also the need for human scale, the advantages of natural materials, the way of generating an apparently erratic and informal shape from a study of the house's activities. At Tigbourne Court in Surrey in 1897 he built for the chairman of the Prudential one of his finest houses, a symbol of the wealth, and skill of

domestic architecture, at the end of the century.

He was probably the most gifted architect of Das Englische Haus. He restored – and virtually recast – the castle on Holy Island that Mackintosh had drawn in 1901. Two years later Edward Hudson of *Country Life*, finding it a ruin, decided to restore it; Lutyens made it into a delightful and original country house, with rooms where there were once magazines, exposing the materials and constructing a suitably exposed ascent by a cobbled ramp.

Witty, irrepressible, inventive, whimsical, Lutyens was a man of enormous comprehensiveness and scope. By the twenties and thirties he was

Early Lutyens. 1 Tigbourne Court, Surrey, built in 1897, a symbol of the wealth and skill of domestic architecture at the end of the century.

seen not merely as a great architect but possibly the greatest architect the country had ever known. Perhaps it was a sign of his success that he more and more abandoned the organic architecture of his youthful years and moved into a rather pompous kind of neo-classicism, for country houses and banks and public buildings – nowhere ultimately more spectacularly in conception or outrageous in scale than in his Government buildings at New Delhi and his design for the Metropolitan Cathedral at Liverpool.

In so far as Lutyens symbolised the spirit of his age, his change of mood and of scale from those early houses to the pompous banalities of the public buildings was a sign that the tide was running against the Arts and Crafts Movement. What transformed the scene and, I suppose, saw the end of the movement as such, was the Great War – the terrible Armageddon that destroyed the kind of society in which the movement grew up and flourished.

By the twenties it must have seemed that the prospect for the arts and crafts was poor. The architectural stage was dominated by Lutyens, now virtually a national monument himself, designer of the new Cenotaph for Whitehall. Away in exile in France, broken by disappointment and drink, Charles Rennie Mackintosh was frittering away his last years doing watercolours. And yet, at the same time, in the cavernous spaces of Westminster Cathedral, a sculptor was carving some Stations of the Cross, which gave a new turn to the tradition of the artist as workman and established the sculptor himself as one of the major personalities of our century.

Eric Gill had worked for an architect in London, but given it up and become a sculptor. He was also a letterer, a typographer, an illustrator and a draughtsman of considerable brilliance. A magnetic personality, wherever he went artists and craftsmen gathered round him. From London he moved to Ditchling in Sussex and set up a workshop. A group of friends joined him and formed a community of craftsmen. After a few years he left it and moved into the Black Mountains in Wales, where he took

Late Lutyens. 2 His designs for the Government buildings at New Delhi. 'Neoclassicism, spectacular in conception and outrageous in scale.'

over the abandoned monastery at Capel-y-ffin built by one of the more colourful characters of the Church of England in the nineteenth century, Joseph Leycester Lyne, usually known as Father Ignatius of Llantony. From there he moved finally to Pigotts in the Chiltern Hills.

Eric Gill was one of the most idiosyncratic and memorable figures of my childhood. He objected strongly to trousers and wore a smock, gathered together at the waist with a leather belt, and bright red stockings. In his studio he wore a home-made paper hat. I can remember him in this characteristic garb, walking about Pigotts, serving Mass in the chapel, walking down the hill to catch the bus. A gifted writer, talker and lecturer, he was a key figure in finding, if not wholly successfully, the link between craftsmanship and the mechanistic world of technology.

Established as a letterer and stone carver, and a declared enemy of mechanisation and mass-production, he was persuaded by the Monotype Corporation to turn his talents to the design of printing types. He was, I suppose, the outstanding typographic designer of his time. For all his condemnation of the machine, he was one of its masters.

In showing how art could master the machine Gill effectively extended the ideology of the Arts and Crafts Movement. Yet he hated the Arts and Crafts Society and thought the movement a failure. He particularly disliked its identification with the middle class, with people who did not really live the kind of life they talked about. He spoke with contempt of garden cities. Nevertheless I see him as a direct descendant of the ideas of William Morris. For he saw the work of the artist as being essentially part of the daily work of Man. 'The artist', he liked to say, 'is not a special kind of man; but every man is a special kind of artist'.

His own work, and his own life, testify to the integrity of his ideal. And none of the homes he made speaks more strongly of the possible unity of art and life than Capel-y-ffin. Its appropriateness is partly its simplicity, the effortless drama of its shape

Eric Gill at work on a sculpture, at Pigotts. The illustration facing is one of Gill's Stations of the Cross from Westminster Cathedral.

and form. But it also arises from the way he used and adapted it. The chapel, for example, was made out of one of the side buildings of the quadrangle – the exposed timber roof structure had lettering applied to it, the pews were left plain, everything was as simple and fundamental as it could be. And therefore very beautiful. 'Look after goodness and truth', said Gill, 'and beauty will look after itself '.

The Arts and Crafts Movement offered a theory of making and living that encompassed everything, from the smallest object to a whole community. It might have become one of the most significant, as well as distinctive, movements in our history – for a time it must even have seemed the dominant movement. It influenced Germany and, especially in the design of furniture and interior fittings, Scandinavia. But it was profoundly at variance with some of the major developments in society, which have almost – but not quite – swept it away.

For one thing, it was based upon craftsmanship,

not machines; and the machines won. For another, it revolved around the individual workman, responsible for his own work; and mass organisation could hardly fail to win. For a third, it was concerned with the discovery of solutions to individual – not mass – problems; and the mass problems were in the end the most important.

Yet in a way, the movement did succeed – not for the workman, not as a piece of social reform, but for the individuals who chose that way of life. It is still a very English approach – to see if one can solve an individual problem, analyse it in detail and from all those solutions generate a whole series of things – objects and works of art and craft – necessary things, both practical and decorative – that will add up to the kind of place in which Man is really the centre of things.

That, essentially, is what the Arts and Crafts movement was about. And because its ideas are so basic they are still around. It might even be that they could inspire the next wave of social thinking and design.

The Englishman's Home: 1 Anne Hathaway's Cottage. 2 Semi-detached at New Malden. 3 Weybridge. 4 Islington, London.

8

HUGH CASSON

DREAMS AND AWAKENINGS

Architecture is a long word for the design of places in which we feel at ease or by which, when occasion demands, we are uplifted. Not surprisingly, therefore, architecture begins at home. Here it is neither a professional mystery nor itemised fodder for guidebooks, but something as familiar and affectionately used as the family teapot. We can approach it of course at different levels. For the expert there are always references and sub-codes to be identified, interpreted and enjoyed, and the more we know – as previous pages have shown – the more we will be rewarded. But for most of us 'architecture' without the capital A is not so much a building as the place where we live, or, more likely perhaps, its familiar image – 'The Englishman's Home', by Georgian vicarage out of Anne Hathaway, small, self-contained, secure, the castle not in the air but on the ground. Most of us settle happily enough for its suburban equivalent, a small house, a gate, a bay window, a hedge, leaded lights, three bedrooms and a fitted kitchen . . . probably built between the wars. Set on a curving road in a semi-rural surround of shrubs and trees (not too urban nor too remote), practical, convenient, comparatively cheap. It meets the shopping list of our requirements – shelter, safety, character and a sense of identity. (It's the same but not *quite* the same as next door.) We know where we are, and what to expect. What are the reasons for its success? There are three.

First, its strong and healthy pedigree – starting with the seventeenth-century small manor house or tradesman's cottage, followed by the eighteenth-century upper-class retreats of the rich and

THE SUBURBS

Because they are so many and the same,
  The little houses row on weary row;
Because they are so loveless and so lame
  It were a bitter thing to tell them so.
And ill to laugh at those who hither came
  Not without hope and not without a glow,
And who, perchance, by sorrow struck or shame
  Not without tears look back before they go.

Here is no place for laughter nor for blame,
  And not for tears, since none shall ever know
What here is done and suffered, nor proclaim
  The end to which these myriad spirits grow.
He understands, whose heart remembereth
  That here is all the tale of life and death.

Humbert Wolfe

SUBURBAN DREAM

Walking the suburbs in the afternoon
In summer when the idle doors stand open
  And the air flows through the rooms
  Fanning the curtain hems.

You wander through a cool elysium
Of women, schoolgirls, children, garden
    talks,
  With a schoolboy here and there
  Conning his history book.

The men are all away in offices,
Committee-rooms, laboratories, banks,
  Or pushing cotton goods
  In Wick or Ilfracombe.

The massed unanimous absence liberates
The light keys of the piano and sets free
  Chopin and everlasting youth,
  Now, with the masters gone.

And all things turn to images of peace,
The boy curled over his book, the young girl
    poised
  On the path as if beguiled
  By the silence of a wood.

It is a child's dream of a grown-up world.
But soon the brazen evening clocks will
    bring
  The tramp of feet and brisk
  Fanfare of motor horns
  And the masters come.

Edwin Muir

educated, and the picturesque illusionism of eighteenth-century landscape design, through the folksy romanticism of the Garden City movement and the well-scrubbed experiments of Victorian philanthropists, right up to the worthy and wide-verged council estates of Wythenshawe and Becontree.

Secondly, its suitability – compact, practical and convenient within; scenic, varied and anarchic without – a perfect background for a tool-shed and sunroom, sundial and lily-pond way of life, friendly and participatory, self-identifying and self-fulfilling.

Thirdly, its simple symbolism, recognisable and familiar. Here the builders and the consumers were as one, the Architecture fitted the dream – the most persistent and successful in England's architectural history – of the small individual cottage home.

The Age of Illusion 1920–1930

Over four million of these homes were built between the wars – most of them by private enterprise. (The architects were for the most part busy elsewhere with banks and town halls and insurance offices.) In the twenties the post-war demand for housing seemed insatiable. There was plenty of cheap land available round our cities, and such little planning control as existed was beyond the competence of the cat's-cradle of small local authorities who tried half-heartedly to administer it. The procedure was simple. The developer, who was not always the builder, bought the land, designed a layout – usually formless or over-formal – put down the infrastructure of roads and services, and sold off

COMING

On longer evenings,
Light, chill and yellow,
Bathes the serene
Foreheads of houses.
A thrush sings,
Laurel-surrounded
In the deep bare garden,
Its fresh-peeled voice
Astonishing the
  brickwork.
It will be spring soon,
It will be spring soon –
and I, whose childhood
Is a forgotten boredom,
Feel like a child
Who comes on a scene
Of adult reconciling,
And can understand
  nothing
But the unusual
  laughter,
And starts to be happy.

Philip Larkin

the plots to the builders. Most of the houses were semi-detached – bungalows were kept for cheaper land – and the favourite style was Tudoresque with individual extras. (New Ideal Homesteads offered tiled bathrooms and oak mantelpieces. Berg's promised leaded lights in the front door, Curton's a pedestal lamp on the newel post.) The customers came from the white-collar class, earning between £5 and £10 a week. The scale of social life was modest, but everyone was climbing up the ladder. Estates of over 200 houses could support a small group of shops – usually placed around the station where the suburban railway system, in particular London Transport, the Metropolitan Railway and Southern Region, was acting sometimes as camp-follower but more often as pioneer.

Virtually no community facilities were provided and not many new churches were built. Mystery and reassurance were sought in the true cathedrals of suburbia – those great cinemas that squatted like jewel-headed toads at the major crossroads. Nobody bothered much about the sides and backs of these monsters, but they did about their fronts and also their insides. Egyptian or Polynesian, Neapolitan or Art Deco. You paid your 9d – or less before lunch – and took your choice. Snug in the gilded belly of the local Odeon some twenty million people spent three hours a week in dreamland, watching Greta Garbo or Mickey Mouse, listening to the Wurlitzer, afterwards perhaps taking tea while seated on the apple-green, gold-dusted cane chairs of the tea-lounge.

MEWS FLAT MONA:
A MEMORY OF THE 'TWENTIES

Mona took a flat in a Mayfair Mews;
To do that then was to be in the news.
        Oh, Mona! it wouldn't be now!

The walls were of glass and the floor of
        pewter,
This was thought 'intriguing', but the
        bathroom was cuter;
On a sofa upholstered in panther skin
Mona did researches in original sin.
        Oh, Mona! they're concluded now!
· · · · · ·

Diamond bracelets blazed on her wrists
(They were not presented by
        misogynists)
And Mona got engaged to a
        scatterbrained peer;
His breach of promise cost him pretty
        dear.
            Oh, Mona! he couldn't pay now!

When she gave a dance she engaged
        three bands,
And she entered the Ritz once walking
        on her hands;
She drove round London in a crimson
        Rolls,
'The soul of every party' – as if parties
        had souls!
        Oh, Mona! the party's over now!

William Plomer

The New Victoria Cinema in London,
designed by W. E. Trent and
E. Walmesley Lewis in 1930.

The Housing Boom slowed down in 1935 and the wave of bricks and tiles broke eventually on the edge of the Green Belt, established in 1938. For the time it was all over, and suburbia was left to consolidate and mature behind its bay-windows, rockeries and shrubs. As a phenomenon, it had been the despair of intellectuals (D. H. Lawrence called them horrid little red mantraps; only Arnold Bennett it seemed had a good word for them) and the butt of the music halls, and it would be dishonest to elevate its achievements higher than its aims. Yet these aims, because they were founded on firmly shared assumptions, are not despicable, and the achievements, because they were expressed in a recognisable language, are worthy of respect. It could be said that suburbia was unbalanced social-ly, that it was pretentious, visually dispiriting, psychologically depressing, and stifling for the young, but for all its faults and failures it exhibited accurately and acceptably the spirit of its times and it gave practical happiness to many millions of people at a remarkable speed and at a price they could afford to pay. Aesthetically, we must admit, it was a lack-lustre and irresolute period – Georgian office blocks, Art Deco factories, ribbon development and thatched filling stations. . . . 'Dear old, bloody old England,' wrote the future Poet Laureate, 'of telegraph poles and tin, seemingly so indifferent and with so little soul to win.'

Apt words in the appalling social and political climate of a period which saw the virtual collapse of major British industry – for twenty years unem-

'New Ways', Northampton. *This house, built in 1926, was designed by the German pioneer architect, Peter Behrens, whose name the client, Mr Bassett-Lowke, had found in an art magazine. It was the first 'international style' house to be built in England. Although what matters always is not who did it first but who did it best, this house was a brave piece of patronage for the time, and it was in its modest dead-pan unseductive way a milestone in the history of 20th-century architecture.*

'High and Over', Amersham. *The first British-designed house in the international style – apart from a small experiment for the Crittall workers at Silver End, Braintree – was completed in 1929. It was the joint enterprise of two young men who had met in Rome – Bernard Ashmole, Director of the British School, and the young New Zealander, Amyas Connell, a Rome Scholar. The locals thought it was brutal, bossy and conspicuous – and said so. The battle to get it built was long and ill-tempered – the first of many such battles to be fought in the following years by those wishing to build anything unfamiliar or experimental. Today the garden is mature, the trees grown up, and the house, ironically enough, is 'listed' for preservation.*

ployment was seldom below two million – the gradual disintegration of the Empire, the rise of Fascism in Europe. It was the time of Hunger Marches and Peace Pledges, of Mosleyites and the Left Book Club, deeply-felt stresses beneath a froth of unusual silliness at all levels – Oxford Bags and Pogo Sticks, Night Clubs and Joynson-Hicks, Horatio Bottomley, Hatry and the Vicar of Stiffkey. The biggest design impact in the home was given by the Paris Exhibition of 1925, which was to influence the appearance of every teacup and cushion for many years to come. For women in particular – who had tasted independence in war work – new opportunities were opening up. The invention of rayon made their clothes lighter, cheaper and prettier. Hire-purchase, vacuum cleaners, smaller families,

paperbacks and magazines, the radio and the roadhouse, and above all increasing car-ownership (the true founder of Women's Lib was the inventor of the self-starter) had made their home life for them more stable but also more varied. No wonder they trotted off so happily to the shops, to the day in town or to the tennis club. (To the question: 'Anyone for tennis?' in suburbia the answer was 'practically everybody'. Football was for the Council estates where the architectural language of private enterprise was spoken more drily and fewer quirks were permitted.)

This language – private or public – was almost totally brick and tile, gable, dormer and hip. But around 1930 a few self-conscious strangers – flat-roofed and white-walled, with wide curving

1 Not all modern buildings were three-dimensional manifestos. This one – the Boots Factory at Beeston, Nottingham, built in 1932 – was, in the view of the engineer and designer, Sir Owen Williams, probably no more than a run of the mill industrial problem. He made it into a masterpiece. It is one of the largest reinforced concrete buildings in the world – four concrete floors stacked above each other and wrapped in a tight envelope of metal and glass. All materials were designed to work to their economic limits and the technology of the time was fully exploited. Like all good buildings it can be comprehended spatially and structurally at a glance.

windows glazed with Vita glass – began to appear behind the forsythia and crazy paving. These – a short-lived experiment launched by a few courageous builders at the trend-setting Ideal Home Exhibitions of the time – were perhaps the nearest that suburbia ever *consciously* got to the Modern Movement, a design philosophy which was within a few years to conquer our schools of architecture and thus, in due course, influence every corner of our environment.

1930–1940

Like most intellectual ideas it came to this country from abroad. Its seed-bed, planted around 1900, and springing earlier in England from the works and teachings of Butterfield, Godwin and Webb, was a growing professional distaste with the style-mongering historicism of the nineteenth century. This in turn led throughout Europe to a wave of self-examination in which the first shoots of social unease (contributed largely from England by the writings of John Ruskin and William Morris) and rationalist realism (contributed largely from France and Germany by Viollet-le-Duc and the Bauhaus) developed into a sort of tiny Common Market of the avant-garde. From Holland came Expressionism, from Italy Futurism, from France Cubism. (Throughout the movement, the influence of painters was deep and lasting. Picasso and Le Corbusier were alike in their need to destroy or to distort form before recreating it.)

The social and political disintegration that fol-

*2 Peter Jones store, Sloane Square, by Slater and Moberly.
W. Crabtree Associate.*

3 Kensal House, Ladbroke Grove, by E. Maxwell Fry and Partners.

*4 A zoo is a good place for architectural experiment – and not just
because the clients can't complain. The architect, Berthold Lubetkin
– a Russian-born cosmopolitan with a strong European feeling for
the Baroque – took the chance in Regent's Park to devise, with the
help of the engineer Ove Arup and his partners in Tecton, a
brilliant outdoor theatre-set for the penguins. More a piece of
sculpture than a building, it is a brilliant tour-de-force in
reinforced concrete and surely one of the most imaginative,
delightful and ingenious structures in the country.*

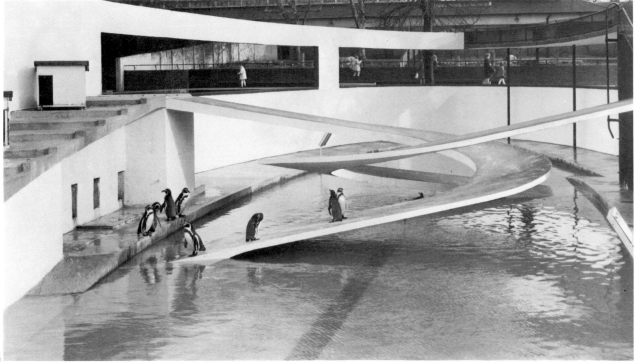

lowed the first great war, the leap forward in technology demanding an imagery to match – the uncon-
vinced eclecticism of the general architectural scene
– mostly commercial Georgian with Pswedish
trimmings – were factors that demanded, it seemed,
a return to those first principles which in England
had been kept precariously alive by Lethaby and
Ashbee. The writings of Le Corbusier first published in England in 1927, and the arrival here a few
years later of many distinguished foreign architects
as refugees from Fascism, were – to young architects in particular, who always like a good moral
reason for a change in taste – turning points in the
development of a new architectural philosophy.

The physical results – both in Europe and in
England – were few, small, scattered, but to
architects profoundly influential. To those not
directly concerned they also seemed self-conscious,
mechanistic, meagre and without joy. After all
Functionalism, as Lord Clark observed, is basically a
materialist doctrine, and if ornament and history
also were to be proscribed, and the literary
metaphors by which most of us judge architecture
dismissed as irrelevant, then it was not surprising
that the modern movement failed to catch the public attention – much less its affection. By 1932 it was
officially banned in Germany and Russia, which had
in 1917 embraced it so enthusiastically, and the
battlefield – guerrilla warfare would be more accu-
rate – moved to France and England. Here, between
1930 and 1940, a handful of pioneers, among them
Connell, Ward and Lucas, Wells Coates, Joseph

1

MIDDLESEX

Gaily into Ruislip Gardens
  Runs the red electric train,
With a thousand Ta's and Pardon's
  Daintily alights Elaine;
Hurries down the concrete station
With a frown of concentration,
Out into the outskirt's edges
Where a few surviving hedges
  Keep alive our lost Elysium –
rural Middlesex again.

John Betjeman

Emberton, Maxwell Fry and the distinguished foreign refugees Lubetkin, Gropius and Mendelssohn, pursued the struggle against public opinion and official conservatism, and left us a handful of remarkable monuments.

None of these made much public impact. Only where it was playful (as by the seaside or at the Zoo) or where it was inarguably appropriate (factories and railway stations) did modern architecture pass successfully through the sieve which the English genius provides for all ideas from abroad, and thus become accepted. It was in London's suburbia – strangely enough the heart of the enemy country – that the modern movement scored perhaps its greatest success, in the handsome, modest and totally functional stations designed for London

Transport under the inspiration of Frank Pick by Dr Charles Holden. Not so surprising perhaps. Although a public art (in that it's always under your nose), architecture is an art only half-sensed by the user or observer. The fact that these logical and discreet buildings, as easy to slip in or out of as an old jacket, are barely noticed perhaps by their daily customers hurrying to and from Arcadia, and who would certainly be surprised to hear them described as 'architecture', is a tribute to their quiet appropriateness.

The Age of Survival 1940–1950

When war came, architecture – of the sort we have been talking about – went either overseas or under-

1 London Transport Station: Arnos Grove. Perhaps the most successful buildings of the 1930s were not the white-walled manifestos of the revolutionaries, nor even the daring structural experiments of the engineers, but the series of small suburban stations designed for London Transport by Charles Holden, the Manchester-trained pupil of C. R. Ashbee. Arnos Grove on the Piccadilly Line is one of the best of these.

The ingenuity and drama of war. 2 A factory making Anderson shelters. 3 Seaforts.

ground. Overseas to America which for twenty years, until challenged ironically enough by its late opponents – the Germans, Italians and Japanese, was to become the design pace-setter of the Western world; and underground into a substratum of non-architecture – huts and hangars, fortifications and air-raid shelters.

Some of these, the off-shore AA towers and the coastal forts, were as strange and dramatic and powerful as Easter Island images. Others, the Bellman hangar, the Bailey bridge, the Morrison shelter, were minor miracles of ingenuity and economy, three-dimensional evidence of man's ability to evolve in order to survive what Edith Sitwell called 'the sad uncomprehending dark'.

The Age of the Herbivores 1950–1960

When it was all over, those who were lucky enough to have survived found that nearly two million houses had been damaged or destroyed – a loss small by European standards but severe enough to demand radical action. It was taken; and by 1946 200,000 families had been rehoused and 40,000 prefabs built. Despite the spivvery and squatting, despite groundnuts and snoek, optimism was in the air. Eros was back on his pedestal: India was free: the New Look – a comforting hint of the past in its promise for the future – had routed Sir Stafford Cripps' attempts to keep the hem-line high. True, of course, the State was taking over. By 1948 the Bank of England, Coal, Steel and the Railways were

1 Coventry Cathedral.
2 The South Bank site from the air.
3 One of the Hertfordshire schools

nationalised, but twenty million a week still visited the cinema and the social revolution was proving not so upsetting as it might have been. (After all the Royal Garden Parties had started again.)

By 1948 with the help of Marshall Aid we had an Education Act, a National Health Service and Family Allowances, as well as a mass of new legislation on housing standards. Bevan's target, almost reached, as Housing Minister was 200,000 houses a year of 'high' standard. (Private building was controlled by licence.) Fourteen New Towns were to be started, new planning legislation introduced. Although the achievement foundered in the economic crisis of 1946/47, when rations of food, fuel and clothes fell below the worst wartime stan-

dards, it was an exciting time when we sensed that things could be better and believed they would be.

Unarguably the architectural star of this decade was the Hertfordshire school programme. In 1946 the County needed 100 new schools ... and quickly. The solution devised by their architects was to go into partnership with industry and to build the schools from a range of standard components to a standard grid. A steel frame was the base but roofs, floors, doors and windows were all brought into the system as well. By 1954 the target was met.

These schools – small-scale, flexible, loose-fitting, informally planned within the modular discipline – looked friendly, unassertive and pleasantly makeshift, almost as if the children had done it all themselves. It was a triumph for all those

Extracts from Dylan Thomas's
broadcast on
The Festival Exhibition 1951

*. . . Here they will find no braying
pageantry, no taxidermal museum of
Culture, no cold and echoing inhuman
hygienic barracks of technical
information, no shoddily cajoling
emporium of tasteless Empire wares, but
something very odd indeed, magical and
parochial: a parish-pump made of flying
glass and thistledown gauze-thin steel, a
rolypoly pudding full of luminous,
melodious bells, wheels, coils, engines and
organs, alembics and jorums in a palace
in thunderland sizzling with scientific
witches' brews, a place of trains, bones,
planes, ships, sheep, shapes, snipe,
mobiles, marbles, brass bands, and
cheese, a place painted regardless, and
by hand. . . .*

South Bank 1951.
The Shot Tower.

1

Greedy of land and expensive to service, the 'prefabs' were technically only a mixed success, but people liked their toy-like scale, and the survival of so many of them to this day is a tribute to the robust ingenuity of their design.

2

3

A resounding apathy greeted the eccentric campaign – launched in 1930 by English don Mansfield Forbes and architect Trystan Edwards – for A Hundred New Towns, and it was not until the last years of the last war that the official new town programme was launched. The first – and probably the least adventurous – was Stevenage, but later models managed to develop more individual versions of the standardised manicured Arcadia, and at Peterlee (3) the idea of visual collaboration with the painter Victor Pasmore proved interesting. The latest and largest of them all – Milton Keynes – may be the last. (The colour illustration shows a detail of plans for the town centre.) The future seems more likely to lie in the expansion of small existing towns.

2 Alton Estate, Roehampton, designed in 1955 by the Architect's Department of the LCC. 3 Peterlee.

concerned, and particularly for those who held to the herbivore values of the immediate post-war period when it seemed to so many of us that radical thinking and rationalised building were the gates to Utopia. Those gates indeed seemed already ajar, for by now nearly all building was officially or semi-officially financed, and half the architectural profession was in 'official' service – the majority school-trained and thus speaking the 'modern language'. In 1951 some of them were given a chance to show what they could do when let off the economic leash.

The Festival of Britain – thought up by Gerald Barry, then editor of the *News Chronicle*, politically mothered by Herbert Morrison and organised by a youngish group of Herbivores – was planned to be nationwide and participatory at all levels. It culmi-

nated in London at the South Bank Exhibition. Here, on twenty-seven acres of derelict, bomb-scarred riverbank, a brief city of steel, aluminium and glass was mounted by an army of architects, engineers, artists, display designers, poets and writers. Eight million people visited it and it was a resounding success. For six months indeed this was the most exciting place to be in England. After the grey austerity of the forties and the ingenious but sometimes depressingly pinched economies of the housing programme, here was a chance for architects and designers to shake a leg, to give a glimpse of what our future cities might be like – full of colour and lively shapes, of trees and water – and of course no cars. (Above all the South Bank exhibition was a place to walk about in.) It was in retro-

HAT

Nothing in my woman's head
didn't worry about that
Took her in to C and A's
and bought her a great big
purple woolly hat

Alan Jackson

MRS MIDDLEDITCH

'A Supermorning, madam,
For Supermarketing!
Our cut-price Superfoods
Are best for each and all,
Our Supergoods await you
On every Supershelf,
So take a Superbasket
And help your Superself!'

William Plomer

spect a demonstration of intelligence – the role of which, said Bertrand Russell, is to find means to reach ends conceived in passion. Stylistically it was no revolution. The designs were mostly from the hands of those who were just qualifying when war broke out, and who therefore spoke the language of that time. But many of their ideas found their way into later use – since under the funny hats there was plenty of serious and progressive thinking. However, this – with the New Town programme – was to be the last heave-ho of the Herbivores. The next two decades were to be the hunting-ground of the Carnivores . . . and they never had it so good.

The Age of the Carnivores 1960–1970

Trading stamps and television, the teenage indus-try, package holidays and supermarkets, the car explosion and the adman's paradise. Architecture once more entered the land of mythology. Six new universities, each perhaps more experimental in its architecture than academically: lumpy glass palaces for princes of industry, shopping-centres like stranded Atlantic liners aground among the roofs of old market towns, local authority housing towers and fantasy hotels . . . the image of a white-hot, quick-moving technological sprint with money as the prize. The nation seemed swept off its feet by the speed of change, and as we bobbed helplessly about in its wake, we searched in vain for the re-assurance of familiar landmarks.

We got little comfort from our newly built en-vironment. To start with, the new buildings looked

1 *Centrepoint, Holborn, by R. Seifert and Partners.*
2 *London boutique.*
3 *Supermarket.*
4 *Commercial Union Building, by Gollins Melvin and Ward.*
5 *Gatwick Airport, by Yorke Rosenberg and Mardall.*

alarmingly different. New needs – airports, container depots, leisure centres, open-plan offices – demanded new forms. Developing technology made the new forms possible. Air-conditioning could make climate irrelevant, windows dispensable, walls non-structural, so that – to quote Dr Nuttgens – a modern building can be upside-down, inside-out and back-to-front. Mass needs and twentieth-century economics – on both sides of the Iron Curtain – seemed to demand mass solutions, an architecture that is centralised, over-large, repetitive, shiny-faced and hard-edged, that could only be handled by specialists and to which we, the consumer, seemed powerless to contribute. Inevitably public disenchantment with what they saw developed into public petulance.

You could argue about the reasons – the death of optimism, the absence of a 'centre' in Western civilisation, the money-manic ethos and confused values of the sixties, but you couldn't argue about the fact that people – who react more quickly and directly to buildings than architects are inclined to admit – looked at what they saw around them and for the most part did not like what they saw. Architecture was in the dock charged with being banal and inhuman and impossible to love. Even the intellectuals who have been described as those who disparage everything and disapprove of nothing managed this time to do both. This disenchantment was shared by architects, torn as always in half by their need to make a living and their wish – presumptuous-sounding but genuine enough – to

1 The National Theatre, by Denys Lasdun and Partners, 2 Roof of the Cambridge History Faculty Library, by James Stirling, 3 The Economist Building, St James's, by Peter and Alison Smithson.

4 *The Cripps Building, St John's College, Cambridge, by Powell and Moya, 5 The Royal College of Art, by H. T. Cadbury Brown in association with Robert Gooden and Sir Hugh Casson, 6 IBM, Cosham, by Norman Foster Associates, 7 UOP factory, Surrey, by Piano and Rogers.*

be of service to society. The principles of the modern movement – a careful and compassionate analysis of needs, and logical solutions economically and precisely expressed in the language of our time – still seemed defensible but the old revolutionaries had become fossilised in myth. The recipes for Utopia – comprehensive redevelopment, social zoning, system building, high-rise housing – now seemed no better than the clumsy weapons of some power-crazed boy-scout.

There were positive sides to this discontent of course, among them a wider and more sophisticated interest among non-experts in the environment and more humble and open-minded attitudes from experts. But the general effect was dispiriting, and the despair, because it ignored the existence of

many fine and exciting new buildings, was often self-indulgent and unthinking. (The British – as Doris Lessing has pointed out – seem to have discovered in analysis and critical discussion a mechanism for impotence and indecision. We are so exhausted by stating a problem that we have no energy left to solve it.)

The Age of Disbelief or Rain Stops Play

Yet the lesson of the sixties had been learned. It would be an exaggeration to describe it as a retreat from rationalism or as the defeat of technology by conservationist and ecological groups and the triumph of the Small-is-Beautiful Do-It-Yourself Co-operative Housing brigades. Yet what could be more irrational than a so-called 'rational' solution to

LANCASHIRE WINTER

The town remembers no such plenty,
under the wind from off the moor.
The labour exchange is nearly empty;
stiletto heels on the Palais floor
move between points of patent leather.
Sheepskin coats keep out the weather.

Commerce and Further Education
won't be frozen. Dully free
in snack bars and classrooms sits the patient
centrally heated peasantry,
receiving Wimpies like the Host;
striving to get that Better Post.

Snow on the streets and Mini-Minors
thickens to drifts, and in the square
from dingy plinths, blind eyes, stone collars,
the fathers of revolution stare,
who, against pikes and burning brands,
built the future with bare hands.

Tony Connor

1 Halifax Building Society Building,
Halifax, by Building Design Partnership.
2 The old Maltings at Snape have been
brilliantly converted by Arup Associates into
one of the finest concert halls in Europe. 2

so complex an organism as a city, more sensible and compassionate than the wish to conserve and make the best of what we've got, and without denigrating the essential part played by the specialist, or investing populist feelings with a fake nobility, to recognise the right of everyone to have a say in and to contribute to the form of his environment?

The Age of the Sceptic 1970–

These were the values and attitudes – sceptical, half-sensed, yet bone-true – that were to be rediscovered in the seventies, and nowhere more recognisably than in the common ground of the home. It is true that beneath the surface of domestic stabilities and normal family life – as writers such as George Eliot and Flora Thompson well knew – lie threatening depths of dislocation, even of social revolution. But here among the familiar surroundings, traditional materials and accustomed rituals the spirit of the age could be identified and cherished. There might be a sailing dinghy in the Californian carport. Fibreglass Georgian doorways may have replaced Tudorbethan gables. But the success and appeal of Arcadia remained as strong as ever, and its image – practical, secure, participatory and fantastic – continued to beguile and to reassure. This is not to say that in these days of radical rethinking and explosive technology our architectural future lies only in Toy Town. That would be baby-talk. It *is* however to say that no architecture – however ingenious or spectacular – can flourish or mature without that respect for human values and

NEW LIGHT ON TERRY STREET

Up terraces of slums, young gum-chewing mothers sit
Outside on their thrones of light. Their radios,

Inside or placed on window ledges, grow hot
With sun and electricity. Shielding their eyes from sun

They talk above music, knitting or pushing prams
Over gentle, stone inches. Under the clawed chairs

Cats sleep in the furry shade. The children bounce balls
Up into their dreams of sand, and the sea they have not
    seen.

Becoming tired the fascination of wheels takes them.
They pedal their trikes slowly through dust in hollows,

Quietly give up cheek to old men, sing with sly voices.
Their mothers go inside to cook. Their fathers come home.

Douglas Dunn

1 Lillington Street Housing, Pimlico, by Darbourne and Darke. 2 Byker – an inner suburb of Newcastle under construction. Declared a slum clearance area ten years ago, it is now being rebuilt to the designs of Ralph Erskine – an Englishman who has spent most of his working life in Sweden – and his partner, Vernon Gracie. Their office – an old corner shop – is on the site, and the locals drop in all the time for information, or to say what they think of what's going on. The local authority took the time and trouble to write a good programme – and to get the right architect (one who devotes as much trouble to the spaces between buildings as to the buildings themselves).

for the importance of the individual in his personal world which is so clearly expressed in Arcadia.

There is still a need, of course, for the occasional monument – for permanence expressed in noble proportions and fine materials. There are still opportunities for the sparky experiment carried out at top technological pitch. More than ever is there necessity for the makeshift and the make-do and mend, to prolong the working life of old buildings by giving them new uses. But the last fifty years have been a rather quietist – not to say mousy – period in the story of British architecture. Not much majesty and very little confidence. Few monuments as spectacular as Hatfield and Chatsworth, Greenwich Hospital or the Palace of Westminster. No architectural giants like Inigo Jones or Vanbrugh, Christopher Wren or Barry. And if the architecture has – with notable exceptions – been clumsy or pretentiously banal, certainly our reaction to it has been unexcited, not to say sulky. You'll be lucky to get more than two cheers for twentieth-century architecture. Yet it's too easy to underrate the value of what has been built since 1920. Easy and wrong. The truth is that these are not the times for monuments. England has never indeed been at ease with them. Houses like Chatsworth and cathedrals like St Paul's are handsome enough, but a bit too bossy for our tastes. What Lutyens used to call 'the High Game' of architecture can only be played by those few designers – rare in any century – who are up to it.

As we all know, England is regarded by other

2

nations as pragmatic and tolerant, happily resigned to a climate of political and cultural compromise which has been the legacy of the Civil Wars. Extremism to the Englishman is a term of censure. Not surprisingly, therefore, he dislikes it in his architecture. He is prepared to accept a certain amount of grandeur as a setting for ceremony in appropriate places – but even there it never approaches the knock-out scale encountered in France or Italy. One of our largest classical buildings, Somerset House, is minute by European standards, and the most powerful man in England, the Prime Minister, lives in a simple brick house in a modest cul de sac.

This attitude has recently become intensified. It is easy to argue that our affection for the play-acting of suburbia is infantile, that our rejection of the modern movement, before we had learned its lesson, was timid, that the tangled squalor of our city centres – and for that matter their edges too – shows not so much a lack of imagination, though that's there too, as lack of will to act. Yet this policy of 'live and let live', this unwillingness to interfere till pushed, this shrinking from cultural rhetoric, is part of our make-up, and it has made the revolution we have undergone a comparatively quiet one for most of us. What has happened, quite simply, and within two generations, is the beginning of a customers' revolt – a refusal any longer to be totally the victims of experts, a growing insistence on having more say in the shape of our surroundings.

The qualities we are beginning to look for in our

architecture are not so often the elegant gestures or strong statements, glad as we are for their occasional appearance, but modesty and common sense, suitability and reassurance, a sense of shared decisions and of the importance of the individual, and a respect for what is already there. The spirit of this age, in my view, is the rediscovery of the truth – often obscured beneath the stylistic nit-picking of experts and historians – that architecture is not just buildings, it is places . . . buildings and spaces and landscape and light and weather and movement and people, all warmed by a concern for human life. This is architecture – 'Work done', as Lethaby said, 'by human beings for human beings', and thus truly expressive of its times.

INDEX

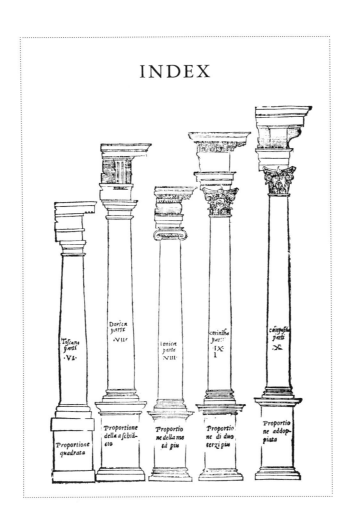